How the California Electricity Crisis Generated a Green Wave

This book provides the definitive account of a decade-long transformation of energy policy in California with rippling consequences. The author, a state government "insider" during much of this period, tells a story informed by personal experience, access to the key actors of the time (both then and now), and extensive research.

California's risky experiment in deregulating the state's electricity market in the 1990s, resulting in manipulation from unscrupulous energy providers and necessitating government action, laid the foundation for a greener grid and greater energy efficiency in the early 2000s and beyond. The book follows the state's energy journey through Democratic Governor Gray Davis's administration and his Republican successor Arnold Schwarzenegger's time in office, providing a detailed behind-the-scenes account. It highlights how this period influenced broader discussions of energy policy in the U.S., culminating in President Barack Obama pledging bold action and securing $90 billion for clean energy programs in the 2009 "stimulus" bill, the largest single "green" investment in history at that point in time. The energy crisis provided a springboard for green growth by discrediting deregulation, elevating public support, and establishing a political pathway for a growing array of sustainable energy advocates.

This book engagingly balances policy considerations and political drama to reveal the untold details of how the electricity crisis paved the way for key climate and clean energy policies and offers unprecedented access to archival material from the Davis administration era. It will be a must-read for energy policymakers, researchers, and environmental historians.

Kurt Schuparra was Senior Policy Analyst in the Office of California Governor Gray Davis and later served as his Deputy Secretary for Policy at the state Environmental Protection Agency. In 2004 he worked in the state legislature as a policy consultant and in 2007 became a government affairs advisor in the private sector.

Routledge Environmental History

The new *Routledge Environmental History* series presents current interdisciplinary research investigating our changing ecological entanglements over time. It draws on diverse time periods, geographical regions, methods, and ideas from subject areas such as history, geography, archaeology, and the natural sciences. It taps into how topical debates such as the roles of non-humans and more-than-humans, social and environmental justice, climate change, and antiracism are shaping environmental histories and shifting approaches to engaging with the natural world.

Comprising edited collections, coauthored volumes, and single author monographs, this collection provides an invaluable resource for advanced undergraduate and postgraduate students and scholars with an interest in the wide-ranging field of environmental history.

For more information, or to submit a proposal, please contact the Commissioning Editor, Grace Harrison (grace.harrison@tandf.co.uk).

A Global Environmental History of Coastal Dunes
Joana Gaspar de Freitas

How the California Electricity Crisis Generated a Green Wave
An Insider's Account
Kurt Schuparra

For more information about this series, please visit: www.routledge.com/Routledge-Environmental-History/book-series/ESREH

How the California Electricity Crisis Generated a Green Wave

An Insider's Account

Kurt Schuparra

Routledge
Taylor & Francis Group
LONDON AND NEW YORK

earthscan
from Routledge

First published 2025
by Routledge
4 Park Square, Milton Park, Abingdon, Oxon OX14 4RN

and by Routledge
605 Third Avenue, New York, NY 10158

Routledge is an imprint of the Taylor & Francis Group, an informa business

British Library Cataloguing-in-Publication Data
A catalogue record for this book is available from the British Library

ISBN: 978-1-032-84321-6 (hbk)
ISBN: 978-1-032-85436-6 (pbk)
ISBN: 978-1-003-51815-0 (ebk)

DOI: 10.4324/9781003518150

Typeset in Sabon
by KnowledgeWorks Global Ltd.

For my daughter Ella, her generation, and the generations that follow

Contents

Acknowledgments

Since the electricity crisis, and especially in recent years, many individuals interested in California energy and climate-change policy have asked me if they could "pick my brain" on these topics and recommend a good book on the crisis and its legacy. These queries came from journalists, legislative staffers, and others in state and local government, academics, and students. I came to realize that as a historian with wide-ranging experience as a key energy policy analyst in the governor's office during the unprecedented crisis and its aftermath, I was uniquely positioned to write that "good book."

***

In January 1999, I had the good fortune to join the administration of Governor Gray Davis—the first Democrat to hold that office in 16 years—and work and interact with many interesting and capable individuals. When the wholesale electricity price spikes began in late May of 2000, some new people joined that mix, and then many more by late fall and the beginning of the new year as the price spikes soared higher, and blackouts loomed as we entered an energy policy twilight zone.

So many years later, I had the good fortune to interact with many of these individuals again as I conducted research for this book and attempted to put all the pieces together. I would like to express my great appreciation to them for the interviews they engaged in with me, as listed in the Appendix.

At the height of the crisis in January 2001, I was already laboring in the trenches to address it; but if the late Nancy McFadden, senior advisor to the governor, had not directed me to meet with two economists early that month, it's less likely that I would be writing this book. These two economists, Severin Borenstein from UC Berkeley and Stanford University's Frank Wolak, helped bring me up to speed in understanding electricity markets in what seemed like a crash-course graduate seminar. I corresponded regularly with them after this first meeting, and by spring I also began corresponding with James Bushnell, then the research director for the University of California Energy Institute (now the Energy Institute at Haas). Though the urgency of addressing the crisis necessitated a deep dive into "competitive" electricity markets and how they can go wrong, this topic and related matters, for some reason still not totally clear, fascinated me and drove my effort to attain extensive knowledge.

I want to thank Frank, Jim, and Severin for their excellent academic work over the years, and especially for their work—and that of other experts such as MIT's Paul Joskow—on the energy matters I dealt with in the Davis administration and, after that, as a consultant in the California legislature. They also provided great feedback on my ideas for this book and reviewed selected chapters. In that regard, I also want to thank UC Berkeley's Ken Alex, Carl Blumstein, Ethan Elkind, and Dave Rapson from UC Davis.

Outside of academia, I want to express my gratitude to Adrienne Alvord and Bob Epstein for their "present-at-the-creation" insights on California energy policy from 2000 through 2010 and for their reviews of several chapters of my book. I also need to give a shout out to Ralph Cavanagh, Mike Florio, Matt Freedman, Annie Notthoff, Jan Smutny-Jones, and V. John White for their invaluable input.

In addition, I want to convey my appreciation to two former Davis administration colleagues, Linda Adams and Susan Kennedy, who went on to become Governor Arnold Schwarzenegger's CalEPA secretary and his chief of staff, respectively. Linda became one of my closest friends from Davis's staff, and that friendship was no doubt nurtured by the two of us having cabins on Donner Summit in the Sierra Nevada Mountains where we had many great barbeques and starry nights with friends years ago. Those fond memories popped up in our more recent discussions about California's energy saga. My engaging and informative interview with Susan focused mainly on her time working for Schwarzenegger during the effort to reach a deal on Assembly Bill 32, the landmark Global Warming Solutions Act of 2006.

Our former boss, Governor Davis, provided me not only the opportunity to work for him but also proved generous with his time when I wrote this book. I had several in-depth discussions with him, and he also granted me access to his gubernatorial records at the California State Archives. My thanks go out to another former Davis colleague, Panorea Avdis, and Nick Warshaw for helping to facilitate that access.

In addition, Garry South, Davis's long-time campaign manager and political advisor, provided recollections of behind-the-scenes discussions and deliberations that proved critical to understanding the political dynamics of the crisis and its near-term aftermath.

I also want to thank two other individuals I worked for: CalEPA secretaries Winston Hickox (under Davis) and Terry Tamminen (under Schwarzenegger). I worked closely with Winston during the crisis, and in 2003 he asked me to be his deputy secretary, which I enthusiastically accepted. He has long been a good friend and provided keen insights while I was writing my manuscript. When Schwarzenegger became governor, Terry kept me on as deputy secretary for several months—not a common occurrence for a high-level appointee of a governor who had just been defeated. During our chat in 2023, we discussed the push-and-pull dynamics in Governor Schwarzenegger's office en route to the enactment of AB 32 and the early efforts to implement the bill.

Reporter Arthur J. O'Donnell provided me with transcripts of interviews (see Appendix) he conducted for a book he wrote about the California Independent System Operator, which manages the state's electricity grid, and helped me during the early days of my project with other materials he had. I also want to express my gratitude to two other reporters, Dan Morain and Nancy Vogel, for helping me frame the crisis.

In addition, I want to thank my developmental editor, Eric Engles, for convincing me how important it was to be a first-person storyteller, and not just a chronicler, of matters large and small in my narrative; and thanks to Stacy Eisenstark for recommending Eric for these consultations.

The now-happily retired editor of my first book, Peter Coveney, provided good advice on preparing my book proposal for submission to a publisher, and I eventually signed an agreement with Routledge. Anyone who's worked with an established publisher on a book that has seemingly countless endnotes and very lengthy references knows how meticulous one must be in that process. My editor, Grace Harrison, and senior editorial assistant, Matthew Shobbrook, have been just that, but also cordial, straightforward, and constructive. I also appreciate that the U.S. Department of Energy and the California Energy Commission provided me with high-resolution images for use in this book.

I can't help but feel that I'm leaving out other individuals I should recognize in this acknowledgment. Suffice it to say that, if I have, it's strictly my oversight. The same is true for any mistakes in my book. I can only hope they are few and minor.

Finally, I want to thank Oliver Dunskus, a fellow jazz guitar player from Dusseldorf, Germany, who I've only met in spirit. He wrote the only comprehensive biography of my ultimate guitar hero, and that of many others, Wes Montgomery—still *The* Master since his untimely death in 1968.

Having (mostly) retired in the summer of 2020 during the Covid pandemic, I felt like I had the time and energy to write a final book; and I was inclined—though not necessarily determined—to write it on the life and incredible guitar style and musicality of Montgomery. When Oliver's book came out in late 2020, that biographic void had been filled. So, I then focused exclusively on my *other* book idea, which centered on the electricity crisis instead of the *sui generis* electric guitar maestro.

My determination to write this book gained steam in 2021 during the recall campaign against California Governor Gavin Newsom. There couldn't help but be comparisons to the recall campaign against Governor Davis, especially given that the state experienced a few unexpected rolling blackouts under Newsom for the first time since 2001. Many of the comments in the media got basic facts about the crisis wrong, and that served as a catalyst for me to finally get this project rolling. I now hope it fills the void in good books on this topic and spurs further research, and perhaps even aspiration.

Abbreviations

AB	Assembly Bill
ACA	Affordable Care Act (aka "Obamacare")
ACR	Assembly Concurrent Resolution
ARRA	American Recovery and Reinvestment Act
BP	British Petroleum
CAISO	California Independent System Operator
CalEPA	California Environmental Protection Agency
CARB	California Air Resources Board
CAT	Climate Action Team
CEC	California Energy Commission
CLECA	California Large Energy Consumers Association
CMA	California Manufacturers Association
CPUC	California Public Utilities Commission
CSI	California Solar Initiative
CTC	Competition Transition Charge
DOE	U.S. Department of Energy
DWR	California Department of Water resources
E2	Environmental Entrepreneurs
EDF	Environmental Defense Fund
EIA	Energy Information Agency
EJ	environmental justice
EO	executive order
EOB	Electricity Oversight Board
ESP	energy service provider
ETS	Emissions Trading System
FERC	Federal Energy Regulatory Commission
GGDR/CSA	Governor Gray Davis Records/California State Archives
GHG	greenhouse gas
IEP	Independent Energy Producers
IOU	investor-owned utility
kWh	kilowatt hour
LADWP	Los Angeles Department of Water and Power
LBNL	Lawrence Berkeley National Laboratory

LCFS	low carbon fuel standard
MIT	Massachusetts Institute of Technology
MOU	memorandum of understanding
MWh	megawatt hour
NAP	national allocation plans
NEG	National Energy Group (PG&E)
NEM	net energy metering
NRDC	Natural Resources Defense Council
PG&E	Pacific Gas & Electric
PPD	preferred policy decision
PPIC	Public Policy Institute of California
PURPA	Public Utilities Regulatory Policy Act
PX	Power Exchange
QFs	qualifying facilities
RPS	Renewable Portfolio Standard
SB	Senate Bill
SCE	Southern California Edison
SDG&E	San Diego Gas & Electric
TURN	The Utility Reform Network
TVA	Tennessee Valley Authority
UC	University of California

Introduction

If California had not undertaken a massive and risky experiment in deregulating the state's electricity market in 1996, shifting the state's energy policy toward a far "greener" and less carbon-intensive foundation would have been a hard sell in the first decade of the 21st century. But that deregulation experiment, pushed by a determined Republican governor and passed unanimously by legislators, failed spectacularly beginning in May 2000 due primarily to manipulation of the electricity market by unscrupulous energy marketers and plant operators. Wholesale power prices rose exponentially as market machinations, driven mainly by intentional reductions of electricity output at newly privatized natural gas generation facilities, destabilized the electricity grid and wreaked economic havoc.

As evidence of the market manipulation grew, Democratic governor Gray Davis and others seized the opportunity to demonize these private generators and traders operating in California as "energy pirates." They forged a new narrative in which diversifying energy resources emerged as the best choice for Californians. As such, the power pendulum began to swing to the green energy advocates who had been largely trampled by the ill-fated deregulation stampede in the mid-1990s. The move toward more environmental sustainability continued under Davis's Republican successor, Arnold Schwarzenegger, and in 2006 resulted in landmark climate-change legislation that made California even more of a champion of green policies and practices. The Golden State, long a leader in environmental stewardship, played a key role in galvanizing the sustainability movement in the U.S. and worldwide. In 2009, the "California effect"[1] coursed through President Barack Obama's determination to direct over $90 billion in the American Recovery and Reinvestment Act (ARRA) to sustainable energy endeavors. He succeeded.

By the end of the first decade of the 21st century, the nascent foundation for environmentally sustainable growth in the U.S., particularly regarding energy, had been established despite a gauntlet of challenges. This book is about how that happened, beginning with its calamitous catalyst, the California electricity crisis.

DOI: 10.4324/9781003518150-1

***

During an interview after the crisis, which had battered his reputation as an effective leader, Davis tersely asserted that "when I ran for governor in 1998, not one human being asked me about electricity."[2] His campaign manager, Garry South, echoed that recollection. He noted that education, the environment, and abortion garnered the most attention and that electricity concerns never came up during Davis's debates with his Republican opponent, Attorney General Dan Lungren, or in press conferences with reporters.[3]

It's somewhat ironic that the topic never came up given that the 1998 state ballot included Proposition 9, an initiative that would have partially repealed the electricity deregulation plan enacted in 1996. However, that initiative, backed mainly by consumer groups unhappy with cost-recovery provisions that benefited large utilities, never polled well and ultimately was rejected by more than 73 percent of voters—one the most lopsided defeats of an initiative in California history. This defeat occurred alongside Davis's landslide victory over Lungren. When Davis became governor in January 1999, the deregulation effort seemed to be going well, and energy concerns were not even on the back burner of the policy agenda. The only serious concerns about potential problems in the new market had been raised outside of the capitol, and they received scant attention.

While not *predicting* significant price spikes, University of California economists Severin Borenstein and James Bushnell presented a California market-simulation paper in 1997 that showed potential wholesale price spikes could be significant. In that presentation at the annual POWER Conference of the University of California Energy Institute in Berkeley, they noted that California's new market, which had yet to launch, might be gamed, particularly during peak demand periods in years when hydroelectric power was limited due to low precipitation. Borenstein and Bushnell maintained that, unlike the state-regulated investor-owned utilities, the market's "competitive" new "firms might have an incentive to restrict output" to raise wholesale prices four or five times, or more, than average. While conference attendees' views varied on the possibility that tactics in the new market might include generators deliberately withholding output, the idea that prices could jump as high as the two economists claimed seemed unfathomable. As one utility executive steadfastly declared at the conference, "prices will never get that high." Later that year, Borenstein, who served on the board of governors for the new market's electricity transaction platform known as the Power Exchange, privately expressed his concern about potential gaming to the board's chair, the nonchalant septuagenarian S. David Freeman. With decades of experience running *regulated* power operations, Freeman assured Borenstein, "don't worry, son; we've got that covered."[4]

Like every other policy staff member in the governor's office, I knew very little about electricity and energy markets prior to the crisis. I had a decent understanding of California politics given that my dissertation for my Ph.D.

in history at the University of Arizona was on the rise of the California conservative movement after World War II, culminating with Ronald Reagan defeating Edmund "Pat" Brown for governor in 1966. My dissertation became a book in 1998, and I parlayed that and an organized labor connection into an opportunity to help Davis during his campaign. I became Davis's senior policy analyst after he took office. The governor and his inner circle considered me to be a quick and reliable study, so when the initial electricity price spikes began, I became part of the small (but growing) team in his office that increasingly focused on the problem over the summer of 2000. By the end of the year, that "problem" had become an unprecedented crisis. The governor's senior advisor, Nancy McFadden, then tapped me—"hey, you've got a Ph.D."—to be the liaison to the energy economists who had identified the potential for manipulation that now seemed to plague the state's restructured market. From then on, I did almost nothing but work at all hours on matters related to the crisis until late summer, when it abated, though its impact lasted for years (and in some ways continues).

***

So, how did the California electricity crisis generate a green wave? It's no surprise that a huge and protracted event like the crisis in California, with roughly 12 percent of the nation's population, would have significant ripple effects and consequences for government policy. Political scientist Roger Karapin has effectively described the impact of the crisis as one of the key "windows of opportunity" for green policy reforms made possible by "the right circumstances converg[ing] to overcome the barriers posed" by "political institutions and certain socioeconomic structures." He rightly attributes California laws enacted in 2002 that increased the state's commitment to renewable energy and to decreasing greenhouse gas (GHG) emissions from motor vehicles as momentous "policy window" achievements that almost certainly would not have happened if not for the crisis. Moreover, he appropriately notes that the "crisis had major short-and-long-term effects on many aspects of California energy policy," especially from 2005 through 2008.[5]

While I generally agree with Karapin's perspective, my deeper dive into the same political battles in California arrives at a different conclusion. Karapin offers a broader and more theoretical assessment of U.S. climate policy up to 2015 whereas I mainly highlight the politics behind California policies that spurred green technology up to 2010—and to significant fruition since then. (Though our emphases and methods diverge, our arguments clearly have a strong nexus.) As such, and understandably, Karapin barely mentions Obama's $90 billion investment in sustainable energy in 2009; but I view that investment as the crest of a great green wave, notwithstanding its subsidence in 2010 during ill-fated efforts to establish a federal program to curtail GHG emissions.

As Joel Jaeger with the World Resources Institute noted in 2020, due to the ARRA funding, the "U.S. was the only country in the world that invested a ton into renewable energy and building efficiency." Joseph Aldy, the lone economist working with Obama's top energy adviser, Carol Browner, to fine-tune the green stimulus package after Obama's election in 2008, noted that "by 2011, we were up to what the U.S. Energy Information Agency [had] forecast" for wind power installations by 2030. "We blew it away."[6] Utility-scale solar energy got a similar big boost. In a July 2023 interview, Obama, who had touted California's sustainable energy and climate policies as a presidential candidate beginning in 2007, acknowledged that action on climate change "is not happening as fast as we'd like, but I constantly remind our young leaders that we've made enormous progress." He noted that when he became president, "the entire clean energy industry was about to collapse in the United States. Now its booming."[7]

As I argue in this book, the genesis of that boom can be traced back to California—even before the electricity crisis given Governor Jerry Brown's embrace of renewable energy (and efficiency) in the 1970s and early 1980s. But by the late 1980s through the 1990s, renewable energy, even in California, began to wither due to cost, political, and practicality concerns. During the latter half of 2000, the crisis breathed new life into green energy, though the resuscitation initially proved modest. In late August, three months after the wholesale price spikes began, the legislature passed a bill to maintain a retail rate surcharge established in the 1996 deregulation legislation for funding renewable technology, energy efficiency, and conservation. The new bill also directed the California Energy Commission "to prepare an investment plan aimed at the development of a fully competitive and self-sustaining California renewable-energy supply."[8] But the bill stopped short of requiring incremental increases in utilization of renewable energy in contrast to laws that did which had already been enacted in Massachusetts and Texas. There simply was not sufficient support for that requirement in the legislature. The most notable energy legislation enacted in 2000 was Senate Bill 970, which established the California Energy Security and Reliability Act to promote clean energy and expedite generation siting and electricity demand-reduction programs. In September, Davis, after signing AB 970 and a few other clean energy bills, emphasized the need to "accelerate the contribution of solar energy and other renewables, and continue to focus on energy conservation, to provide affordable, reliable energy."[9]

By mid-October the monthly average wholesale price for electricity dropped substantially below the summer month peak, but it was still well above the cost in early May before the price spikes had begun. As we headed into the cooler and lower electricity demand months, everyone—from utility executives to energy economists to government staffers like me—wondered if the average price would soon settle at some semblance of "normal." But, after five months of exceedingly high prices and unprecedented market volatility, uncertainty ruled the day. With the seasonal dip in demand in mind, that collective uncertainty yielded somewhat to expectations that prices would come down further—not necessarily to what they were prior to the May price spikes, but at least lower than in mid-October. But by early December, to the disbelief of most everyone, the average wholesale price soared past its peak summer average to a stratospheric level. And the crushing costs continued day after day into the new year.

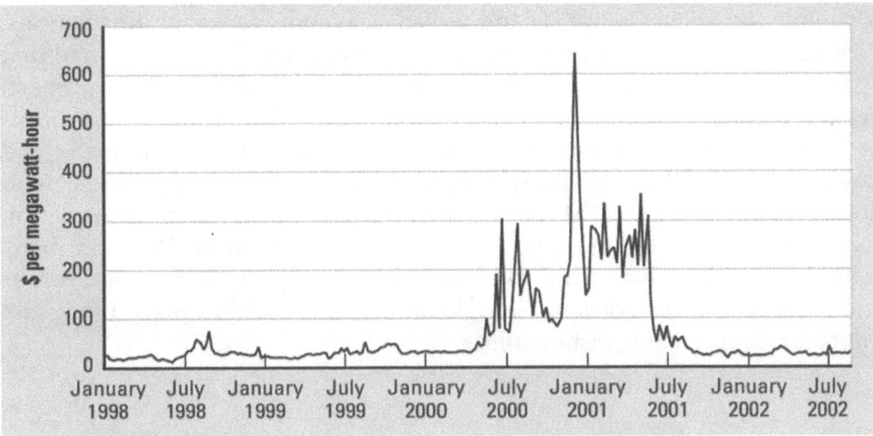

Figure I.1 Weekly average peak electricity prices in West Coast spot markets, 1998–2002

Source: Graphic excerpted from *California's Electricity Market: A Post-Crisis Progress Report,* by Carl Pechman, 2007. Public Policy Institute of California.

As the crisis raged into 2001, the Federal Energy Regulatory Commission, which had the authority to curtail the "unjust and unreasonable" costs, continued to refrain from doing so in California and neighboring states despite ample evidence of market machinations. Moreover, there were glaring indications of manipulation in the supply of natural gas in southern California. More than fed up with the obvious and long unabated fossil-fuel-driven exploits behind the electricity crisis, by the summer of 2001, Davis endorsed the establishment of a renewable energy requirement for electricity that would increase incrementally. (He didn't do so reluctantly as Karapin and others have asserted.[10]) And the following year, Californians widely supported the legislation that ultimately established this requirement in state law along with another landmark bill to cut GHG emissions on the state's roadways.

After Schwarzenegger ousted Gray Davis in the recall election of 2003, the former actor used his immense celebrity to promote green goals. However, as a disciple of the free-market economist Milton Friedman, he also wanted to give deregulation another try, as did many of his key supporters and staff members. His effort to do so did not go over well with the Democrats who controlled the legislature and had endured the crisis. Moreover, the public had no appetite for revisiting deregulation either. It took Schwarzenegger a while to accept that, and he suffered some significant political bumps and bruises when he tried to strong-arm his broader conservative agenda, especially in 2005. By the end of that year, he decided to move in a different direction and to cooperate more with Democrats on green policies. This tactical shift resulted in his crowning achievement, the Global Warming Solutions Act of 2006, which established a program to reduce GHG emissions across economic sectors in California and served as a model for other jurisdictions.

When Obama became president in 2009, pundits and media reported that Schwarzenegger might become his energy "czar," but that never went much beyond speculation. Nevertheless, "Arnold" and Obama jointly sought, as best they could, to promote, establish, and bolster green technologies and standards in 2009 as the transformative decade for energy policy wound down. During and after 2010, the movement to build on that transformation encountered much tougher political terrain in Washington, DC, and many states.[11] Still, deep blue California forged ahead, albeit with varied results and prospects, as America and our global village labored through a long and difficult slog to greater sustainability.

Notes

1 The "California effect" is a descriptor coined in 1995 by David Vogel, a political scientist at the University of California, Berkeley. In a recent book, Vogel stated that he came up with this "geographic designation" after "learning how California's stringent regulation of automotive emissions had strengthened those of Germany…." Vogel, *California Greenin': How the Golden State Became an Environmental Leader* (Princeton, NJ: Princeton University Press, 2018), ix.

2 Davis interview in the documentary by Alex Gibney, Matt Houser, and John McCullough. *Enron: The Smartest Guys in the Room* (USA, 2005).

3 Interview with Garry South, July 1, 2021.

4 Severin Borenstein and James Bushnell, "An Empirical Analysis of the Potential for Market Power in California's Electricity Industry," *The Journal of Industrial Economics*, Vol. XXVLI, No. 3 (September 1999): 319-20; interview with Severin Borenstein, July 18, 2021.

5 Roger Karapin, *Political Opportunities for Climate Policy: California, New York, and the Federal Government* (New York: Cambridge University Press, 2016), 11, 139.

6 Jaeger and Aldy quoted in Shannon Osaka, "Obama's Recovery Act Breathed Life into Renewables. Now They Need Rescuing," *Grist*, June 1, 2020.

7 Obama interview with Christiane Amanpour, *CNN*, June 27, 2023. https://www.rev.com/blog/transcripts/former-president-obama-interview-with-cnns-christiane-amanpour-transcript. High interest rates tied to a jump in inflation created challenges for clean energy projects during the latter half of 2022 and the following year.

8 Senate Bill 1194, Senate Floor Analysis, August 31, 2000.

9 Governor Davis, "Governor Davis Signs Legislation to Promote Renewable Energy," Press Release, September 21, 2000.

10 Karapin and fellow political scientist David Vogel—in their books cited in endnotes 1 and 5—claim that Davis was disinclined to promote green policies, but that's not true. Prior to becoming governor, Davis had served as Governor Jerry Brown's chief of staff, and Davis shared Brown's affinity for conservation and renewable energy. It is fair to say that Davis was not a crusader in this regard, but he was a solid supporter.

11 For an insightful account of the often-successful pushback by business interests against green policies in certain states during this time, see Leah Cardamore Stokes, *Short Circuiting Policy: Interest Groups and the Battle over Clean Energy and Climate Policy in the American States* (New York: Oxford University Press, 2020).

1 Prosperity Fades into a Power Crisis

Four months into the year 2000, California was enjoying the best of times. "[T]his cheerful spring," opined George Skelton, an often-crusty political columnist for the *Los Angeles Times*, "hills are green, reservoirs are full" and, due to a $12.3 billion budget surplus, the state "never had so much money to give away." Crime and unemployment rates were lower than they had been in several decades and Silicon Valley's technology boom had created what Democratic Governor Gray Davis called "the best economy in the history of man."[1]

In Sacramento, Governor Davis, a primary political beneficiary of this "fiscal phenomenon," basked in the bounty.[2] For much of the previous year, a reporter for *The New York Times* observed, the governor's actions had been defined by "a string of media superlatives, legislative achievements, fiscal luck, political popularity and, yes, success."[3] Davis was sitting on top of the political world, and staff in the governor's office, myself included, were sitting there behind him. We were on such a roll that it seemed nothing could go wrong.

At the end of May, Davis's chief political advisor, Garry South, received a phone call from Bob Foster, a senior vice president of Southern California Edison (SCE), an investor-owned utility (IOU) that provided electricity to millions of customers in the state. Foster told South that the cost of wholesale electricity in the market in which Edison purchased power for its retail customers had spiked on May 22 and had inexplicably remained very high since then.[4] The spike began on a day that was unseasonably warm, even in the usually cool San Francisco Bay Area, causing millions of Californians to run their air conditioners. Within a couple of days, temperatures throughout the state had returned to seasonal norms and power demand had dropped, but electricity prices had not come down accordingly.

Foster and South met for lunch at the City Club in Los Angeles to further discuss the problem, and Foster brought brightly colored charts and graphs to help make his points. South listened intently, especially given that the cost and supply of electricity had not been an issue in Davis's 1998 gubernatorial campaign or first year in office. Not one to beat around the bush, Foster informed South that Edison, along with the even bigger

DOI: 10.4324/9781003518150-2

California IOU to the north, Pacific Gas & Electric (PG&E), were unavoidably buying wholesale power at a price higher than they could charge their retail customers. They were unable to pass along the higher cost because a retail rate freeze was in effect until early 2002.[5] Foster's company was hemorrhaging cash every day and he was worried the situation wasn't just a temporary glitch.

The rate freeze had been included in Assembly Bill 1890, which, after it had been passed and signed in 1996, had "deregulated" the wholesale electricity market in California and restructured other key elements in the operation of the state's power grid. Undoing that rate freeze, which had helped secure a unanimous legislative vote for the bill, was not politically tenable. Both Edison and PG&E—two of the largest regulated energy utilities in the nation—had made handsome profits during the first two years of the restructured market that they helped create and had agreed to the freeze. If the wholesale cost problem persisted, it would surely become a major political and policy quagmire.

South soon talked with Davis, his chief of staff Lynn Schenk, and deputy chief of staff Susan Kennedy, and briefed them on his discussions with Foster. He warned of the troubles that might ensue if wholesale electricity costs did not return to normal. Invoking the legislation that everyone knew to be at issue, Davis was quick to note that he had never endorsed AB 1890 when it was being debated while he was lieutenant governor[6] (an elected position separate from the office of Republican governor Pete Wilson, who had strongly backed the bill). Moreover, he reminded his staffers, he had campaigned in 1998 as the "education governor" who would restore the state's once-envied public school system with increased funding and technological innovations from Silicon Valley—"to recapture California's rightful place at the head of the class," as he declared in his State of the State Address in 2000.[7] He did not want to be sidetracked from that mission.

In addition to having policy priorities that did not include utility reform or energy, the circumspect Davis practiced a centrist politics that constrained how he was prepared to act in response to mounting problems in the wholesale electricity market. As a "New Democrat," he supported business and limited government, in addition to being tough on crime, "family-friendly" on social issues, and a steady steward of California's environment and splendid natural geography. "Of all the candidates I have ever worked with," South, a veteran strategist, told *The New York Times* in early 2000, "Gray is the most anomalous blend of conservative beliefs and progressive instincts."[8] In that sense, Davis resembled President Bill Clinton, the quintessential New Democrat, but without the latter's charisma or deft communication skills. The governor proved quick to publicly joke about his staid ways, and I and other staffers privately joked that he had a closet full of the same neatly tailored, navy-blue Armani suit that he seemed to always be wearing. Prim, proper, and cautious, Davis turned his bland presence into a workmanlike asset. He approached the mid-point of his second year in office with a

62 percent approval rating,[9] four points higher than the vote percentage he had received in his landslide victory in 1998. He was well on his way to replicating, and perhaps even exceeding, the remarkable success of his first year. Nevertheless, it was apparent to everyone in the room that day that the brewing problem in the electricity market might shake up Davis's mission and challenge his political instincts.

On June 14, with the governor and legislators on the verge of a state budget agreement, the temperature in San Francisco reached a then-record 103 degrees. For the first time since World War II, about 100,000 PG&E customers in the city and a few other areas on the San Francisco peninsula experienced planned rolling blackouts as the operators of the state's electricity grid, known as the California Independent System Operator (CAISO), sought to avoid a wave of larger uncontrolled blackouts that could shut down the entire grid.[10] The record heat proved to be much bigger news than the blackouts given the general understanding that the former precipitated the latter. Once again, however, wholesale electricity prices spiked and then remained extremely high after the heat event despite a 48-hour high temperature drop of more than 40 degrees in San Francisco and a corresponding drop in electricity demand throughout northern California.

The events of June 14 and the persistence of high electricity prices quickly became a topic of broader and more intense discussion in the governor's office and elsewhere in the capitol. Indeed, just a day later, Davis directed the president of the California Public Utilities Commission (CPUC), Loretta Lynch, and the chair of the state's Electricity Oversight Board (EOB), Michael Kahn, to "investigate the circumstances" and reasons behind the state's escalating electricity problems. "Ensuring a reliable electric system is central to the health and safety of every Californian as well as California's continued economic growth," the governor declared. "Existing generation capacity simply must be available to use when Californians need the power."[11]

As we headed into July, shortcomings in the electricity market created by AB 1890 became increasingly clear as I reviewed a report from the CAISO's independent Market Surveillance Committee. Arguing that the state's electricity market lacked competition, the report asserted that "it makes little sense to attempt to run a competitive market for electricity in California for the current configuration of the California grid and set of available generation capacity."[12] Another research paper by two University of California economists maintained that in the restructured market, certain power generators "might have an incentive to reduce output to raise price" due to their "market power," a reference to the ability of one or more firms to raise and maintain prices above the level that would result under true competition.[13]

I discussed these studies with Staff Director John Stevens and Deputy Cabinet Secretary Vincent Harris who, along with me, were the point staffers in our nascent effort to get our arms around the electricity enigma. We soon came to grips with the fact that there was no AB 1890 contingency plan—or authority, as we rather shockingly learned—to remedy, or even significantly mitigate, insufficient market competition. The governor publicly acknowledged that reality. "When California deregulated the electricity market in 1996," he lamented on July 27, "consumers were promised that competition in the marketplace would be mature enough to ensure stable, if not reduced, prices. That is clearly not the case in California. The result is uncontrolled price spikes with no end in sight."[14]

***

To the extent any near-term relief might come, it would have to be from the Federal Energy Regulatory Commission (FERC). Pursuant to AB 1890, the FERC had become the regulator of the state's wholesale electricity market. Established in 1977 as part of the newly created Department of Energy and successor to the Federal Power Commission, the FERC began pushing hard in the 1990s to "restructure" electricity markets that were dominated by highly regulated utility "monopolies." In pursuit of lower costs through competition and greater operational efficiency, this effort gained momentum after the deregulation of seemingly similar monopolies such as the natural gas industry in the 1980s. In addition, the FERC was following the guidance established in the federal Energy Policy Act of 1992, which provided a long-term vision for the nation's electric services that embraced greater reliance on competition and market mechanisms.[15]

The FERC had encouraged and facilitated the restructuring of California's market, and the performance of that market would loom large given its size and reliance on mostly unfettered competition in wholesale transactions. Given the commission's functions and duties, Chairman James Hoecker announced in July that the FERC would investigate the high electricity prices in the West and California in particular. Shortly thereafter, Davis sent Hoecker a public letter lauding his action:

> Under the Federal Power Act [of 1935], FERC has an affirmative obligation to ensure that wholesale power rates under the jurisdiction are just and reasonable. I applaud your initiative to undertake an investigation into wholesale power rates. I am requesting that the Commission order immediate refunds to customers if this investigation determines that these rates are not just and reasonable.[16]

Prior to the price spikes, few Californians had even heard of the FERC, and far fewer understood the key role it now played in the state's electricity market. But now the commission was increasingly in the news and on the minds of those of us in the governor's office.

In early August, the CPUC and EOB released the report Davis had requested. It made clear the critical importance of the FERC's role, which had been the state's jurisdiction prior to AB 1890. The report noted that the FERC permitted power plant owners to sell wholesale power at unregulated "market-based rates" even though "California markets are not now competitive," and there was "very little evidence to support those rates as just and reasonable." Instead, power plant owners were garnering profits that went far beyond a "fair" return on the firm's cost of production. "FERC's assumption that the market will discipline wholesale prices," the report concluded, "is not a reasonable one at this time in California."[17]

The 70-page CPUC/EOB report proved to be very helpful for understanding the state's electricity problems and how we got into our predicament. Outside of John Stevens, who had served as chief consultant for the Assembly Transportation Committee, no one in the governor's office had any notable energy experience, let alone expertise. Frankly, prior to the May 2000 wholesale price spikes, there had not appeared to be a need for such expertise because energy stakeholders had not raised significant concerns about the cost and supply of electricity with our office or the legislature, and the market seemed to be performing reasonably well.

On March 14, the state Senate Energy and Utilities Committee had held an informational hearing on energy supply and related preparedness "for Summer 2000 and beyond" that included testimony from IOU representatives and top state energy officials. The CAISO's chief operating officer, Kellan Fluckiger, told the committee members that, barring an aberrant reduction in electricity generation available to the state's grid, "we will likely be able to meet normal summer peak" demand. The committee's "Issue Overview," which reflected the discussants' broad perspective, observed that although electricity demand had increased in recent years and that on "several occasions" the state's operating reserve had dipped below the required margin of 7 percent, 11 new power plants were scheduled to come online over the next two years. The Overview concluded that while the grid could be strained when major heat events and peak demand spikes occurred, "the overall demand for power has yet to outstretch the supply."[18]

In keeping with that sanguine observation about the supply of electricity, we learned not long after the June 14 rolling blackouts that they likely would have been avoided if several generation facilities had not shut down for unscheduled maintenance issues. Nevertheless, we knew we needed a significant action plan to address the growing challenges. The CPUC/EOB report provided initial action recommendations but at the same time explained how and why the state's options were limited—mainly due to the FERC's laissez faire approach to wholesale market prices and the inability to quickly add more electricity generation capacity to the grid.

Coinciding with the release of the CPUC/EOB report on August 2, Davis announced that he had requested Attorney General Bill Lockyer to investigate "possible manipulation in the wholesale marketplace." To address other potential factors in the crisis, he also issued executive orders directing state agencies to "streamline the review process for siting new power plants without compromising environmental laws or public health and safety protections," and to take "immediate emergency actions" to conserve electricity during power alerts from the CAISO. He also created the California Energy Reliability Task Force, "modeled" after the president's National Security Council, to coordinate steps taken by the state's energy agencies.[19]

Comprising agency secretaries and other top administration officials, the Task Force focused on increasing power generation and enhancing transmission, particularly along the often-congested Path 15 transmission corridor that linked northern and Southern California. The Task Force met for the first time on August 10, and I and most of the attendees struggled to find firm footing on this still relatively new and exceedingly complex terrain. It initially seemed as though we were operating from the CliffsNotes version of an electricity market textbook, assisted by a few energy policy veterans from the CPUC, EOB, and California Energy Commission who awaited further direction on the game plan. I could not help but note the irony that these energy officials were part of the very bureaucratic gauntlet that the governor aimed to bypass in approving and building power plants and transmission infrastructure. But these were among the few things we had any control over, and we needed all the help we could get.

***

In addition to providing an overview of the state's electricity woes, the CPUC/EOB report detailed how, in the summer of 2000, San Diego Gas & Electric (SDG&E) customers, by a twist of legislative fate, lost the retail rate-freeze protection that still insulated PG&E and Edison customers. Compared to the previous summer, SDG&E customers saw their bills nearly double. While that burdened all the utility's ratepayers, it proved especially perilous to the viability of many businesses. A San Diego restaurant owner demanding state action to rein in the sky-high costs noted that her rate-freeze protected bill of $5700 in June had jumped to $10,204 in July after the freeze was lifted.[20]

Spurred by the SDG&E ratepayer dilemma, Davis spoke by phone with President Bill Clinton on August 10 about the urgent need for the FERC to take quick and effective action. "Time is of the essence, Mr. President," the governor noted in a public letter to Clinton after the call. "San Diego consumers have paid an enormous price for deregulation in a market that no one believes is functionally competitive." He excoriated "the outrageous wholesale prices being charged by out-of-state generators" and thanked the president for his "support in requesting that the FERC accelerate its investigation and ultimately recognize that the market is dysfunctional."[21]

AB 1890 permitted the removal of an IOU's rate freeze after the utility recovered all its "stranded costs"—which critics preferred to call "bad investments." This provision served as a *quid pro quo* for the IOUs to recoup the cost of certain assets through a customer surcharge that would otherwise not likely be recovered in the "competitive" market established pursuant to AB 1890. In return, the IOUs agreed to cede control of the power grid to the

CAISO and, to promote competition, sell their natural gas-fueled generation plants to private "merchant generators" subject only to FERC jurisdiction.

That *quid pro quo* notwithstanding, when AB 1890 was enacted the prospective removal of the rate freeze was envisioned by supporters, including the utilities, as a positive development because the IOUs would then *decrease* their rate-based revenue requirement after fully recovering their stranded costs through the surcharge. The bill's authors even "anticipated" another 10 percent rate reduction after the surcharge was eliminated by no later than early 2002.[22] But the electricity market reality in the summer of 2000 had transmogrified that expectation into a burgeoning consumer nightmare with huge political and financial implications.

How did SDG&E manage to fully recover its stranded costs well before SCE and PG&E? Major cost overruns for the construction of two nuclear plants in the 1960s and 1970s, along with many above-market-cost contracts for renewable and other "alternative" energy projects in the 1980s, had burdened Edison and PG&E with immense debt. In contrast, the smaller SDG&E only had a limited stake in one of the nuclear plants and few costly alternative energy contracts. So, after SDG&E fully recovered its more manageable stranded costs in summer 1999, its rate freeze came to an end. In accordance with AB 1890, PG&E and SCE had until early 2002 to recover all their costs, but the freeze would remain in place.

The SDG&E rate shock sparked a "ratepayer rebellion" led by Michael Shames, the executive director of the San Diego-based Utility Consumers' Action Network. "SDG&E has become the corporate equivalent of the gang that couldn't shoot straight," he maintained. Throughout the 4200 square miles of SDG&E territory, company employees experienced verbal and physical abuse. For its part, SDG&E maintained that it was merely passing along higher costs so it could remain solvent. "I wish we had foreseen this market spike," the company's CEO said apologetically. "We didn't."[23]

The shockwaves of the ratepayer revolt could be felt far to the north at the CPUC in San Francisco, and particularly in the state capitol in Sacramento. Consumer groups and politicians representing SDG&E customers initially appealed to the CPUC to impose a retail rate cap for SDG&E customers, but that effort fell short by a vote of 3–2 due to opposition from the three pro-deregulation commissioners who had been appointed for fixed-terms by Governor Wilson. The commission approved a much more modest proposal that critics widely panned. Democratic State Assemblymember Susan Davis and Senator Dede Alpert, who represented districts served by SDG&E, warned of the likelihood of a severe economic recession in the region if businesses shut down or scaled back operations and laid off employees to avoid high electricity costs.[24] They vowed to pass and send to the governor AB 2290 (S. Davis), which would re-impose the rate freeze on SDG&E retroactive to June 2000. The bill had already passed in the Senate but faced significant Republican opposition in the Assembly.

The challenge of passing the bill in the Assembly with the required two-thirds majority vote for it to take effect immediately proved daunting, and that was not lost on me and other newly minted energy staffers in the governor's office. Chief of Staff Lynn Schenk, who had served one term in the U.S. House of Representatives for constituents in San Diego's 49th district, made sure of that.

AB 2290 was "held" in the Assembly Appropriations Committee, so three days short of adjournment of the legislative session, Assemblymember Davis had to find a different bill that she could "gut and amend"—that is, delete and replace the contents of one of her other bills with the rate freeze provisions—and secure the support of Democratic legislative leaders to pass it. This process, while not uncommon, created, at the session's 11th hour, a tougher task to secure the votes for passage. On the second-to-last day of the session, Schenk directed me and chief deputy legislative secretary, Linda Adams, to go to the Assembly Speaker's office and help round up the 54 votes for Davis's new bill, AB 265. And so we did. Amid other scrambles and bill drills that were part and parcel of the end-of-session clamor, AB 265 received a bipartisan 58 "aye" votes, while 14 Republicans cast all the "no" votes. With the governor's signature, the SDG&E ratepayer rebellion ended.[25] But the wholesale cost calamity continued.

***

Peak electricity demand in California is tied to increased air conditioner use from June through September. In early August we learned that peak demand had actually been lower in 2000 than in 1999 during the highest wholesale cost days.[26] With that in mind, there was a mix of hope and expectation in the governor's office that prices would come down by October when daytime temperature highs moderated. Though the average price for wholesale electricity did come down that month to its lowest point since June, it was still more than twice as high as it had been during October of the previous year. Then in November, one of the lowest demand months, the average price soared higher than it had gone in any of the summer months.[27] This jump was the strongest indication yet that there was a disconnection between price and consumer demand. Despite increasing evidence to the contrary, many supporters of the deregulated market, including prominent economists, continued to maintain that the cost problem was tied to the state's lack of electricity plants and capacity to meet the growing customer demand.

That contention seemed to be contradicted by the FERC in early November when it found ample evidence of market power. "There is clear evidence," the commission opined, "that the California market structure and rules provide the opportunity for sellers to exercise market power when [electricity supplies are] tight and can result in unjust and unreasonable rates."[28] While we were glad that the FERC made this finding, we knew that even when the electricity supply was not tight, wholesale costs remained bafflingly high, strongly indicating not just market power but deliberate and largely hidden manipulation.

Whatever faith we had in the FERC dissipated when the commissioners cited a legal technicality that FERC attorneys maintained prevented the commission from ordering any refunds from merchant generators from late May to early October of 2000. Though California Attorney General Bill Lockyer "vigorously disputed" that position,[29] the FERC also contended that there wasn't enough evidence against any individual power supplier to justify ordering a refund.[30] As frustrating as that position was, we were hoping that the FERC would at least stop the bleeding going forward. However, the commission refused to impose a region-wide wholesale price cap in the West. Adding insult to injury, the exorbitant wholesale costs went even higher.

Given the FERC's inaction, retail rate increases seemed to be the only near-term way to potentially bring down the high wholesale prices. The increases would exert this effect by reducing demand, but that hardly appeared to be a sure thing given the persistence of high costs during lower demand periods. Moreover, for the governor and legislators, the prospect of revoking the rate freeze and consequently enabling a significant rate hike held no appeal whatsoever as that would violate the resounding promise of lower rates made by Governor Wilson and legislators in 1996.

With its solvency now threatened, PG&E took legal action in federal court on November 8 to bypass the rate freeze, despite having agreed to that provision in AB 1890. "The wholesale power costs which the utility has incurred," PG&E maintained, "are included in filed rates which FERC has authorized and approved, and under the United States Constitution and numerous federal and state court decisions, such costs cannot be disallowed by state regulators."[31] As both the stakes and the complexity of the crisis grew, it seemed more intractable than ever. Heading into the holidays, the mood in the capitol was anything but festive.

On December 6, Governor Davis and First Lady Sharon Davis, joined by a seven-year-old boy from Bakersfield, kept a 70-year tradition by pressing a button to light the 56-foot state Christmas tree on the Capitol Lawn. Half an hour after the 4000 bulbs on the white fir tree began glistening for the merry crowd, they went dark. The governor, seeking to lead by example with energy conservation, had turned the lights off during yet another power alert. "Tonight, while some Californians are going without power," Davis told the holiday revelers, "let the light in our hearts represent the true spirit of the season." Right before he turned out the lights, he wryly noted, "We're going to send FERC a picture of the tree going dark."[32]

Two days later, the cost crisis went from oppressive to almost unfathomable when the CAISO's CEO, Terry Winter, removed the wholesale price caps that had been in place for various types of power purchases since July 1998. And he did so without the knowledge of Davis, the CAISO Board of Governors, or the FERC, though the latter quickly concurred with the decision.

Winter maintained that CASIO could no longer purchase enough electricity with the cap in place, and he had no choice but to accept power at any price provided that the sellers could justify the costs. Touting the "accountability" his action would bring "for these outrageous costs," he maintained that "my people were making phone deals—10 to 15 an hour—when I needed them running the grid. We had a gun to our head." While the governor certainly agreed that the costs were outrageous, he blasted Winter's action: "This ruling, issued in the dark of night without notice to anyone in California, is an outrageous assault on the consumers and businesses of California by a federal agency answerable to no one and an unaccountable [state] entity that acted without the authorization of its board of directors." He vowed to fight to rescind the decision and threatened to "dismantle the current CAISO and reconstitute it in a way that will be responsive to Californians."[33]

The removal of the price caps at a time when wholesale costs already dwarfed the prices paid during the summer jarred everyone in the administration working on energy policy. The electricity expense ledger boggled our minds: When Davis became governor, the average wholesale cost of electricity was around 3 cents per kWh—or about $30 per MWh.* By December 2000, average wholesale costs had jumped to well over $300 per MWh, more than double the already exorbitant average cost during the summer months when demand, and especially peak demand, was higher.

The FERC-approved price caps—which ranged from $250 to $750 per MWh—had been put in place by CAISO and its board early on to protect against stratospheric price spikes while the market "matured" to the point that inflated costs would be squeezed out by robust competition. But now, two-and-a-half years after the imposition of the first cap when those spikes were short and infrequent, and on the heels of the FERC finding "clear evidence" of uncompetitive market power, and with the average cost of electricity much higher than ever, the price caps were being removed? That decision added a giant lump of coal to our holiday headache as we grasped for coping mechanisms and policy prescriptions in an energy twilight zone that held yet another twist.

On December 13 Vice President Al Gore conceded to George W. Bush, the Republican governor of Texas, in a hotly contested presidential election in which Gore won the popular vote but lost the electoral college tally after the Supreme Court ended a Florida vote recount in Bush's favor. Gore had campaigned for Davis in 1998, attended his inauguration ceremony, and beat Bush in California by a 12 percent margin. Davis strongly endorsed Gore's presidential candidacy and campaigned for him. "We have very few differences," the governor noted. "We both served in Vietnam. We are both longtime public servants. Neither of us wins elections on charisma alone," he joked.[34]

* Retail prices are expressed in cents per kilowatt hour (kWh). A megawatt hour (MWh), which is the standard measure for utility-scale wholesale costs, is equal to 1000 kWh.

The coup de grâce the Supreme Court delivered to Gore's presidential ambitions also dealt a blow to our prospects of bringing the electricity crisis under some semblance of control in the near term. The Clinton-Gore administration had not been as helpful as we had hoped in addressing the crisis, but even the modest assistance we did receive was more than we could reasonably hope for from Bush, a former Texas oilman who had strong support from the energy industry. Those supporters included Texas-based companies, such as Enron Corporation, that were running California's IOUs through the wholesale cost wringer. Enron's founder and CEO, Ken Lay, who had a long and close relationship with the Bush family, had donated more than $500,000 to Bush's political coffers, and as a member of the governor's Business Council, he extoled deregulation and excoriated price caps. Bush remained silent on California's crisis but tipped his hand when he appointed Lay to his transition team for energy policy and made it known that a number of others with energy industry ties were in line for high-level appointments.[35]

***

In stark contrast to the ebullience of the 1999 gathering, Governor Davis's Christmas party for his staff and cabinet members in 2000 was subdued, though everyone tried to keep their chin up. After months of rate increase defiance, Davis and legislative leaders became merely reticent, and finally, just in time for Christmas, essentially acquiesced to rate hikes. There was no other realistic option. Whereas the end of the previous year posed the enviable prospect of government leaders being purveyors of the perks of unprecedented prosperity, at the end of 2000 Davis acknowledged that consumers would have to "bear some of the burden" to save the utilities from bankruptcy and the grid from potential collapse.[36] Consumer groups sharply criticized the pending state government actions as a utility "bailout" while everyone with a dog in the hunt—and there were many—girded for battle in the new year with renewed resolution.

The media captured this milieu with insightfully scathing synopses of the deregulation debacle. *Los Angeles Times* reporter Nancy Vogel declared that "deregulation" was supposed to reduce electricity costs but "instead shifted billions of dollars from utilities and consumers to energy companies and electricity brokers." This epic "miscalculation," she maintained, "was the result of critical misjudgments by the California Public Utilities Commission and the state Legislature." Davis did not escape criticism. Vogel's colleague, Dan Morain, described the months-long buildup of the crisis as "a little like a car crash in slow motion." While he noted that Davis was not directly responsible for the crash, he highlighted the "increasing chorus of critics" who maintained that the governor couldn't make tough decisions "and has dwelt too long on his rhetorical attacks."[37]

The State of State Address that the governor would deliver on January 8, 2001, was not only keenly anticipated by many Californians but also attracted national interest and media coverage given the dire circumstances California faced. The calamity had largely eclipsed the many accomplishments of Davis's first two years in office, and the Silicon Valley-based "tech bubble" that had produced the budget surpluses of those years had begun to burst. Now a big portion of the remaining surplus dollars were going to have to be used by the state to rescue the IOUs and, so it seemed, one of the fundamental necessities of modern life.

The speech was the biggest moment of Gray Davis's governorship, and many pundits thought it was his best opportunity to take the reins of the crisis and wrest some degree of control over it. However, his press secretary, Steve Maviglio, sought to lower expectations. "People need to understand the limitations on his powers," said Maviglio. "The governor has no power to control rates charged by the generators. That's up to FERC."[38] Maviglio was correct, but that incantation had worn so thin that most people didn't want to hear it anymore. In addition, Davis had broad executive powers, including the authority to take steps to buy transmission lines and commandeer power plants, which the Democratic leader of the state senate and some consumer groups were now advocating. That was a tall order for a moderate who took pride in not deviating too far from the center on any issue. But the electricity crisis had long since ceased being just another big issue. Like it or not—and he loathed it—the governor's response to the crisis in 2001 would dictate his legacy.

After a perfunctory declaration that state's economy was "fundamentally strong," the governor in his address called deregulation a "colossal failure" in which we had "lost control over our own power." He claimed that California had "surrendered the decisions about where electricity is sold—and for how much—to private companies with only one objective: maximizing unheard-of profits." Worst of all, he inveighed, "there's evidence that some generators may be purposely withholding electricity from the California grid to create artificial scarcity which in turn drives up the price astronomically." After enumerating a long list of policy objectives to "regain control" of the grid, he trumpeted the big stick approach: "If I have to use the power of eminent domain to prevent generators from driving consumers into the dark and utilities into bankruptcy—then that's what I will do." In perhaps the only conciliatory note of the speech—and in contradiction of much of it—he maintained that "I'm not here to point fingers or assign blame, and I assume the proponents of deregulation really did envision lower energy costs and smaller electricity bills. They certainly didn't plan for this mess."[39]

Indeed, the "proponents of deregulation" had great expectations for the "magic" of the market to revamp a much-maligned utility system that seemed dated and bloated. But those expectations rested on an inordinate faith in the promise of a restructured market and obscured the unique complexities of electricity conveyance and transactions. Ultimately, as we came to understand in the governor's office, the enactment of AB 1890 had launched a highwire act that failed to provide a net.

Notes

1 Davis quoted in Todd S. Purdum, "Tug-Of-War on Budget Threatens California Governor's Near-Perfect Record," *The New York Times*, January 10, 2000.
2 George Skelton, "A Welcome Task: Divvying Up the State's Bounty," *Los Angeles Times*, May 18, 2000.
3 Skelton, "A Welcome Task: Divvying Up the State's Bounty."
4 Interview with Garry South, July 1, 2021.
5 Interview with South.
6 Interview with South.
7 Governor Davis, State of the State Address, January 5, 2000.
8 Paul Van Slambrouck, "California's Brightest Star Is, Well, Gray," *The Christian Science* Monitor, April 17, 2000; South quoted in Purdum, "Tug-Of-War on Budget Threatens California Governor's Near-Perfect Record."
9 Van Slambrouck, "California's Brightest Star Is, Well, Gray."
10 Don Knapp, "San Francisco Heat Blamed for Deaths, Blackout," *CNN*, June 15, 2000.
11 Governor Davis, "Letter to President Lynch and Chairman Kahn," Press Release, June 16, 2000.
12 Frank Wolak and James Bushnell, "Reliability Must-Run Contracts for the California Electricity Market," April 2, 1999, 2–3. http://web.stanford.edu/group/fwolak/cgi-bin/sites/default/files/RMR_Report_Bushnell.pdf. Wolak, an economics professor at Stanford University, was chair of the MSC. Bushnell, an economist with the University of California Energy Institute, was not yet a formal member of the MSC. He would join the committee in early 2002.
13 Severin Borenstein and James Bushnell, "An Empirical Analysis of the Potential for Market Power in California's Electricity Industry," *The Journal of Industrial Economics*, Vol. XLVII, No. 3 (September 1999): 319–21.
14 Governor Davis, "Gov. Davis Calls for Wholesale Price Caps, Electric Bill Refunds," Press Release, July 27, 2000.
15 Carl Blumstein, L.S. Friedman and Richard Green, "The History of Electricity Restructuring in California," *Journal of Industry, Competition and Trade* (January 2002): 6.
16 Davis, "Gov. Davis Calls for Wholesale Price Caps, Electric Bill Refunds."
17 Michael Kahn and Loretta Lynch, "California's Electricity Options and Challenges: Report to Governor Gray Davis," August 2, 2000, 29.
18 Senate Energy, Utilities and Communications Committee, "California's Energy Supply: Preparing for Summer 2000 & Beyond," Agenda and Issue Overview, March 14, 2000. Fluckiger quoted in a digital video of the hearing.
19 Governor Davis, "Governor Davis Acts to Stabilize Electricity Prices, Reduce Demand," Press Release, August 2, 2000.
20 Nancy Vogel, "PUC Caps Electric Bills of Some San Diego Users," *Los Angeles Times*, August 22, 2000.
21 Governor Davis, "Governor Gray Davis Calls on President to Speed Electricity Investigation," Press Release, August 11, 2000.
22 AB 1890, Chapter 854 of 1996.
23 Shames and SDG&E CEO quoted in Nancy Rivera Brooks, "Sempra Still Feeling the Heat," *Los Angeles Times*, September 17, 2000.
24 Vogel, "PUC Caps Electric Bills of Some San Diego Users."
25 SDG&E opposed the bill due to its "vague" language on the company's ability to ultimately recover the wholesale costs that couldn't be passed on. According to a SDG&E spokesperson, "A significant under-collection issue still remains." Quoted in *NGI* Staff, "San Diego Power Prices Capped Through 2003," *Natural Gas Intelligence*, September 4, 2000.

26 Kahn and Lynch, "California's Electricity Options and Challenges," 26.
27 Blumstein, et al., "The History of Electricity Restructuring in California," 20.
28 Southern California Edison, "FERC Finds that California Electricity Prices Are 'Unjust, Unreasonable'," Press Release, November 1, 2000.
29 The legal technicality was over the interpretation of the federal "Filed Rate Doctrine." For a detailed discussion of this issue, see Attorney General Bill Lockyer, "Attorney General's Energy White Paper: A Law Enforcement Perspective on the California Energy Crisis," April 2004, 28–41.
30 Scott Thurm, Robert Gavin and Mitchel Benson, "As Blackouts Hit California, Traders Manipulated the Market," *The Wall Street Journal*, September 16, 2002.
31 Pacific Gas & Electric, "PG&E Asks Federal Court to Affirm Company's Cost Recovery Rights under Federal Law," Press Release, November 8, 2000.
32 Davis quoted in Nancy Vogel, "Crisis Darkens State Christmas Tree," *Los Angeles Times*, December 6, 2000.
33 Winter quoted in Rebecca Smith, "California Energy Officials Discontinue Price-Cap System, in a Surprise Move," *The Wall Street Journal*, December 11, 2000; Governor Davis, "Statement of Gov. Gray Davis on FERC Ruling Lifting Price Caps on Electricity," Press Release, December 8, 2000.
34 Davis quoted in Rone Tempest, "Davis Endorses Gore, Says He's Right for California," *Los Angeles Times*, September 17, 1999.
35 Edwin Chen and Judy Pasternak, "Bush's Ties to Enron Chief Attract Growing Scrutiny," *Los Angeles Times*, February 11, 2001.
36 Davis quoted in Barbara Whitaker, "A Lightning Rod in California," *The New York Times*, December 24, 2000.
37 Nancy Vogel, "How Consumers Lost with Electricity Deregulation," *Los Angeles Times*, December 9, 2000; Dan Morain, "Davis Faces Growing Criticism on Power Crisis," *Los Angeles Times*, December 31, 2000.
38 Maviglio quoted in Morain, "Davis Faces Growing Criticism on Power Crisis."
39 Governor Davis, State of the State Address, January 8, 2001.

2 The "Deregulation" That Paved the Way to Disaster

Assembly Bill 1890 received a great deal of media scrutiny—in late 2000 and in 2001, several years after its enactment. Journalist Dan Morain, who covered the deliberations on the bill and its enactment in 1996 for the *Los Angeles Times*, aptly observed 25 years later that "no one really got it." Not even the legislators, who voted unanimously for it. *The Wall Street Journal* reporter Rebecca Smith conducted interviews with many of them after the bill passed. She lamented that the number of legislators with a "full understanding" of the bill could be counted "on one hand."[1] That said, the vast majority of legislators knew at least that its implementation was not without challenges. But notions that the Federal Energy Regulatory Commission (FERC) would fail to take action against market manipulation, and particularly that the new market could then catastrophically collapse, were all but nonexistent, even among industry experts. To the extent that something might go wrong in the new market, there seemed, by and large, to be an article of faith that the market itself, with perhaps a tweak or two by minimalist regulators, could remedy any issues. And, in the mid-1990s, an abundance of cheap electricity in California obscured those potential issues because the excess supply showed how the "market" pushed wholesale costs down. So, an advantageous time for "deregulation" appeared to be at hand.

***

In November 1991, a *Time* Magazine cover feature on California's "endangered dream" declared that the "land of golden opportunity was becoming a land of broken promises." Iconic images of sun-drenched surfers, the Golden Gate Bridge, and towering redwoods gave way to those of clogged freeways and polluted beaches. Moreover, an increase in poor air quality, unaffordable housing, and crime evoked comparisons to the dystopian Los Angeles depicted in the 1982 science-fiction film *Blade Runner.* The primary problem underlying this "malaise," according to *Time* columnist Jordan Bonfante, was that "the state is attracting far more people than it can cope with" while job opportunities shrank along with the robust economic growth during most of the previous decade.[2]

DOI: 10.4324/9781003518150-3

Many Californians, including some journalists, scoffed at the *Time* critique and maintained that it was just another hyperbolic parable in a regular cycle of bashing the state. California native Jay Matthews, the Los Angeles bureau chief for *The Washington Post*, highlighted "more than two decades of journalistic efforts to defame and distort life in my state" due mainly to the critics' repressed envy of that life.[3] However, it was not hard to find Californians with an unsettled notion that this time the critics might be right, particularly regarding the economy, which had been bolstered for decades by federal defense spending.

Though the state's population and economy grew rapidly in the 1980s, manufacturing—a cornerstone of post-war economic growth and prosperity—declined by 18 percent, as many companies moved from California to other states where costs were lower.[4] The fall of the Berlin Wall in 1989, the end of the Cold War in late 1991, and the decline in federal defense expenditures greatly contributed to a recession in 1990–1991, and that downturn hit California particularly hard. During this time a trend of supplanting high-paid manufacturing jobs with low-paid and less-skilled ones began in earnest, especially in Southern California. For example, while almost as many apparel jobs were created in Los Angeles County as were lost in the aerospace industry, the median annual pay was $17,000 in garment work compared to $45,000 in aerospace. The hit taken by workers in the lowest income quartile statewide during this recession was considerably greater than that experienced by those workers nationwide and especially compared to higher income Californians.[5]

The drop in state tax revenues due to the recession proved immense, and that problem landed in the lap of the newly elected Republican governor, Pete Wilson, and the state legislature. The 1991 budget forged by Wilson and legislative leaders covered a $7 billion deficit with new sales and upper bracket income taxes along with slowed increases in state wages and social services outlays. California and its state government had weathered earlier recessions better than this one, including the 1981–1982 recession, which had hit the rest of the country harder. But not this time. As defense spending declined, so did California's economic vitality. The looming 1992 state budget deficit was projected to be twice that of 1991, and the prospective tax increases to cover that yawning gap were almost certain to add to the exodus of companies that already were being lured to other states with lower business costs, fewer regulatory hurdles, and more affordable housing. Regarding this growing quagmire, Wilson warned, "We have to face the fact that California is no longer irresistible to business."[6]

Among the high costs of doing business for energy-intensive industries in California was the cost of electricity. In 1991, the average electricity rate charged by California's Investor Owned Utilities was 30–50 percent above both national average rates and the competitive cost of additional electricity, and much higher than in neighboring Western states.[7] Residential and commercial customers also paid higher rates, but due to numerous and effective energy efficiency programs, and the relatively mild climate in the state's major cities, the combined residential and commercial per capita consumption of energy was less than in any other state,[8] and their electricity bills were therefore lower than those of many counterparts outside California. While this low-energy consumption dynamic certainly did not make residential and commercial customers indifferent to high rates, the loudest complaints by far came from big industries that lobbied hard to reform the state's electricity market.

Wilson heeded those complaints and embraced the reform effort. Deregulating the electricity market to make it competitive instead of an Investor Owned Utility monopoly, Wilson and others reasoned, would lower rates and help the state recover more robustly from the deep recession by attracting new industry and creating jobs. In 1992, he directed the California Public Utilities Commission to begin formal proceedings to "restructure" the market.

The CPUC, whose five commissioners were appointed by the governor, had the responsibility for setting and approving IOU rates. Established in 1911 by a state constitutional amendment as the Railroad Commission, the legislature expanded the commission's authority by passing the Public Utilities Act in 1912 to include regulation of natural gas, electric, telephone, and water companies as well. The primary reason for the establishment of the commission was to rein in the pervasive political influence of the Southern Pacific Railroad. As railroads increasingly gave way to other transportation modes, the Railroad Commission was renamed the Public Utilities Commission in 1946, and the CPUC's bureaucracy grew rapidly during the state's post-war population boom.

By the mid-1970s, the fallout from the Arab oil embargo prompted California electric utilities to switch from oil to natural gas generation for their fossil-fuel plants. They also began to utilize costly nuclear power and, in the late 1970s, "alternative" energy, mainly as a hedge against natural gas price volatility.[9] However, in the 1980s oil and gas prices dropped and stabilized while California's electricity rates began to climb well above the national average as that hedge looked more and more like a bad bet. In addition, the commission was often chided by consumer and business representatives for being "cozy" with the IOUs and too acquiescent to their rate-increase petitions.

CPUC President Daniel Fessler, a former UC Davis law professor appointed by Wilson and, like the governor, a "committed free marketeer," led the restructuring effort with the support of fellow commissioner and kindred spirit P. Gregory Conlon. The latter maintained that competition "puts the customer in the decision-making responsibility," and that "regulation is just a surrogate for competition."[10]

In September 1992, the CPUC directed its Division of Strategic Planning to undertake a meticulous review of the state's regulated electricity industry and to consider and recommend alternative market-based structures. This review led to the release in February 1993 of *The Yellow Book* (named for its cover color) which included recommendations largely pursuant to directives in the federal Energy Policy Act of 1992 to minimize regulation.[11]

***

The desire to bring competitive market forces into sectors that were heavily regulated or otherwise non-competitive was not just a fixation of free-market Republicans. During this period, academics, pundits, and elected officials of every ideological stripe subscribed to the idea that government, along with highly regulated entities such as utilities, would function more effectively if they incorporated more of the principles driving private enterprise.

Published in 1992, the book *Reinventing Government: How the Entrepreneurial Spirit is Transforming the Public Sector*, became popular with moderate Democrats, including presidential candidate Bill Clinton and his running mate, Al Gore. After he became president, Clinton appointed Gore to lead the National Performance Review which, according to a Performance Review official, targeted "the overhead costs, not the organizational structure, of agencies." The main goal was to incorporate private sector efficiency techniques so government would be more results-oriented and less costly.[12] In California, however, Wilson went a good deal further than that. His office released a report in 1995 titled "A Competitive Government Plan for Less Bureaucracy and More Results." A Wilson administration official explained that the plan was based on the "phone book test"—that is, if you could find a service listed in the Yellow Pages, "you have to ask whether there's any compelling reason for government to be doing it."[13]

Wilson, Fessler, Conlon, and likeminded others did not harbor any illusions that government electricity regulators would soon be out of their jobs; after all, in a restructured market, the IOUs would still at least own the electricity transmission and distribution system, and regulators would still be needed to oversee that monopoly and potential market manipulation. Nevertheless, as *Los Angeles Times* reporter Michael Parrish observed, the commissioners did want to "substitute market forces wherever possible for traditional command and control regulation."[14]

Regardless of party affiliation, most everyone agreed that the electricity market in California needed major changes, but certain stakeholders viewed *The Yellow Book* with trepidation. Ralph Cavanagh, energy policy director of the Natural Resources Defense Council (NRDC), explained that "it's not a debate about whether to have competition. The environmental community has promoted competition for years. It's over how competition should proceed." For Cavanagh and other green energy advocates, that essentially meant that until renewable energy technologies matured and became cost competitive with fossil-fuel-based generation, these technologies should compete with each other for subsidies to ultimately yield the best technologies in terms of cost and environmental benefits.[15]

The Yellow Book served as the initial basis for dialogue on regulatory reform between all interested parties and the commission, and it proved to be the first serious effort by state-level policymakers to take on a significant restructuring of the entire electricity sector.[16] While it recommended market-oriented reform, all but the last of the four options it offered were fairly restrained in that regard. However, that last option, the "Restructured Utility Industry," was a rough blueprint of a complete transition to a competitive market environment in which the IOUs would act as common electricity transmission carriers while most of their generation assets would be divested and customers could choose non-utility energy providers. While this approach was clearly the overhaul of the market favored by Fessler and Conlon, Edison balked at the idea of having energy service provider alternatives to the utilities. In addition, environmental groups chafed at the prospect of market forces squeezing out more expensive renewable energy from IOU portfolios.[17]

These concerns notwithstanding, in April 1994, after considerable deliberation, the CPUC issued *The Blue Book* in which it announced its intention to begin formal hearings for the rulemaking procedures to restructure the industry to a market-based system. This process launched a long and contentious debate between a multitude of stakeholders and the commissioners, and it was not pre-ordained to succeed. But Fessler and Conlon were committed to finalizing a market-based plan and confident in getting the one other commissioner they needed to approve it. They favored the energy market "deregulation" that had been instituted in the U.K. under former Prime Minister Margaret Thatcher, an icon of conservative free marketeers. That system created a "transparent" transmission "pool" in which generators bought power directly from the pool at the hourly market price with the aim of optimizing the cost benefits of real-time competition for their retail customers.[18]

For Fessler and Conlon, preparation for their effort included a trip to the U.K. to examine the operation firsthand. The excursion was sponsored and paid for by the California Council for Environmental and Economic Balance, headed by former Edison President Michael Peevey and backed mainly by business interests but also organized labor. Other trip participants included the California Senate Republican Caucus chairman Bill Leonard and top executives from Edison, PG&E, and SDG&E, as well as senior CPUC staffers. Meeting with ranking Thatcherites, conservative members of Parliament and other free-market acolytes, Fessler—who enjoyed affecting a British accent—took great pleasure in his company and edification.[19]

As reporter Bill Bradley would later observe, "Fessler opposed government efforts to promote conservation, and regarded renewable energy skeptically. To him, the price signal was all that was needed to spur greater energy efficiency," and government needed to get out of the market's way.[20] Invited to share his views at a congressional energy committee hearing in Washington, D.C. shortly after his U.K. trip, Fessler drove home this point and expressed concern about potential government obstacles. He took issue with the testimony before him of a former Maine utilities commissioner who had stated that "the movement to a competitive market is being and should be led by regulators." In a rather ironic diminishment of his own position, Fessler declared, "Mr. Chairman, I respectfully disagree."

> I believe that if the movement was ever centered in government aspirations or leadership, it has long since moved to the marketplace and is in the custody of those men and women who are the multifaceted industry. Given this perspective, I find greater accuracy in the remark of [business] Professor William Hogan before the committee that, 'the forces in motion are powerful and will sweep over those who ignore them.'[21]

The Blue Book widely reflected Fessler's embrace of the market, though less dogmatically, by proclaiming that "California must shy away from proposals which simply *maintain* the current level of economic activity, and we must opt instead for a strategy that fosters economic *growth*, enhancing the state's competitiveness, and increasing business opportunities."[22] The market restructuring proposal, which highlighted the U.K. approach, was repeatedly referred to as "our vision," which would "build upon existing competition in the [wholesale] electric services industry to foster a truly competitive market for California." According to the self-congratulatory commission, "the vision we propose and the strategy to achieve it mark the end of one era and the beginning of another."[23]

Arguably the most critical element of "the vision" was the opportunity for "California consumers to gradually enjoy *direct* access to non-utility electricity suppliers." Initial eligibility would be for larger business energy consumers, but all ratepayers, including residential customers that the commission pledged to protect, could reap the benefits "of the competitive marketplace" by January 1, 2002. That meant, theoretically at least, that all IOU customers could choose to get their electricity from another energy provider, though the IOUs would still provide transmission and distribution services through the "poles and wires" they already owned. However, to promote true competition, the commission—and later, the legislature—would all but require the IOUs to divest most of their generation facilities outside of their nuclear and hydroelectric operations. The vast and complex ambition of the restructuring plan was not lost on the commission as it acknowledged in *The Blue Book* that "the Legislature can *assist* [emphasis added] in the timely implementation of our proposal...to take the important first steps in revitalizing California's energy policy."[24]

A number of prominent legislators had long been leery of the broad authority vested in the CPUC through the state's constitution, and they made clear to the commission that the legislature would do more than just "assist" in the restructuring process. Passed on the last day of the 1994 legislative session, Assembly Concurrent Resolution 143—which did not require the governor's signature—"urge[d] that the Public Utilities Commission issue no interim, final, or effective order in specified proceedings relating to the regulation of the electric services industry, until it has held evidentiary hearings and made specified reports to the Legislature and the Governor in that regard." The ACR established the Joint Committee on Lowering the Cost of Electric Services "to ensure that the proposals made by the commission meet certain standards." In a direct shot at Fessler and his unabashed free-market cohorts, the ACR maintained that "witnesses before the CPUC expressed concern that the commission had not developed a sufficient factual record on the potential adverse and beneficial impacts on all ratepayers, utilities, independent power producers, and the environment and resource diversity of the proposals in order to make a reasoned decision on whether or how to restructure the electric services industry." Nevertheless, the ACR made clear that "it is in the public interest to reduce electric rates and costs for all customers of investor-owned utilities in the near term to stimulate California's economy and to strengthen the state's competitive position."[25]

While the CPUC provided some leeway in how to establish a competitive electricity market, the "long-term vision" clearly tilted toward the "UK-style transmission pool" for wholesale transactions—or "PoolCo," as it came to be known in California's restructuring deliberations. The competition among electricity wholesalers engaged in PoolCo transactions was expected to cut costs and accelerate the introduction of new generation technologies to replace old utility power plants. PoolCo would operate as a "spot market," in which wholesale electricity would mainly be purchased at its price the day before or the day of its delivery, and not through fixed prices in long-term bilateral contracts. Edison and its senior vice president, Robert Foster, became the most ardent advocate of PoolCo, mainly because it provided a relatively clear way to track and secure the money the IOUs needed to recover their stranded costs.[26]

After the release of *The Blue Book*, the stock prices of the IOUs plunged, and that prompted them to dig in their heels and ratchet up their considerable political clout in Sacramento to demand full recovery of those costly past investments during the transition to a competitive market in which they could lose customers. IOU executives maintained that, over many decades, major investments in their vast network of power plants and transmission systems to meet their "obligation to serve" customers with safe and reliable power were part of their "regulatory compact." To the extent that retail competition would render some of these investments uneconomic under competitive market rates, the IOUs argued they should still be able to recover the cost of these stranded assets pursuant to the compact.[27]

* * *

Chaired by Democratic Assemblymember Byron Sher, a respected champion of the environment and alternative energy, the Joint Committee on

Lowering the Cost of Electric Services created by ACR 143 held its initial hearing on October 28, 1994. Sher noted that the legislature generally supported the cornerstones of restructuring highlighted in *The Blue Book*, including "fair competition and customer choice in the generation and purchase of electricity through [open] transmission access and utility and ratepayer indifference to the ownership of the source of the electricity."[28] However, that support didn't necessarily extend to the IOU's recovering all their stranded costs.

As the first witness testifying before the committee, University of California economist Severin Borenstein stated that determining "who should cover those stranded investments is probably the most controversial issue this committee will face." According to Borenstein, the stranded costs were primarily tied to "decisions to build nuclear power plants that have, after the fact, turned out to be extremely costly." In addition, pursuant to the state's implementation of the federal Public Utilities Regulatory Policy Act (PURPA) in the 1980s, the CPUC required the IOUs to sign many expensive power contracts with relatively small "Qualifying Facilities" that generated power through renewable energy and other alternative technologies. Due mainly to the debt service on these investments, the retail cost of electricity under California's regulated prices was 6–7 cents per kWh, while the wholesale cost was only about 2.5 cents per kWh.[29] Therefore, Borenstein maintained, the cost benefits from a shift to a competitive market would be diminished while consumers were on the hook for that IOU debt, which Sher emphatically reiterated. And counter to the claims of many deregulation advocates, Borenstein opined that if a "surcharge were placed on electricity to make the [IOU] shareholders whole our rates would not drop to close to the national average."[30]

Appearing on behalf of Fessler, the commission's general counsel, Peter Arth, defended the "competition transition charge" (CTC) that was established in *The Blue Book* to allow IOUs to recover stranded costs either in whole or in part. In regard to those costs, Arth declared that Fessler strongly disagreed with those who "view the issue as a new burden which may be imposed on ratepayers as a consequence of the Commission's restructuring effort." Arth rightly noted that those costs "are a burden and an opportunity cost on California's economy which we seek to recognize and address. We did not create them and the abandonment of this restructuring effort cannot make them go away."[31] Nevertheless, Arth did not directly address, nor did Sher ask him about, the observation that the recovery of stranded costs from ratepayers would necessarily reduce the retail price benefits widely expected from competition until those costs were paid off. Other witnesses generally skirted or downplayed this matter as well.

Most stakeholders believed there would indeed be benefits from competition and focused on ensuring that the benefits would be equitable for all ratepayers, generation resources, and providers, as reflected in the testimony of other witnesses before the committee. Large energy consumers were concerned that the PoolCo approach favored by Edison would leave the IOUs with too much market control and therefore dampen competition. PoolCo supporters maintained that the pool would be an independent entity regulated by the state, and that the divestment of IOU natural gas generation facilities would promote competition at both the wholesale and retail levels. There was almost no discussion about the possibility that a restructured market, with divested power plants that would no longer be under the CPUC's jurisdiction, could become seriously dysfunctional and a haven for manipulators.

But Jan Smutny-Jones, the head of the Independent Energy Producers (IEP) Association which represented the qualifying facilities, did make a prescient observation in response to a question from Sher about the potential for "market power" in the PoolCo proposal. Noting that market power could be exercised, Smutny-Jones believed that this potential problem "is really not looked at in the discussion of PoolCo." He offered this admonition:

> You will need to superimpose some sort of regulatory process over that. I think one of the questions we need to ask ourselves and you as a legislator specifically need to ask is, does basically supplanting the existing PUC regulatory structure with basically a regulatory structure that would be dominated by the Federal Energy Regulatory Commission, is that necessarily in anybody's best interest, and the answer from my way of thinking is probably no.[32]

A decentralized wholesale electricity market, as proposed in *The Blue Book*, would be regulated by the FERC under authority granted by the Federal Power Act. This meant that if California restructured its market in accordance with the CPUC's plan, including the divestment of generation plants owned by the IOUs to private "merchant generators," those generators would then be under the FERC's jurisdiction instead of the CPUC. Curious about the prospective new dynamic between the FERC and the CPUC, Assemblymember Gwen Moore asked Arth if there was "some thought about how we reconcile what's going on at the federal level with what goes on at the state level?" "We are optimistic," he said reassuringly, "that this is going to be done on a cooperative basis rather than a tug-of-war."[33]

Arth's optimism reflected a broader acceptance, though not an embrace, of the FERC having the upper hand in the state's wholesale electricity market restructuring. The reasons for this acquiescence are not hard to understand. There was a strong consensus that regulated prices were too high. Also, as noted earlier, the *Reinventing Government* zeitgeist crossed party lines, and the generally successful deregulation of the telecommunications, natural gas, and airline industries were trumpeted in *The Blue Book* as precursors to electricity restructuring's success. Moreover, simply put, California's glut of power in the mid-1990s made the notion that the state faced any shortage of power in the foreseeable future seem far-fetched, and so did the potential need for significant action by the FERC.

However, as some experts pointed out, this power glut—generally measured by the megawatt "capacity" of the state's generation network compared to customer demand—was not necessarily the best measure of being able to meet the state's electricity needs. Equally, if not more, important was potential transmission congestion based on locational constraints in the transmission system which could facilitate the exercise of market power. IOU transmission systems were designed for regional operation and reliability, not for the reliability needs of the statewide grid under the PoolCo plan.[34] The UC Energy Institute noted in several restructuring analyses that "a decentralized electric power market may create problems relating to network reliability and the abuse of market power," and that there was "evidence from the UK" that its pool market "is vulnerable to manipulation." But these market power warnings were "mainly theoretical" and didn't receive much attention.[35]

* * *

Citing California's plethora of power in February 1995, the FERC overruled the CPUC and determined that the CPUC had violated federal law by requiring the IOUs to purchase power from certain independent alternative power producers when cheaper power was available from other independent suppliers. Edison and SDG&E had challenged the CPUC's approval of these contracts, and Edison claimed that the agreements essentially forced the company to buy more than $1 billion of "unneeded" power between 1997 and 2003. In its ruling, the FERC questioned the need for this capacity as well. The most ardent supporter of renewable energy in the state legislature, Byron Sher, declared that the FERC had made a "serious mistake" by second-guessing "California's actions in this regard [to] preclude parties from proceeding with their low-cost, clean-energy projects."[36] Indeed, the FERC's decision was a major blow to environmental and clean-energy advocates who had labored for years to secure IOU purchase agreements for a large amount of new renewable generation as opposed to just renewing contracts for existing facilities.[37] Moreover, the decision did not bode well for the future of renewable energy resources in a restructured wholesale market governed primarily by the FERC.

A spokesperson for Fessler expressed tepid disagreement with FERC's decision,[38] but by then Fessler and his fellow commissioners were in the thick of the proceedings and deliberations to draft and release for stakeholder comment a "proposed policy decision" for restructuring. Under intense pressure from Edison, the commission voted 3 to 2 in May 1995 in favor of a proposal backed by Fessler and Conlon that was largely consistent with the IOUs' insistence on the full recovery of their stranded costs and with Edison's desire for wholesale transactions to be confined to the centralized market under PoolCo. Commissioner Jesse Knight, one of the two dissenting votes, had proposed a competing plan, backed by large energy consumers, built around a more unfettered direct access market. It did not require purchases to be made from the pool, which supporters of Knight's proposal believed would limit the new market's potential benefits.[39]

The approval of the Fessler-Conlon draft plan escalated the disagreement over PoolCo between Edison and the big energy consumers, led by the California Manufacturers Association (CMA). As Foster had asserted during the October Joint Committee hearing and continued to maintain, the manufacturers and power marketers "want to go out there and lock up the most efficient generators. I mean, that's the reason they want direct access" and oppose PoolCo.[40] PG&E, the state's largest IOU, accepted direct access as an inevitable outcome in the growing deregulation juggernaut, but they locked arms with Edison and SDG&E to get full recovery of their stranded costs. The California Large Energy Consumers Association (CLECA) continued to push hard for direct access and insisted that the IOUs relinquish control of transmission operations to a new transmission entity that would be outside of the PoolCo power exchange, which PG&E accepted but Edison did not. The standoff between Edison and the CLECA and its allies became so intense that Governor Wilson directed his chief of staff, George Dunn, and top economic advisor, Phil Romero, to broker an agreement. "It was analogous to the Arab-Israeli peace talks," Romero later recalled.[41]

Representatives from consumer and environmental groups were not invited to participate in these negotiations, but these groups tended to join Edison in support of PoolCo because they disliked the potential of direct access to shift higher IOU costs to residential and small business consumers. In addition, these groups worried that a decentralized direct access market would likely create problems for maintaining energy efficiency programs and renewable energy procurement.[42] By July 1995, while Romero and Dunn continued their heated negotiations, a broad coalition including consumer and environmental groups announced support for the Fessler-Conlon proposed policy decision to develop "a 'pooled' wholesale electricity market that would give all customers the benefit of a competitive market." Jim Conran, president of Consumers First, stated that "the CPUC's majority proposal is a balanced policy. It allows all consumers to benefit, it emphasizes safety and reliability, it maintains quality service, and it offers protection to consumers." Ralph Cavanagh added that the NRDC believed that "the commission majority has identified a formula that will work for both the economy and the environment—including, in particular, the energy-efficiency and renewable energy resources that are crucial to a sustainable energy future."[43]

In the talks between Edison and the large energy customers, the latter maintained that if the IOUs were going to be allowed the opportunity to fully recover their stranded costs, there had to be a significant *quid pro quo*. The CLECA and its allies, including the IEP, demanded that the control of the grid and the power pool had to be separated. As IEP Executive Director Smutny-Jones later recalled, "we were clearly in the camp with the large industrials that were very suspicious of PoolCo" as they believed this would enhance the market power of the IOUs and "control over where the markets would go." John Fielder, an Edison senior vice president, said that a single entity would better guard against "costly" market gaming opportunities by energy suppliers and traders because each "hand" would be more aware of what the other was doing. But such concerns did not assuage the fear of IEP and the "industrials" that the IOUs, and especially Edison, were seeking greater control by having the grid and the power pool controlled under one roof. The coalition that joined with the CLECA and the IEP, which included the energy marketer Enron, delivered an ultimatum that if there was going to be power pool, it had to be separate from the control of the grid, contrary to the single entity under the Fessler-Conlon plan. And if Edison didn't accept that, the coalition maintained, then perhaps the ability of the IOUs to recover their stranded costs should be revisited.[44] Not wanting to jeopardize the IOUs' highest priority, Edison ultimately conceded to this demand.

In September 1995 the CPUC received a Memorandum of Understanding (MOU) from Edison, the CMA, CLECA, and IEP that recommended two new and separate entities: The Power Exchange (PX), which would handle the spot-market electricity transactions, and the California Independent System Operator (CAISO) to schedule transmission and maintain reliability. The recommendations also included direct access for large energy consumers utilizing bilateral contracts but sought to ensure there was no way for those big consumers to bypass or transfer costs to small business and residential customers. Most importantly for the IOUs, the non-bypassable costs included the prospective recovery of all their stranded investments through the "competition transition charge" in customer bills.

Though the MOU essentially retained Fessler's prized power pool in the creation of the PX, he was apparently completely blindsided by the separation of the CAISO and the PX in the MOU and the allowance of bilateral direct access contracts for large energy consumers outside of the PX. According to Smutny-Jones, "Fessler was in Sweden...when all of this came down. And when he got back—he was normally a very formal guy—he apparently erupted at people and swore at them up and down the aisle." However, Wilson quickly endorsed the deal, as did PG&E.[45] The commission could have rejected the filing of the MOU, but that was not politically realistic given Wilson's support of it. The MOU became the cornerstone for the commission's Preferred Policy Decision (PPD), and the governor made sure that it provided the basis for the legislative restructuring effort in 1996.[46]

On December 20, 1995, the CPUC brought the primary restructuring proceeding that began with release of *The Yellow Book* in early 1993 to a close by voting 5–0 to approve the PPD. Despite his apparent misgivings about the MOU-based PPD, upon its passage Fessler touted it as a seminal achievement: "With the decision today we open the door to the broadest array of choice in which former ratepayers can function as informed customers. The variety of customer choice which we seek for Californians after January 1,

1998, is currently unavailable anywhere in the world." He called upon the FERC to partner with the state through "cooperative federalism" to lay the cornerstones for "a California Consensus."[47]

The PPD was essentially a mishmash of something for everyone—to like and to dislike. While this decision deviated from the Fessler-Conlon majority proposal in May 1995 by separating the CAISO and PX, its key market feature was Fessler's power pool.[48] At the same time, the large energy consumers got direct access options, though not as many as they would have preferred and expected; but they did prevail in separating the CAISO from the PX. While unhappy about the full recovery of IOU stranded costs and the direct access provisions in the PPD, environmental and consumer advocates still got concessions. The latter had argued that smaller customers should be able to aggregate their electricity needs to prevent cost shifting by providing some degree of consumer parity with the purchasing power of larger energy customers. To that end, the PPD allowed "community aggregators" to facilitate larger "bundled" electricity transactions and related services for residential and other smaller consumers. Environmentalists had sought a commitment to renewable energy that they feared could dissipate in the more open restructured market. The PPD included an escalating "minimum renewables purchase requirement" proposed by the American Wind Energy Association for participants in the new market, including direct access providers. However, there also was a less ambitious option for a smaller surcharge-funded renewables program to support existing and new renewables in the state but without any minimum purchase or portfolio growth requirements.[49]

***

In 1996, the main venue for restructuring shifted from the CPUC in San Francisco to Sacramento, where Governor Wilson leaned on the state legislature to pass legislation enacting the PPD. In a letter to the FERC that was shared with state lawmakers, Wilson declared, "I will necessarily oppose any legislation which seeks to alter the [CPUC's] basic framework or timeline."[50] But the brainy and sardonic Democratic Senator Steve Peace bristled at that prospect. As a member of the Senate Energy and Utilities Committee, Peace had closely followed the CPUC restructuring proceedings, did not trust Fessler, and had major misgivings about the commission itself. After a late December storm knocked out power for many northern Californians, Peace contended at a legislative hearing that "as I watch deregulation unfold, there's an apparent lack of focus and attention to issues other than sweeping statements from the commission," and he questioned Fessler about whether the CPUC had sufficiently considered system reliability and public safety. Fessler responded that "safety and reliability concerns aren't being changed at all" by the PPD.[51]

Fessler's reassurance notwithstanding, and pursuant to the concerns raised by ACR 143 and the bipartisan joint committee the resolution created, Peace and Republican Majority Leader Jim Brulte formed a bipartisan conference committee to consider restructuring bills. In what came to be known as the "Steve Peace Death March," the senator relentlessly pushed the legislative process forward and, as best he could, "special interests" aside. "As noble as the representatives of these economic interests may be, the public process is frankly served better by them not engaging in what is often self-delusion of higher purpose," Peace pontificated at a committee hearing. "Any time someone tells me, 'I'm just trying to do God's work here,' that is when lawmakers should step in. Our job is to do God's work." The quintessential dynamics of the death march were deftly described by reporter Art O'Donnell, who closely covered the legislative proceedings for *California Electricity Markets*: "Part of the Peace strategy was to reduce adversaries to ashes with his withering wit and to brow beat parties to a submissive state where they would agree to almost anything just to end the torture."[52]

The chances of getting a renewable energy procurement mandate in the restructuring bill diminished in the face of opposition from large energy consumers and the IOUs. While the latter were generally supportive of maintaining some degree of commitment to California's environmentally beneficial energy programs, the costly alternative energy contracts of the previous decade put a damper on that support because they accounted for a significant portion of the IOU stranded costs. Simply put, the cost of renewable energy could not compete straight up with the cost of electricity from most generators utilizing natural gas, and hydroelectric power cost even less. Alternative energy advocates touted "the values that renewables bring to the system" such as resource diversity and cleaner air and sought to monetize these values in avoided healthcare costs and environmental damage. However, these arguments did not gain much traction for a renewable energy procurement mandate, the resistance to which was buttressed by a growing discomfort with mandates as the economy moved to a more deregulated structure. In addition, some environmental groups believed that too much attention was being given to renewable energy at the expense of other more targeted environmental protection programs for clean air and water.[53]

Nearing the end of the death march, alternative energy advocates were not spared the Peace treatment. In yet another late-night committee hearing, Peace told the renewable energy stakeholders—which included renewable energy opponents such as the Manufacturers Association and the CLECA—that they had 15 minutes to come back to the committee with an agreement on a renewable energy program. While there was some disagreement among renewable supporters, the majority agreed they should take what they could readily get: $540 million collected through a customer bill surcharge to pay for the above-market costs of existing and *perhaps* additional renewables through the year 2001.[54] There would be no mandate for escalating procurement targets.

As the grinding legislative process drew to a close, the IOUs, and Edison in particular, mounted and maintained an intense lobbying effort to ensure that the restructuring legislation, Assembly Bill 1890 by Assemblymember Brulte (and numerous coauthors), provided for the recovery of the utilities' stranded costs through the competition transition charge (commonly referred to as the CTC). *Los Angeles Times* reporter Dan Morain maintained that "the bill has been the focus of the largest lobbying effort of the year, possibly of the 1990s." Utility employee labor unions managed to get a fair amount of job protection and $100 million for retraining and severance benefits for any laid-off workers. Non-industrial large energy users such as the Bay Area Rapid Transit District, the University of California, and agricultural interests in the San Joaquin Valley received CTC exemptions that amounted to about $200 million.[55] To seal the deal for the passage of AB 1890 with unanimous support from legislators, a retail rate freeze was added so that "no customer shall pay a higher rate for electricity than they paid on June 10, 1996." In addition, residential and small business customers would receive "no less than a 10% rate reduction beginning January 1, 1998, and lasting until March 31, 2002." John Rosza, a consultant for the Senate Energy and Utilities Committee, stated that "these rate reductions [were made] possible by creating a unique financing mechanism that will permit 'securitization' of a portion of the CTC amounts that are already being paid by customers."[56] In fact, that "unique financing mechanism" was essentially the authorization for the IOUs to issue $7 billion in "rate reduction bonds" so that ratepayers would cover whatever losses the utilities would incur due to the reduction. Lost in the celebratory statements on the rate reduction was that the bond debt service would effectively reduce the 10 percent rate cut for customers to about 3 percent.

At the end of August and the 1996 legislative session, both the state assembly and senate unanimously passed AB1890, and Senator Peace hailed the bill as the culmination of "the most complex transition of an industry done anywhere in the world." Upon signing the bill in September, Governor Wilson declared that "we've pulled the plug on another outdated monopoly" and had taken "a major step in our efforts to guarantee lower rates, provide consumer choice and offer reliable service, so no one literally is left in the dark." Not everyone agreed. Consumer advocate Lenny Goldberg, who represented Toward Utility Rate Normalization (TURN), presciently observed that "the whole thing is a shot in the dark."[57] And despite Peace's declaration of a monumental achievement, "the most complex transition" now moved from a rather static policy prescription to the much more daunting nuts-and-bolts market implementation and launch.

***

All the ballyhoo aside, the restructured market could not help but be a major gamble, and the biggest market players bet heavily on its success. In accordance with their commitment to divestiture, the IOUs sold almost all their natural gas-powered generation by the end of 1998, mostly to five companies that paid top dollar for the facilities, which gave them the capacity to provide 30–40 percent of the state's power. Importantly, none of these companies would own more than 6–8 percent of California's generation capacity.[58]

These companies needed the FERC's authorization to sell their wholesale power at "market rates"—that is, without a price cap tied to a regulated profit margin or index price. They were clearly aware that the FERC's "test" to determine whether or not they could exercise market power was based on the contention that a firm with less than a 20 percent market share could *not* do so. However, the FERC's methodology, which was strongly and rightly criticized by CAISO representatives and economists, did not account for the fact that electricity must be delivered to retail customers over the existing regionally oriented transmission grid, and that transmission "congestion"—much like cars stuck in a traffic jam unable to get from point A to point B—at times limits the number of generators able to sell power into congested regions like the San Francisco Peninsula. That gave generators located in certain geographic areas prime market power opportunities, the CAISO contended. Fatefully, the FERC did not agree with that assertion, nor did it concur with the argument that during peak periods of electricity demand, even companies owning far less than 20 percent of generation capacity can exercise significant market power by holding out for the highest price if their generation is needed when virtually all the other available generators are already running to meet demand.[59]

The California legislature had also made short shrift of market power concerns, though it appears that legislators believed the CPUC still had some enforcement authority in that regard. A 1997 CPUC informational briefing noted that AB 1890 "authorizes the CPUC to allow plant divestment to mitigate market power." However, the briefing made clear those divested facilities "will be operated according to market-based influences and will no longer operate under the traditional CPUC regulatory system."[60] That observation notwithstanding, the bill itself declared that the commission still had a duty to "ensure that facilities needed to maintain the reliability of the electric supply remain available and operational, consistent with maintaining open competition and avoiding an overconcentration of market power."[61] Regardless of the legislature's directive that the CPUC had this duty, the reality was, as the commission recognized, that its authority to rein in market power had been ceded to the FERC.

***

The separation of the PX and CAISO created operational challenges in structuring the new market, particularly for the computer technology interface that the two entities needed to run the complex system effectively. The PX could not even be located in the same building as the ISO, which added both time and additional costs during implementation of the market apparatus. Moreover, the PX and CAISO enlisted separate vendors that bundled data differently. Due to mounting technical problems, the initial dry-run market simulations failed in late 1997. Though CAISO and PX officials downplayed the extent of their operational problems, a week before the market's scheduled launch date of January 1, 1998, they jointly announced that the launch would be delayed for three months so they could identify and correct software problems and perform further tests and simulations.[62]

The new market launched on March 31, 1998, and during its first two years, it provided relatively low-cost electricity and reliable service. Prices remained low enough to easily maintain the rate freeze and reduction for residential and small business customers mandated by AB 1890, and to allow the IOUs to recover their stranded costs and even pass on considerable profits to their parent companies. As one prominent energy economist later observed, "a strong case could be made that, according to a number of standard metrics, the California market outperformed all of the wholesale markets in the U.S." in 1998 and 1999.[63]

But as the new century loomed, all was not as well with that market as the metrics indicated given design flaws that invited manipulation almost from the beginning of its operation. After a particularly alarming wholesale price spike in July 1998, CAISO's independent Market Surveillance Committee informed the board that "it makes little sense to attempt to run a competitive market for electricity in California for the current configuration of the California grid and set of available generation capacity."[64] Such admonitions, along with recurrent problems, compelled the board and staff to seriously seek remedies for the design flaws.[65] However, because *average* wholesale prices remained relatively low during the market's first two years, the manipulation, while concerning, could easily be viewed more as episodic profiteering than a portent of the epic meltdown to come. The optimism that drove the deregulation effort in the mid-1990s generally remained, but the energy glut that existed then and kept average wholesale prices low was coming to an end. The purportedly competitive market for electricity in California began to be exposed as a house of cards in the latter half of 2000 and by the end of year toppled into hallways, hearing rooms, and offices in the capitol.

Notes

1 Interview with Dan Morain, August 3, 2021; Smith cited in Joe Fitzgerald Rodriguez, "What Lessons Can California Learn From Its Energy Crisis 20 Years Ago," *KQED*, July 17, 2021. https://www.kqed.org/news/11881207/what-lessons-can-california-learn-from-its-energy-crisis-20-years-ago
2 Jordan Bonfante, "The Endangered Dream," *Time*, November 18, 1991.
3 Jay Mathews, "The Endless Bummer," *The Washington Post*, November 17, 1991.
4 Bonfante, "The Endangered Dream."
5 Sarah Bohn and Eric Schiff, "The Great Recession and Distribution of Income in California," Public Policy Institute of California, December 2011.
6 Wilson quoted in Bonfante, "The Endangered Dream."

7 Carl Blumstein, L.S. Friedman, and Richard Green, "The History of Electricity Restructuring in California," *Journal of Industry, Competition and Trade*, Vol. 2 (2002): 9–38.
8 Allan Chen, "Myth: California is an Energy Hog Ranking Low in Energy Efficiency," *Sciencebeat*, Lawrence Berkeley National Laboratory, March 5, 2001. https://www2.lbl.gov/Science-Articles/Archive/energy-myths1.html
9 Nick Zanjani, "A Brief History of the California Public Utilities Commission: Examining the Past to Help Shape the Future." CPUC Executive Division, August 15, 2014, 20–25.
10 Conlon quoted in Michael Parrish, "PUC Pushing Free-Market Revolution," *Los Angeles Times*, May 8, 1994.
11 Blumstein, et al., "The History of Electricity Restructuring in California," 17.
12 David Osborne and Ted Gaebler, *Reinventing Government: How the Entrepreneurial Spirit is Transforming the Public Sector* (Boston: Addison-Wesley, 1992). Charles S. Clark, "Reinventing Government – Two Decades Later," *Government Executive*, April 26, 2013. https://www.govexec.com/management/2013/04/what-reinvention-wrought/62836/
13 Wilson official quoted in Staff, "Getting the Best Value," *Washington Technology*, November 7, 1996: https://washingtontechnology.com/Articles/1996/11/07/Getting-the-Best-Value.aspx
14 Parrish, "PUC Pushing Free-Market Revolution."
15 Cavanagh quoted in Parrish, "PUC Pushing Free-Market Revolution"; interview with Ralph Cavanagh, July 16, 2021
16 Christopher Weare, "The California Electricity Crisis: Causes and Policy Options," Public Policy Institute of California, 2003.
17 Blumstein, et al., "The History of Electricity Restructuring in California," 19; Xi Wang, "The Emergence of the Renewable Portfolio Standard in the U.S.: A Case Study of Negotiating Power in California," Master's thesis, Department of Environmental Studies, University of Colorado, 2014, 25.
18 For a detailed analysis of *The Blue Book* and the proposed "pool," see James Bushnell and Carl Blumstein, "A Reader's Guide to the Blue Book: Issues in California's Electric Industry Restructuring and Regulatory Reform," PWP-021, UC Energy Institute, June 1994. https://haas.berkeley.edu/wp-content/uploads/pwp021.pdf
19 Bill Bradley, "Master of Disaster," *LA Weekly*, February 14, 2001.
20 Bill Bradley, "Master of Disaster."
21 Fessler testimony before the Subcommittee on Energy and Power of the Committee on Energy and Commerce, U.S. House of Representatives, One Hundred Third Congress, Second Session, July 14, 1994.
22 CPUC, *The Blue Book* (R.94-04-031), April 20, 1994, 6.
23 CPUC, *The Blue Book*, 13.
24 CPUC, *The Blue Book*, 27.
25 California Assembly Concurrent Resolution 143, enrolled on August 31, 1994. Because the CPUC is a state entity established in the constitution, the legislature could only "urge" the CPUC to comply with its requests as opposed to directly demanding that they do so. However, the legislature by and large controlled the CPUC's budget through the state's annual budget process, and noncompliance with legislative "requests" could have negative fiscal consequences for the CPUC.
26 Arthur J. O'Donnell, *The Soul of the Grid: A Cultural Biography of the California Independent System Operator* (New York: iUniverse, Inc., 2003), 10, 14–15.
27 Assembly Joint Oversight Committee, "Assembly Joint Oversight Committee on Lowering the Cost of Electric Services" (October 1994). California Joint Committees. Paper 48. http://digitalcommons.law.ggu.edu/caldocs_joint_committees/48
28 Assembly Joint Oversight Committee.

29 Borenstein quoted in Assembly Joint Oversight Committee, 7; price data in Steve Isser, *Electricity Restructuring in the United States: Markets and Policy from the 1978 Energy Act to the Present* (Cambridge, UK: Cambridge University Press, 2015), 233.
30 Borenstein quoted in Assembly Joint Oversight Committee, 9.
31 Arth and Borenstein quoted in Assembly Joint Oversight Committee, 18.
32 Smutny-Jones and Borenstein quoted in Assembly Joint Oversight Committee, 86.
33 Moore, Arth, and Borenstein quoted in Assembly Joint Oversight Committee, 22.
34 O'Donnell, *The Soul of the Grid,* 101–2.
35 Blumstein and Bushnell, "A Reader's Guide to the Bluebook." Severin Borenstein, James Bushnell, Ed Kahn and Steve Stoft, "Market Power in California Electricity Markets," *Utilities Policy*, Vol. 5, No. ¾ (1995): 236; interview with Severin Borenstein, July 18, 2021.
36 Sher quoted in Jonathan Marshall, "U.S. Tells Utilities to Buy Cheaper Power," *San Francisco Chronicle*, February 23, 1995.
37 Interview with V. John White, June 28, 2021.
38 Marshall, "U.S. Tells Utilities to Buy Cheaper Power."
39 Peter Navarro, "Electric Utilities: The Argument for Radical Deregulation," *Harvard Business Review*, January-February 1996; O'Donnell, *The Soul of the Grid*, 14.
40 Foster quoted in Assembly Joint Oversight Committee, 63; Navarro, "Electric Utilities: The Argument for Radical Deregulation."
41 O'Donnell, *The Soul of the Grid*, 15; Romero quoted in Ron Russell, "Dim Bulbs," *SF Weekly*, March 7, 2001. https://www.sfweekly.com/news/dim-bulbs/
42 Interview with Cavanagh; Cavanagh to Harvard Electricity Policy Group, May 8, 1994.https://hepg.hks.harvard.edu/files/hepg/files/cavanagh_memo_1994.pdf?m=1523367138
43 PR Newswire, "New Coalition for California utility Restructuring Formed," July 10, 1995; https://www.consumerwatchdog.org/sites/default/files/2018-05/Cavanagh-Right-Formula-Dereg.pdf
44 All quotes in O'Donnell, *The Soul of the Grid*, 16.
45 Smutny-Jones quoted in Georg Rilinger, *Toward a Sociology of Economic Engineering: The Creation and Collapse of California's Electricity Markets between 1993 and 2001*, Doctoral dissertation, Department of Sociology, University of Chicago, August 2020, 374.
46 Smutny-Jones quoted in Georg Rilinger, *Toward a Sociology of Economic Engineering,* 375.
47 Fessler quoted in Ed Smeloff and Peter Asmus, *Reinventing Electric Utilities: Competition, Citizen Action, and Clean Power* (Washington, DC: Island Press, 1997), 88.
48 Blumstein, et al., "The History of Electricity Restructuring in California," 29.
49 Smeloff and Asmus, *Reinventing Electric Utilities*, 88-89; Kevin Porter, "A Summary of the California Public Utilities Commission's Two Competing Electricity Restructuring Proposals," Golden, CO: National Renewable Energy Laboratory, November 1995, 14–15; Ryan Wiser and Charles Allen Goldman, "California Renewable Energy Policy and Implementation Issues: An Overview of Recent Regulatory and Legislative Action," Lawrence Berkeley National Laboratory, Energy and Environment Division, September 1996, 18–19.
50 Wilson quoted in Russell, "Dim Bulbs."
51 Peace and Fessler quoted in O'Donnell, *The Soul of the Grid*, 20.

52 Peace and Fessler quoted in O'Donnell, *The Soul of the Grid*, 21.
53 Wiser and Goldman, "California Renewable Energy Policy and Implementation Issues," 16, 18–19.
54 Interview with Cavanagh; interview with Smutny-Jones.
55 Dan Morain, "Assembly Oks Bill to Deregulate Electricity," *Los Angeles Times*, August 31, 1996; Russell, "Dim Bulbs."
56 Assembly Bill 1890, Senate Floor Analysis (by John Rosza), Senate Rules Committee, August 27, 1996.
57 Peace quoted in Nancy Vogel, "How State's Consumers Lost with Electricity Deregulation, *Los Angeles Times*, December 9, 2000; Wilson quoted in Dan Morain, "Deregulation Bill Signed by Wilson," *Los Angeles Times*, September 24, 1996; Goldberg quoted in Morain, "Assembly Oks Bill to Deregulate Electricity."
58 Severin Borenstein, "The Trouble with Electricity Markets," *Journal of Economic Perspectives*, Vol. 16, No. 1 (Winter 2002): 195.
59 O'Donnell, *Soul of the Grid*, 101–102; Rilinger, *Toward a Sociology of Economic Engineering*, 200.
60 CPUC, "Pacific Gas & Electric Company's Divestiture of Electric Assets: Environmental Review," Decision 97-10-058, October 22, 1997, Attachment B, https://ia.cpuc.ca.gov/environment/info/esa/divest-pge-one/chapters/attachb.htm
61 AB 1890, Chapter 854 of 1996.
62 Staff, "Imbalance of Power: Competitors Say Delay in Electric Deregulation Helps PG&E, Other Utility Monopolies," *SF Weekly*, December 31, 1997.
63 Frank Wolak, "Diagnosing the California Electricity Crisis," *The Electricity Journal* (August/September 2003): 12.
64 Frank Wolak and James Bushnell, "Reliability Must-Run Contracts for the California Electricity Market," April 2, 1999, 2–3. http://web.stanford.edu/group/fwolak/cgi-bin/sites/default/files/RMR_Report_Bushnell.pdf
65 Rilinger, *Toward a Sociology of Economic Engineering*, 292.

3 The State Takes Over as the Market Implodes

As trying as the final months of 2000 had been, 2001 would bring unprecedented challenges and chaos to every facet of the state's electricity operations, literally from day one. In a January 1 conference call, senior Davis staff members ratcheted up ambitious and complicated plans for buying the IOU's transmission system and having the state's Department of Water Resources (DWR) negotiate long-term energy contracts in place of the IOUs, which now dangled by a thread from insolvency.[1] The mood in the governor's office dimmed along with the lights in the hallways and offices as the governor began promoting energy conservation as never before. It became clear that the effort to alleviate the crisis would no longer be handled primarily by entities outside the capitol given the growing scope of the problems and need for major legislation to resolve them. Adding to the challenge, those bills had to move through the legislature and be passed relatively quickly to help the state prepare for increased electricity demand in the summer and, of more immediate concern, before the rapidly rising tide of IOU debt and desperation put Californians into an electricity freefall.

***

On January 16, Assembly Speaker Robert Hertzberg left a Democratic Caucus meeting in the capitol while it was still in progress and steadfastly headed downstairs to the governor's office to hand-deliver him a letter. In the letter, Hertzberg noted that he had tried calling the governor first but was informed he was on a plane. He decided to dictate and personally deliver the letter when he didn't promptly receive a return call from the governor's chief of staff, Lynn Schenk. The speaker explained that his staff and experts "have been on the phone all morning with various creditors who have the capacity to force the investor-owned utilities into involuntary bankruptcy." He implored the governor to "immediately make an appropriate statement with respect to this crisis to stave off involuntary bankruptcy. With the default this morning of Southern California Edison and the corresponding downgrades in the [credit] ratings, the markets need some confidence that we have a process to stabilize this situation."[2]

DOI: 10.4324/9781003518150-4

While the governor did have an ever-evolving plan, the growing gravity of the problems he needed to address made planning very difficult and hamstrung efforts to instill confidence, especially after the CAISO lifted wholesale price caps on December 8th. CAISO CEO Terry Winter had maintained then that he could no longer purchase enough electricity with the caps in place, but CAISO still had problems getting enough power without caps even as prices set records. Davis and Senator Diane Feinstein highlighted that fact in a joint statement on December 13,[3] and that same day U.S. Energy Secretary Bill Richardson used his emergency authority to order generators to sell power to California until early January. Commenting on the need for this intervention, Kellan Fluckiger, the CAISO's chief operating officer, stated that the "credit limits of utilities and what markets are willing to sell us have been reached and surpassed in many cases. That has come to a head today."[4]

Everyone agreed that California's market was "broken" as unpaid debts mounted for both Edison and PG&E and wholesale prices skyrocketed with no end in sight. PG&E announced on January 2 that it might run out of cash by the end of the month without a significant rate increase or additional financing.[5] That same day, the utility's president, Gordon Smith, informed EOB Chair Michael Kahn that Canadian electricity and natural gas suppliers—which were outside the reach of Richardson's emergency order—"are just not taking any orders from us."[6] On January 5, a particularly tumultuous day for PG&E and Edison stock, *The Wall Street Journal* reported that the two IOUs "have together spent $11 billion more for wholesale power than they have been allowed to bill their customers as a result of a retail price freeze they originally supported." A number of utility critics, including senate leader John Burton, maintained that the IOUs would not be in their financial squeeze if they hadn't transferred billions in profits to their parent companies during the first two years of the new market.[7]

Nevertheless, by early 2001, California's unprecedented energy crisis required extraordinary action, and the governor, Burton, and Hertzberg absolutely needed to "stabilize this situation," as the speaker urged Davis to do in his letter. As such, after consultations with the two legislative leaders, Davis declared a state of emergency on January 17 amid rolling blackouts in parts of Northern California. "Unanticipated and dramatic increases in the price of electricity have threatened the solvency of California's major public utilities," Davis said, "preventing them from continuing to acquire and provide electricity sufficient to meet California's energy needs." He directed the state's DWR to take over the energy procurement process, including negotiating and signing long-term contracts, in place of the IOUs.[8] The previous day an assembly bill had been amended with provisions to fully enable the DWR to execute its procurement duties. The bill's author, Democrat Fred Keeley, the speaker pro tempore of the Assembly, noted that the legislature only had a few weeks to get the bill passed to keep the utilities out of bankruptcy and to placate generators and markets by ensuring that the full faith and credit of the state of California would be behind DWR transactions.[9]

***

Shortly before the state of emergency proclamation, Lynn Schenk convened an all-hands-on-deck meeting for everyone in the governor's office who had a role in dealing with the crisis, in addition to most cabinet secretaries and representatives from the CPUC, EOB, and California Energy Commission (CEC). After some semblance of a pep talk on the urgent need to tackle the energy enigma with newfound determination, Schenk and Deputy Chief of Staff Susan Kennedy gave everyone marching orders and we broke into several groups. The main task was to devise new or expanded energy conservation and efficiency programs, along with renewable energy incentives. The governor had already directed state agencies and college campuses to reduce their electricity consumption by at least 5 percent to comply with Secretary Richardson's request for this reduction in exchange for an extension of his emergency order requiring generators to sell power to the state. While the state achieved that goal expeditiously,[10] we endeavored to devise the best ways to achieve similar demand reductions in the much larger and more unwieldy residential and private sectors.

During the first two months of 2001, the organizational structure to deal with the energy crisis in the governor's office grew significantly in size and expertise and included more "teams" to promptly address a multitude of complicated and vexing problems as SCE and PG&E receded further into life-support modes. The governor enlisted the consultative services of former SCE President Michael Peevey and the current head of the Los Angeles Department of Water and Power, S. David Freeman, who together had many decades of energy industry experience. As the state prepared to spend billions of dollars on power and possibly purchase the IOUs' transmission infrastructure, the administration engaged two Wall Street investment firms, Saber Partners and the Blackstone Group. To further assist the state in its energy operations, the administration also hired Navigant Consulting and McKinsey & Company for management assistance and program design.[11] Combined with the energy crash course that I and other staffers received in 2000 (in addition to Davis himself), the new experts helped prepare the governor's office for the even greater trials of our energy odyssey in 2001, while the crash course continued on the next level.

For me, the next level included getting a better grip on how electricity markets worked and, specifically, a deeper understanding of the ways California's market provided ample opportunities for market power. Though the "success" of deregulation in other industries, including natural gas, had been a driving force behind the state's restructuring effort, the electricity industry—and electricity itself—was (and is) not the same as natural gas. Electricity could not be stored cost-effectively or on a large scale, and surges in instantaneous electricity demand at the flick of a switch at times provided significant price leverage to generators and traders to dictate spot-market prices. However, with electricity, the exercise of market power is generally episodic and relatively brief; that is, there are certain times that one or more sellers can take advantage of these dynamics before the price soon drops and these firms, in economics terms, become price takers instead of price makers. Defying this pattern, by December of 2000, wholesale electricity prices in California reached stratospheric heights and didn't come down much when demand significantly dipped.

Despite this anomaly and the "clear evidence" of market power identified by the FERC, the notion that the high prices stemmed mainly from market power by generators and marketers was downplayed or dismissed by many, including the country's top economic officials. Treasury Secretary Larry Summers, who maintained that price caps would "distort the market," and the chair of the Federal Reserve, Alan Greenspan, met with Davis in Washington, DC, on December 26th. They told the governor that, to the extent that California's market was being manipulated, it was due to the state's poor market design, especially the retail rate freeze that shielded consumers from high wholesale costs that could've moderated electricity demand. They urged him to lift the freeze, ratchet up conservation, and stop criticizing marketers and merchant generators.[12] Richardson agreed that the market was California's self-made mess and supported a rate hike but, unlike Summers and other high-level Clinton administration officials, favored FERC intervention. He spent his final six months as secretary trying to get a region-wide price cap in the West but to no avail as he had no direct control over the FERC and was a lone voice among Clinton's senior advisors.[13]

Two weeks later, and only days after the CPUC raised residential and industrial rates in an emergency vote for 90 days by 9 percent and 14 percent, respectively, Summers convened another meeting with California officials in Washington, DC, that included Ken Lay. Speaking with Davis, Hertzberg, and Burton, and minority leaders Jim Brulte and Bill Campbell, the Enron CEO reinforced the need for market-based solutions in California (though he had publicly acknowledged that the state's market "invites gaming"[14]). After pedantic commentary on how markets worked, Summers firmly asserted that the state, a creditworthy entity, needed to negotiate long-term contracts with the merchant generators, and he made clear once again that the administration would not support price caps. At the end of this browbeating and comeuppance, Michael Kahn, who had sat next to the governor during the meeting, recalled that "Hertzberg was peppy" while Burton "slumped in his chair" and Davis "tried to behave with dignity" as the door slammed on the last best hope for FERC intervention at the end of the Clinton administration.[15]

Prominent energy experts and economists outside of government echoed the advocacy of Summers and Greenspan for a significant retail rate hike and for increased conservation and other energy demand reduction efforts—but no wholesale price caps. On January 26, UC Berkeley's Institute of Management, Innovation & Organization released a "manifesto" on the urgent need to address California's "unprecedented electricity crisis, which threatens to wreck its economy and cause collateral damage throughout the West." Signed by 31 "experts in regulatory and energy economics," including two Nobel laureates, the paper warned that "either retail prices go up, or the frequency of rolling blackouts will accelerate." The group, contrary to Clinton officials, also warned against making the DWR the major purchaser of electricity and authorizing it to sign long-term contracts—two key components of Assemblymember Keeley's bill that was moving swiftly through the legislature—and instead advocated restoring the creditworthiness of the IOUs. The manifesto "urge[d] FERC, the CPUC and the CAISOs Market Surveillance Committee to work together to gather and analyze the information necessary to identify" and fix possible market power problems, but "we must not let this debate detract from dealing with" the fundamental absence of demand elasticity and sufficient supply.[16]

Around this time, I met with two well-regarded economists who chose not to sign the manifesto, Severin Borenstein of UC Berkeley and Stanford University's Frank Wolak. As the chair of CAISO's Market Surveillance Committee, Wolak had been warning the CAISO's Board of Governors and managers since the early months of the new market that it lacked sufficient competition and fostered market power. Borenstein, the head of the Energy Institute at the Haas School of Business, frequently collaborated with Wolak on research and shared his views on market power in California. Borenstein had spoken with Davis about the state's energy woes several months earlier at a meeting of the Western Governors Association, and he and Wolak had come to the governor's office to follow up on those issues amid even more dire circumstances. They agreed with other experts who argued that retail rates needed to be raised significantly which, at this point, almost everyone acknowledged, however reluctantly. But unlike the manifesto signatories and other notable economists such as Summers, these two did not gloss over the exercise of market power in California, which they found to be a "significant factor" even in the summers of 1998 and 1999.[17]

Borenstein and Wolak gave me a draft of their working paper (coauthored with Energy Institute research director, Jim Bushnell) that showed a lack of competitive pricing that resulted in good part from electricity *supply* being well below normal compared to the amount of electricity *capacity* online. They also highlighted a separate paper by economists Paul Joskow and Ed Kahn analyzing "forced" generation plant outages for unplanned repairs or maintenance—that is, those outages that are not "scheduled" or "planned" and therefore couldn't be accounted for in advance by the CAISO. Both papers cited and analyzed data from the National Electricity Reliability Council and other generation information. The two papers provided ample evidence that the growing number of forced outages in California—which in the latter half of 2000 came to be known as the "sick plant" syndrome—was so frequent and incidental to high demand periods that they simply could not be considered "random events." Focusing more specifically on this issue, the Joskow and Kahn paper stated that though "it is impossible to prove that any given generating unit declared as a forced outage could have been available, the incentive to withhold is powerful and the observed behavior exceeds historic outage norms."[18]

Short of "smoking gun" evidence (which was yet to come), the studies bolstered the case that the exercise of market power in California was pervasive, and Borenstein and Wolak became notable and authoritative advocates in 2001 for region-wide wholesale price caps in the West. They, along with Joskow and Alfred Kahn (no relation to Ed), both key figures in deregulation policy, argued into the spring for the FERC to impose caps, and each of them would cogently make that case in a publicized letter to Bush and in a key congressional committee hearing. But on that January day when Borenstein and Wolak first met with me, price cap prospects looked exceedingly dim. Indeed, all signs indicated that the nascent Bush administration opposed price caps even more than Clinton's and might not even extend Richardson's emergency order to palliate the growing quagmire.

* * *

On January 12, the energy industry publication *Natural Gas Intelligence* reported that the "bizarre behavior" of California's electricity market "for more than a month turned into outright insanity" the previous day when the CAISO "declared a Stage Three power alert and narrowly avoided rolling blackouts." Stage Three alerts were triggered when the CAISO determined that its power reserves were going to drop below 1.5 percent. "An unprecedented one-third (15,000 MWs) of the capacity usually available was offline," *NGI* noted.[19] On January 16, the same day that Keeley introduced his DWR bill, AB X1,* the CAISO issued another Stage Three power alert, and that would be followed by 31 straight days of Stage Three alerts and numerous rolling blackouts.[20] On top of everything else that had occurred from early December to mid-January, it now seemed like the Golden State, home to the information technology revolution and the world's sixth largest economy, had the electricity grid of a developing country.

The DWR began buying power on the spot market for SCE and PG&E on January 19 and utilized a $400 million appropriation authorized in an urgency bill, SB X7, by Senator Burton enacted that same day.[21] However, that purchasing authority would expire on February 1, providing just enough time, everyone hoped, to work out a longer term plan for DWR contracts and spot-market purchases in Keeley's bill. The exceedingly complicated and controversial elements of that effort ensured that negotiations would go down to the wire and made the ultimate outcome uncertain, particularly in the assembly.

* The shorthand designation for the legislature's First Extraordinary Session of 2001 was "X," and it began in January to deal with the energy crisis.

Figure 3.1 Governor Gray Davis signs SB X7 on January 19, 2001, as Assembly Speaker Robert Hertzberg reviews the bill.

Source: Photo: Paul Sakuma/AP.

A personable and able policymaker from a small town surrounded by redwoods in Santa Cruz County, Keeley agreed to author the DWR bill because Hertzberg had made him "chief operating officer" for the crisis, even though he had no energy policy experience. Hertzberg also enlisted the services of two financial experts to help draft AB X1,[22] along with economist Carl Pechman. Keeley was ably assisted by his chief consultant, Guy Phillips, who had helped promote renewable energy as an appointee of Governor Jerry Brown. Representing the DWR, attorneys from Hawkins Delafield & Wood drafted most of the amendments to the bill after Keeley's initial version. Regardless of all the experts who came together to work on the bill, the task proved extremely daunting. As Keeley later recalled, the effort to draft and amend the bill, and then get it passed with a two-thirds majority vote in two weeks, was akin to "trying to fix a flat tire on a car while it was still moving."[23]

By January 31, Keeley's bill had been substantially amended in the senate three times in six days before the senate voted, with a modicum of rancorous debate, to send the legislation to the assembly for final approval. Reporters for the *Los Angeles Times* aptly described the bill as a "multi-paged monster jampacked with technical and financial language."[24] The governor was as eager to sign the bill as Hertzberg and Keeley were to get it to him but, after further amendments in the assembly, they did not have the votes. The only Democrat refusing to support the bill, Barbara Matthews, who represented a San Joaquin Valley district, voiced concerns about the potential impact the bill would have on farmers in her region. On the other side of the aisle, Republican leader Bill Campbell, who supported the legislation, could only corral one other Republican vote while needing at least two more even if Hertzberg managed to get Matthews to change her mind.

As the evening wore on, Matthews received calls asking for her support from the governor, Feinstein, and PG&E Corporation CEO Robert Glynn Jr., but she resisted those pleas. Republicans criticized the bill's authorization for the state to sell up to $10 billion in bonds to cover the DWR's energy procurement instead of using the state's multibillion-dollar surplus to shield consumers and warned that large rate hikes would be necessary to service the bond debt. After much hand wringing and arm twisting, Hertzberg called for a final vote to pass the bill at 2:47 a.m. but to no avail,[25] leaving the DWR's ability to continue purchasing energy up in the air and pushing SCE and PG&E to the razor's edge of insolvency. The IOU-dependent PX trading platform, which both SCE and PG&E owed hundreds of millions of dollars, had shut down on December 31 given those unpaid debts, and the DWR did not seek to revive the PX for its transactions. The CAISO, which was designed to have a small power purchasing role mainly for grid reliability needs, helped fill the large void created by the PX's demise.

After an 11-hour break, the assembly reconvened to take up the bill once again, pursuant to the "reconsideration" of the legislation (which is customarily granted on a bipartisan basis to bills that fail to pass). During the break, Hertzberg had promised Matthews that legislation addressing agricultural concerns would be taken up after AB X1 passed, and she then agreed to support Keeley's bill. To get the final two votes, Davis and Hertzberg targeted Republicans Rod Pacheco and Anthony Pescetti. Following a conversation with Davis, Pacheco said his rate-hike concerns had been abated and he decided to vote "aye." Pescetti maintained that he changed his mind on the bill after learning that Enron had stopped providing power to some of its large industrial customers by unilaterally pulling out of their direct access contracts. "We have to protect industry in this state," he noted.[26] In the wake of another round of Republican invective against the bill on the assembly floor, it finally received the 54 votes it needed to get to Davis's desk. He signed it later that same day.

Ironically, the new U.S. Energy Secretary, Republican Spencer Abraham, cited the passage of the bill as evidence "that California can stand on its own" without meddlesome price caps, though he did extend Richardson's emergency order, for one time only, to February 7th. Some legislators asserted that if the CPUC had approved earlier IOU requests to allow them to enter long-term contracts, the legislature would not have needed to pass a bill giving the state the same authority. "If the PUC had addressed this problem last summer," Republican Bill Leonard maintained, "all this could have been avoided."[27] However, Leonard—who had accompanied Daniel Fessler on the CPUC's free-market fest to the U.K. in 1994—skirted the reality that Keeley's bill was not a second-tier remedy for the CPUC's alleged inaction during the summer of 2000; rather, it was for the serious missteps by the commission and legislators during restructuring.

***

The CPUC did not authorize the IOUs to enter into long-term contracts for electricity during the Fessler-led restructuring of California's market, and the legislature let that de facto "ban" stand in AB 1890. That ban has long been widely and rightly recognized as an egregious error and principal cause of the crisis.[28] There are a number of reasons why Fessler and his colleagues chose to not allow such contracts, but his view that "the competitive model to me means that electricity is a commodity to be traded in an open, transparent market"[29] indicates he believed such contracts would bypass the cost-cutting and liquidity benefits of much shorter term competitive pricing and trading. Others clearly shared that perspective, including, in their formal filings with the commission, the merchant generators that would eventually purchase the power plants divested by the IOUs.[30] A contract law expert, Fessler, also stated that a restructured spot market "substantially reduced" his "fears of a threat" to reliability "in the face of inevitable contract failure."[31] In addition, the costly long-term contracts that the CPUC had required the IOUs to sign with Qualifying Facilities in the 1980s pervaded the restructuring discussions like a bad hangover as many stakeholders cited the above-market and stranded costs these agreements created.

However, Fessler did not succeed in blocking bilateral contracts outside of the PX between private energy service providers (ESPs) and direct access customers that did not directly involve the IOUs outside of their transmission and distribution services. Ironically, many of these direct access agreements ultimately did result in "contract failure" during the crisis and had serious cost ramifications for wholesale electricity procurement by the IOUs in the latter half of 2000 and for the long-term contracts that DWR signed in 2001.

These direct access contracts tended to be structured as short-term deals lasting a number of months, and sometimes even shorter, as opposed to a number of years. As a primary contact in the governor's office for both ESPs and their large customers, I learned that these short "agreements" were preferred for several reasons, but mainly for the flexibility and financial advantage they provided to both parties.

As energy market analyst Robert McCullough noted when California's restructured market commenced in 1998, the IOUs "*must* bid all [their] generation into the PX and purchase all energy needs out of the PX." On the other hand, direct access ESPs "have the *option* whether to bid into and buy out of the PX" (emphases added). In most cases, beating the frozen-rate retail price of the IOUs left little, if any, margin for profit for the ESPs in the direct access market. As McCollough observed, "the dilemma for [ESP] suppliers in this market is: why should I sell energy to direct access customers at a discount off the power exchange [price] when I can make more money selling into the exchange?"[32] The short answer was that ESPs wanted to establish an early foothold in the direct access market with limited profits in numerous instances but with prospects for significant returns in the future as that market matured. But when wholesale prices began to soar in mid-2000, and particularly during and after December, the temptation grew for ESPs to sell power at wholesale for a much higher price to the PX and the CAISO than what they were getting from retail direct access customers under fixed-price contracts. Therefore, the short-term contracts, which generally provided wiggle room on ESP service obligations, enabled the ESPs to maneuver between sales to their retail customers and to the PX and CAISO when transactions with those two entities proved much more lucrative.

What financial advantage did this arrangement provide to direct access customers? In the retail market, larger industrial customers, which unlike IOU residential customers did not receive the 10 percent rate reduction in AB 1890, usually could find an ESP offering at least a somewhat better rate than the IOU. In addition, customers could also benefit from demand-side energy management services, which usually provided additional revenue for the ESP as well. However, the biggest benefit for both parties, but more so for the ESPs, was the leeway the ESPs had in moving their customers back to IOU service—and presumably back to direct access when the two parties eventually chose to do so.

In a meeting with representatives from the California Large Energy Consumers and the California Manufacturers & Technology Association, I asked how such maneuvering by the ESPs didn't constitute contract abrogation if the ESP unilaterally pushed retail customers back to IOU service before the expiration of their contracts. The rather sheepish response was that these contracts entailed an "understanding"—implicit, it appeared—that the customer would just accept being returned to IOU service because that customer was still entitled to the frozen fixed rate from the IOU without penalty or fee upon return. As such, ESPs maintained that unilateral contract abrogation didn't "harm" their customers because the customer safety net was that they would only have to pay the rate that they would've paid if they had never left the IOU, so customers would take their direct access savings while they could and bite their lips if they were abruptly returned to IOU service by an ESP. As the *Silicon Valley Business Journal* noted in early 2001, "despite hard feelings toward these energy companies for abandoning contracts, large businesses hope to have them back."[33] In the summer of 2000, this problematic direct access dynamic was not as clear and pronounced as it became when DWR began negotiating contracts in 2001. Nevertheless, by August 2000, less than three months after the price spikes began, 25 percent of direct access customers had returned to IOU service, which meant that the IOUs had to buy even more wholesale power at high costs that could not be fully passed on to those new retail customers.[34]

That same month, the CPUC voted to allow the IOUs to sign long-term contracts. However, the utilities also wanted the commission to wave any "unreasonable" cost penalties that might be imposed after its retrospective "reasonableness review" for such contracts, a practice that dated back to the commission's inception. The reviews were conducted roughly two years after contracts were initiated and were deemed necessary to protect ratepayers from IOUs passing their power purchase costs on to their customers unconditionally while at the same time being guaranteed a fixed rate of return on those purchases. There needed to be an incentive for the utilities to negotiate good deals, and because the review helped provide that, the CPUC chose not to exempt the IOUs from it. Nevertheless, even though the review had been in place for almost 90 years, the media and numerous stakeholders described the CPUC's decision (then and since) as one that *denied* the IOUs the opportunity to sign long-term contracts. Quite simply, the IOUs *chose* not to sign long-term contracts. As Edison's Bob Foster explained in October 2000, "you have to get to a point where you get prices down in this market before you can do long-term contracts."[35] Moreover, for whatever reason, Edison, and particularly PG&E, didn't even make full use of the authority provided to them by the commission in 1999 to enter into semi-long-term agreements—known as block-forward contracts—for power purchases to cover up to one-third of their electricity through the PX that were not subject to retrospective reviews.[36]

The IOUs did not want to sign contracts that were retrospectively reviewable because in the extremely volatile market, the power prices locked in by those contracts could be considerably higher than the spot and long-term prices in the months and years ahead. If that happened, the CPUC could rule that those contracts were not reasonable and prohibit an IOU from fully recovering the contract's costs in retail rates. In other words, the CPUC might use the review to help protect IOU customers from costs that they thought resulted from "unreasonable" market speculation by the utilities.

Though actions concerning the review were the province of the commission, Davis and legislators did not believe that residential and small business customers should have to assume that risk given that, unlike the IOUs and large energy consumers, they had not been active proponents of the restructured market that created the current dilemma. The IOUs' decision to not sign long-term contracts also showed that, as of late summer and early fall of 2000, they were as uncertain as we were in the governor's office of what electricity prices would be heading into the cooler and lower demand months. We all harbored hopes and cautious expectations that costs would continue to trend down. No one predicted that the average price in those months would more than double the average summer price. That just did not seem possible.

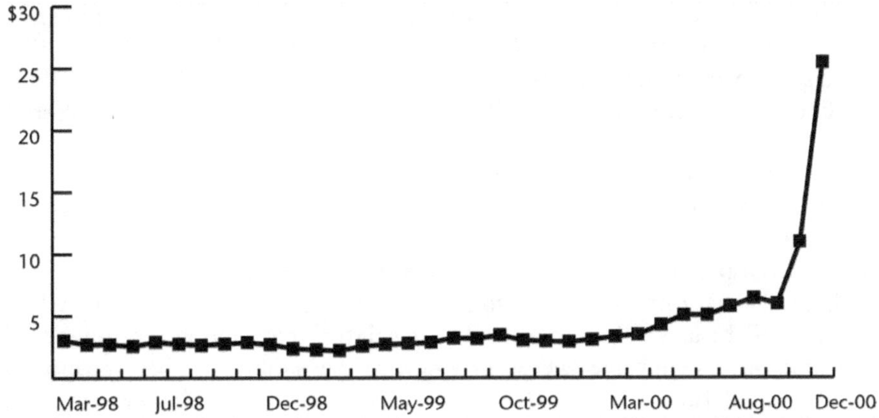

Figure 3.2 Spot price of natural gas ($/Mcf: Dollars per thousand cubic feet): March 1998 through December 2000. (The spot price represents the price at the state's main delivery point at the Southern California border with Arizona.)

Source: California Independent System Operator.[37]

As DWR representatives began negotiating contracts with merchant generators, we began to learn about potential manipulation of California's natural gas market by El Paso Natural Gas coinciding with huge gas and electricity price spikes that began in November, which prompted an investigation by Attorney General Bill Lockyer in early 2001.

While those allegations provided some semblance of an explanation for the price spikes, that proved to be cold comfort as the investigation would surely take months, if not years. The biggest near-term consequence of this alleged manipulation was higher costs for the DWR's spot-market purchases and contracts. Moreover, the big price jump led to the return—by choice or not—of almost all the direct access customers to IOU service by March, which meant that the DWR had to purchase power for them as well. That dynamic set up an eventual showdown between the state and direct access purveyors and customers regarding the latter's obligation to still pay for their share of the DWR's power purchase bills if they wanted to leave IOU service when short-term retail prices dropped in the latter half of 2001 and beyond.

***

The DWR contract negotiations paralleled the extraordinary effort to ramp up energy efficiency and demand reduction programs to help stabilize the market and prepare for escalating electricity use in the summer. On the same day he signed AB X1, the governor announced an $800 million "campaign to reduce demand and improve efficiency" to "crackdown on blackouts and reduce our energy bills." The "Flex Your Power" campaign, launched with help from the Advertising Council, featured, for demonstrative ease, an illustrated image of a finger flicking off a light switch, and this image soon became ubiquitous. For example, McDonald's printed 4 million tray-liners with it for its 1100 California locations, and the liners also offered conservation tips. "Californians have tremendous power as consumers," the governor proclaimed,[38] while I, with advice from the Energy Commission and other efficiency experts, began to work with legislators and their staff on how to get the best "bang for the buck" by summer from the programs in the $800 million proposal and possibly competing alternatives.

These discussions came to include renewable energy proposals when Davis, on February 14, announced a legislative package containing "the most ambitious renewable energy program in the nation."[39] These proposals mainly helped fund residential and small business-scale solar systems but also other alternative technologies such as cogeneration, which produced both electricity and thermal energy from a single fuel source. This effort built on legislation Davis had signed the previous summer when he pledged to "accelerate the contribution of solar energy and other renewables" to improve electricity affordability and reliability.[40] The most notable of these bills, AB 970, the California Energy Security and Reliability Act of 2000, created the Governor's Clean Energy Green Team and a CPUC program that subsidized the purchase of commercial and industrial-scale solar systems from 30 kW to 1 MW. While the renewable and cogeneration energy initiatives would not provide benefits as immediate as conservation and many efficiency efforts, they grew the state's "green" energy commitment and gained broad public support.[41]

I worked closely on this legislation with Senator Sher and his chief advisor and staff director, Kip Lipper, and with Burton's energy advisor, Brian Kelly. Sher's bill, SB X5, had been introduced in January and contained numerous provisions that were in the governor's proposal. Christine Kehoe's AB X29 emerged as the Assembly's companion bill to Sher's, and it expanded and accelerated efforts to replace inefficient appliances, especially refrigerators and air conditioners, with highly efficient "Energy Star" models, with performance standards certified by the U.S. Environmental Protection Agency. Deliberations on this effort included possibly enlisting the California Conservation Corps and private contractors to do this replacement on a very large scale. However, serious logistical challenges, including possible labor and product supply constraints, reeled in this ambitious proposal, though the Conservation Corps did get funding for a Mobile Efficiency Light Brigade. After two months of extensive and often testy debate and negotiations with legislators and stakeholders alike, we finally approached agreement on a package in the two bills that totaled just over $1 billion. But one major problem remained.

Assembly Democrats representing powerful agricultural interests in the vast Central Valley insisted on appropriating at least one-third of the funds for agriculture energy needs, and they informed me that they would not vote for either bill short of that amount. I told Assemblymember Dennis Cardoza, a Democrat from Turlock who became the lead negotiator for valley legislators, that agriculture only accounted for 5 percent of the state's annual electricity use. Cardoza then "reminded" me that Hertzberg, inferentially with Davis's blessing, had promised Assemblymember Matthews that her concerns for agriculture would be addressed in return for her vote for AB X1, though that promise lacked specifics, including a dollar amount. Nevertheless, with summer fast approaching, and with the negotiations having dragged on longer than expected, something had to give—and quickly. At the end of March, the CEC estimated that for every day the state delayed enactment of SB X5 alone, it missed the opportunity to save 20 MW of electricity.[42] With signoff from Mike Gotch, the governor's legislative secretary, I offered Cardoza 15 percent of the funds, which matched agriculture's energy use during its warmer peak consumption months when food processing ramped up. Cardoza and other valley members agreed to that, and we closed the deal with a reluctant commitment from the CPUC to work with large agricultural energy consumers on a voluntary demand reduction program similar to one offered to large industrial customers.

The total cost to the state's general fund for the two bills as passed in the legislature was just under $1.1 billion, but Davis exercised his line-item veto authority to trim that amount to $850 million pursuant to recommendations from me and the Department of Finance to eliminate funding for programs that provided little to no benefit during the summer. Upon signing the bills on April 11, he noted that the programs would trim about 2000 MW from electricity demand in California.[43] Key expenditures included $120 million for low-income residential weatherization; $70 million for an agriculture load-reduction program and $50 million for load-reduction in other sectors; $50 million for Energy Star appliance rebates and the same amount for local building efficiency projects, in addition to $60 million for commercial lighting; and $65 million for distributed generation such as solar panels. The two bills, combined with a new program to provide 20 percent bill rebates to IOU customers who reduced their electricity use compared to the previous year by 20 percent during the coming summer, reflected policymakers' faith in these efforts to be cornerstones in the enormous endeavor to significantly mitigate market volatility and potential blackouts.

***

While Davis lauded the signing of the two bills as a "big day" for ratepayers who received major "financial tools to help them conserve power," that accomplishment was partially eclipsed by the reverberations of PG&E's voluntary and unexpected bankruptcy filing five days earlier. Indeed, during his press conference to tout the conservation package, half the questions from reporters were about the bankruptcy and its implications. When asked why he thought PG&E filed for bankruptcy, the governor, who felt blindsided and betrayed by it, said he believed "they're trying to fashion a world for them that is at least as good, if not better, than it would have been if deregulation had worked out the way they hoped when they supported it back in 1996."[44]

PG&E began to "fashion" that world in a 2000 lawsuit against the CPUC by insisting that because its wholesale procurement and transmission of electricity fell within the exclusive jurisdiction of the FERC, the federal Filed Rate Doctrine, along with the Interstate Commerce Clause, barred the CPUC from setting rates at a level that precluded the utility from recovering its wholesale costs.[45] Therefore, PG&E maintained, those federal provisions superseded conflicting state laws, such as the statutory rate freeze in AB 1890 (to which PG&E had agreed) and regulatory decisions like the CPUC's refusal to raise rates (pursuant to AB 1890) for the IOU's cost recovery. Though SCE had filed a similar suit shortly after PG&E's, the latter's executives made the corporation's suit and self-perceived omnipotence a high horse to dictate demands to restore its creditworthiness and recover under-collections in deliberations with the governor's office in early 2001. "There was no room for negotiation," Press Secretary Steve Maviglio observed after the bankruptcy declaration. "It was my way or the highway."[46]

Six weeks before PG&E's bankruptcy filing, *The New York Times* profiled the 96-year-old San Francisco firm with a lede declaring that "Pacific Gas and Electric has long been a company that Californians love to hate." The profile noted PG&E's explosive growth after World War II which made it the largest electric utility in the U.S. by the 1980s, when ubiquitous bumper stickers declared: "Welcome to California. Owned and Operated by PG&E." The company "has not always had its way," the *Times* maintained, "but it has not been shy about trying to use its resources to wear down opponents."[47] Dramatically reinforcing that assertion, the film *Erin Brockovich*, which shamed PG&E for its indifference to and obfuscation of the company's dumping of cancer-causing chemicals into ponds in the 1940s that seeped into a Mojave Desert town's water supply, received five Academy Award nominations right before the *Times* feature ran. Ed Masry, the attorney who—with feisty legal clerk Brockovich's help—ultimately won a $333 million settlement from the company for residents of the town of Hinkley in 1996, observed in the profile that "there's a lot to dislike about PG&E."[48]

One would think, as we did in the governor's office, that the newly publicized Hinkley debacle and the collapse of deregulation would at least temper the approach of PG&E Corporation, the utility's parent company, in its negotiations with the state. To the contrary, as highlighted in a confidential February 28 PG&E memo obtained by the *San Francisco Chronicle*, the corporation's audacious demands included allowing the utility's $9 billion wholesale cost under-collection to "be fully recovered in retail rates without further CPUC review for prudence or any other purpose." PG&E also insisted that virtually all the restrictions on IOU actions in AB 1890 be overturned and that, going forward, the CPUC's oversight needed to be significantly reduced. Harvey Rosenfield, the head of the Foundation for Taxpayer and Consumer Rights, described PG&E's demands as "breathtaking in their level of self-delusion."[49]

The utility's bankruptcy filing surprised Wall Street and California officials alike because it was voluntary, not forced by creditors, and there were no overt indications it was forthcoming. However, the corporation arguably tipped its hand in January when, through a FERC filing, it began to build a financial "wall" around itself and another subsidiary, PG&E National Energy Group (NEG), based in Bethesda, Maryland. This strategic action, known as "ring-fencing," appears to have been finalized in early March when a senior corporation executive informed one of Davis's attorneys that it had borrowed $1 billion "to avert the possibility of a bankruptcy filing against the holding company" (i.e., the corporation) and "to support its non-utility activities," specifically NEG.[50] Of utmost importance, the ring-fencing also helped shield from the utility's bankruptcy proceedings the $4.6 billion it had transferred to the corporation since 1997. In other words, those profits most likely could not be used to offset the $9 billion under-collection that PG&E sought to recover through ratepayers alone.[51]

Incensed by the bankruptcy declaration, Davis called it a dishonorable act and "a real slap in the face to California" and his administration's good faith negotiations.[52] PG&E's CEO, Robert Glynn Jr., stated right after the filing that talks between the two parties had broken down weeks earlier but later told *The Washington Post* that a "handshake" agreement had been reached by the end of March.[53] Neither of these conflicting assertions was correct. The administration's negotiators, who had talked with PG&E counterparts two days before the filing, viewed PG&E's "my way or the highway" demands as solipsistic salvos that in time would yield to more realistic and reasonable discussions. The administration's communications with PG&E, including a conversation between Davis and the corporation's chief financial officer, Peter Darbee, shortly before the bankruptcy announcement, provided no ominous indications of that pending action.[54] Of all the media commentary on PG&E's bankruptcy calculations, *San Francisco Chronicle* reporter David Lazarus proved perspicaciously succinct and correct. Citing inside "observers," he wrote that PG&E "seized the opportunity to declare bankruptcy Friday so it could lay blame on the governor while also staying ahead of a breakthrough in Davis's separate bailout talks with Southern California Edison—a deal that worked against PG&E's financial interests."[55]

The Edison discussions proved contentious at times and suffered setbacks, but those problems paled in comparison to the row with PG&E and its bankruptcy which *Newsweek* described as "a full-fledged political soap opera."[56] Moreover, as Lazarus foreshadowed, Davis's negotiators, led by Chief Counsel Barry Goode, were on the cusp of an agreement on a memorandum of understanding with SCE. Determined to announce the MOU deal within a few days of the bankruptcy declaration, the governor and John Bryson, the CEO of SCE's parent company, Edison International, held a joint press conference in Los Angeles on April 9 to do just that. Though he never mentioned PG&E by name, Davis called the company out when he contended that the SCE MOU "proves that good things can happen when the parties are responsible, resolute, and remain at the table." The agreement "assured" ratepayers "of 10 years of low-cost power" and required SCE to sell its transmission lines to the state and dismiss lawsuits that "threatened to double" rates.[57] While the fate of PG&E and its shareholders and ratepayers now largely resided with a judge in bankruptcy proceedings, SCE's destiny would rely on the MOU and the unpredictable legislative process that ensued to approve it.

***

Another critical component of the state's strategy to stabilize the market took shape in late December when CPUC President Lynch informed the governor's office that Burton planned to introduce "a Power Authority bill to enable California to build and provide more generation on a cost-of-service basis," and to potentially operate the IOUs' transmission system if the state purchased it. Unlike Davis, Lynch had a good relationship with Burton, but she did her due diligence on the Power Authority proposal by noting its potential benefits and disadvantages, including possibly creating "bloated bureaucracies" and raising "expectations on which California may not be able to deliver."[58] Nevertheless, for state politicians looking for a way out of the power crisis, moving in the opposite direction of the market fixation that had driven the restructuring movement five years earlier held considerable appeal.

On January 6, state Treasurer Phil Angelides, the chief architect of the Power Authority concept, held a press conference and declared that it was time to "take control of our own destiny" by creating the Authority, and Burton announced he would introduce a bill to establish it. The plan was based on the New York Power Authority which was established in 1931 and once headed by the LADWP's David Freeman, who had consulted with Angelides on the plan's provisions. Freeman soon had the governor's ear as one of his top energy advisors, and he encouraged him to get firmly behind the proposal while Freeman continued to work with the treasurer and others to fine-tune it. The plan proved controversial, particularly with business groups; but legislators knew, as polls showed, that voters approved of the state getting more involved in supplying power. A spokesperson for Duke Energy, which had purchased four divested plants, opposed the plan with a terse rhetorical question: "Is this America or what?"[59] But such comments generally fell flat as concerns grew that private generators could not be counted on to build new plants to meet the state's growing energy needs and to charge reasonable prices.

Edison CEO John Bryson supported an expanded state role in the energy sector but advocated gaining control of "the generating plants that are causing the current financial problem" instead of purchasing the IOUs' transmission lines.[60] Seizing the divested plants would require the state to exercise its eminent domain powers pursuant to the governor's authority to seize private property under the state's Emergency Services Act. The governor held out the possibility of this action in his State of the State address "to prevent generators from driving consumers into the dark." Nevertheless, while the prospect of seizing plants proved popular with and cathartic for a wide swath of Californians seething with anger at the merchant generators,[61] taking over private plants was at the bottom of Davis's list of last resorts for one major reason: Such drastic action would likely create a self-fulfilling prophecy regarding the private sector's reluctance to invest in new California power plants (and perhaps in other sectors) by giving companies the biggest reason of all not to do so. But that concern didn't stop talk of "commandeering the plants," even from the governor, as exorbitant wholesale prices persisted into spring.[62]

The Burton bill, SB X6, passed out of the senate in late February after a succession of incremental amendments to fine-tune the Power Authority's duties, management, and governance. The assembly continued this process in March and April in accordance with the governor's desire "to get this bill right."[63] Freeman had managed to get him firmly behind the establishment of the Authority and, on April 16, Davis appointed Freeman to be his chief energy advisor and put him in charge of the state's conservation programs. That same day, the *Los Angeles Times* reported that Los Angeles Mayor Richard Riordan said that Davis told him he would appoint Freeman to head the Authority once the legislation had passed, and that Freeman had informed city officials he would be stepping down as head of the LADWP.[64]

The 75-year-old Freeman had a storied career in public sector energy management which began in the 1950s as an engineer and subsequently a lawyer for the Tennessee Valley Authority, a massive federal electric utility, and in 1978 President Jimmy Carter appointed him chairman of the TVA's board. He became the head of the LADWP in 1997 after serving in the same capacity at the New York Power Authority and the Sacramento Municipal Utility District. Known for his native Tennessee drawl and trademark cowboy hat, Freeman reminded me of an older version of actor Sam Elliott's laconic cowboy interlocutor and narrator in the 1998 comedy noir and cult-classic film, *The Big Lebowski*. Freeman had a similar cadence in his easy-going yet self-assured voice, and his folksy observations about "a blind pig in a poke" and the like tapped the same rusticity as Elliott's cowhand quips about a steer's "tookus." A meeting with Freeman almost always came with sagebrush witticisms. That was part of his argumentative charm which, along with his vast experience and shrewd ability to get things done, earned him the confidence of Davis, Burton, and other state officials.

In early May the legislature approved SB X6 on strictly partisan votes in both houses, and two weeks later Davis held a signing ceremony for the bill in Sacramento along with Burton and the secretary of the California Resources

Agency, Mary Nichols. The secretary noted that she had the "opportunity to work" with Freeman in New York and "saw how a public utility could maneuver and compete, and help keep the cost of the private sector down." Burton trumpeted that the bill "will have the longest and most lasting impact on California getting into the position to control its own destiny against the energy pirates." The governor warned the merchant generators that "if they don't want to see their plants seized, they should make sure their plants are up and running this summer to get us through what everyone acknowledges will be a difficult period."[65]

All the pieces that the state had control over were in place, as best they could be, for what we all hoped would not be an endless summer of blackouts and perhaps even higher wholesale prices. But a big price had already been paid, and not just in dollars. After several hefty spring retail rate hikes, which were needed in good part to pay DWR's power bills, and months of wear and tear on Californians, Davis's approval rating plummeted. A poll by the Public Policy Institute of California found that while the state's residents didn't blame him for causing the crisis, his job-approval rating in May had dropped to 43 percent, down from 62 percent in January.[66] In addition, though the Clinton administration's helping hand had been far from firm, President Bush's representatives, led by Vice President Dick Cheney, effectively just extended their middle fingers from afar. The White House had become Texas on the Potomac, and the energy companies, contrary to Davis and other California representatives, always found a welcome mat at its door.

Notes

1 "Follow-Up, 1/1/01 Conference Call," Chief of Staff Files, Archive Box 144/ Unit Box 12, Office of Governor Gray Davis Records (GGDR), California State Archives (CSA).

2 Robert M. Hertzberg to Gov. Gray Davis, January 16, 2001, Archive Box 144/12, GGDR/CSA.

3 Davis and Feinstein, "Governor Davis and Senator Feinstein Issue Statement Regarding California Energy," December 13, 2000. http://gray-davis.com/ ViewLibraryItem.aspx?ID=9272

4 Fluckiger quoted in a WSJ.com News Roundup, "Richardson Orders Emergency Action As California Power Crunch Worsens," *The Wall Street Journal*, December 13, 2000.

5 WSJ.com News Roundup, "PG&E Expects to Run Out of Cash by Late January or Early February," *The Wall Street Journal*, January 2, 2001.

6 Gordon Smith to Michael Kahn, "Electricity Crisis," January 2, 2001. Archive Box 144/12, GGDR/CSA.

7 Brian Melley, "California Utility Is Broke after Making Billions," *Las Vegas Sun*, January 30, 2001.

8 Governor Davis, "Governor Davis Proclaims a State of Emergency," Press Release and Proclamation, January 17, 2001.

9 James Sterngold, "California Governor Offers a Plan to Save State From Energy Crisis," *The New York Times*, January 9, 2001.

10 U.S. Department of Energy, "Energy Secretary Extends Emergency Power Order for California," Press Release, January 5, 2001; Governor Davis, "California Meets Five Percent Conservation Goal," Press Release, January 17, 2001.
11 Other firms and outside advisors were hired, but those listed in this paragraph were regularly present in the governor's office and interacting with staff. Others were not.
12 Alex Gibney, "Larry Summers' Enron Problem," *Daily Beast*, November 12, 2008.
13 Richardson interviewed by PBS *Frontline* and *The New York Times*, April 10, 2001 for "Blackout," a documentary on California's electricity crisis. https://www.pbs.org/wgbh/pages/frontline/shows/blackout/interviews/richardson.html
14 Richardson interviewed by PBS *Frontline* and *The New York Times*; Lay quoted in James Flannigan, "Texas Power Suppliers Shun Bad Guy Label," *Los Angeles Times*, January 14, 2001.
15 Arthur O'Donnell interview with Michael Kahn, January 9, 2003, provided to the author in 2021 by Energy Overseer/Arthur O'Donnell.
16 David Teece, et al., "Manifesto on California's Energy Crisis," Institute of Management, Innovation & Organization, UC Berkeley, January 26, 2001. https://silo.tips/download/manifesto-on-the-california-electricity-crisis; and Peter G. Gosselin and Dan Morain, "Power Crisis a National Threat, Greenspan Says," *Los Angeles Times*, January 26, 2001.
17 Borenstein, Bushnell and Wolak, "Diagnosing Market Power in California's Restructured Wholesale Electricity Market," National Bureau of Economic Research, Working Paper 7868 (September 2000): 35. https://www.nber.org/papers/w7868
18 The draft paper I received from Borenstein and Wolak was further fine-tuned and then published in 2002: Borenstein, Bushnell and Wolak, "Measuring Market Inefficiencies in California's Restructured Wholesale Market," *The American Economic Review*, Vol. 92, No. 5 (December 2002). Similarly, Joskow and Kahn "improve[d] the data" in their analysis, and it was published in summer 2001: Joskow and Kahn, "Identifying the Sources of Market Power: Refining the Estimates," July 5, 2001 (Quote on p. 3.): https://economics.mit.edu/sites/default/files/2022-09/Identifying%20the%20Exercise%20of%20Market%20Power%20Refining%20the%20Estimates.pdf
19 *NGI* Staff Reports, "California Hits Stage Three; Narrowly Averts Blackouts," *Natural Gas Intelligence*, January 12, 2001.
20 O'Donnell, *Soul of the Grid*, 231.
21 SB X7, Chapter 3 of 2001.
22 Miguel Bustillo, "Wall St. Firm Calls Blackouts a Tactic to Raise Rates," *Los Angeles Times*, January 25, 2001.
23 Interview with Fred Keeley, December 17, 2001.
24 Jennifer Warren and Miguel Bustillo, "GOP Wields Muscle in Crisis Session," *Los Angeles Times*, February 2, 2001.
25 Jennifer Warren and Miguel Bustillo, "GOP Wields Muscle in Crisis Session."
26 Jennifer Warren and Miguel Bustillo, "GOP Wields Muscle in Crisis Session."
27 Abraham quoted in Sam Howe Verhovek, "Energy Secretary Rejects Request to Cap Electricity Price," *The New York Times*, February 3, 2001; Leonard quoted in Greg Lucas, "State OKs $10 Billion for Power," *San Francisco Chronicle*, February 2, 2001.
28 For example, see the "Manifesto on California's Energy Crisis," 2.
29 Fessler quoted in Rilinger, *Toward a Sociology of Economic Engineering*, 405.
30 Fessler quoted in Rilinger, *Toward a Sociology of Economic Engineering*, 109.
31 Bushnell and Blumstein, "A Reader's Guide to the Blue Book," 12.

32 Robert McCullough, "California's Electricity Market: Are Customers Necessary?" *Public Utilities Fortnightly*, July 15, 1998.
33 Andrew F. Hamm, "Energy Firms Fight to Leave Room for Return to California," *Silicon Valley Business Journal*, March 18, 2001.
34 Three months after the price spikes began, the percentage of DA customers that went back to IOU service—by choice or not—declined from 16 percent to 12 percent (of total IOU service load). https://www.cpuc.ca.gov/-/media/cpuc-website/divisions/energy-division/documents/direct-access-implementation-activity-reports/statewide-da-load-graph-8_30_2021.xlsx
35 Foster quoted in *NGI* Staff Reports, "CAL-ISO to Consider Imposing Wholesale Caps," *Natural Gas Intelligence*, October 4, 2000.
36 Wolak, "Diagnosing the California Electricity Crisis," 17–18.
37 CAISO data cited in California State Auditor, "Energy Deregulation: The Benefits of Competition Were Undermined by Structural Flaws in the Market, Unsuccessful Oversight, and Uncontrollable Competitive Forces," March 2001, 54.
38 Governor Davis, "Gov. Davis Outlines $800-Million Energy Efficiency and Demand-Reduction Program," Press Release, February 1, 2001.
39 Governor Davis, "Governor Davis Announces Bill Package To Increase Renewable Energy, Distributed Generation And Co-Generation," Press Release, February 14, 2001.
40 Governor Davis, "Governor Gray Davis Signs Legislation To Promote Renewable Energy," Press Release, September 21, 2000.
41 In a July 2001 poll, the PPIC found that "two in three Californians say they would favor developing more solar and wind power, even if it meant higher electricity prices." PPIC, "Californians Galvanized By Energy Crisis," Press Release, July 19, 2001.
42 Jennifer Warren and Carl Ingram, "Raft of Bills Aimed at Energy Conservation," *Los Angeles Times*, March 30, 2001.
43 Governor Davis, "Governor Gray Davis Signs Landmark Energy Conservation Package," Press Release, April 11, 2001.
44 Governor Davis, "Governor Gray Davis Signs Landmark Energy Conservation Package."
45 Lockyer, "Attorney General's White Paper," 46.
46 Maviglio quoted in David Lazarus, "PG&E Took Hard Line, Dooming State Talks," *San Francisco Chronicle*, April 15, 2001.
47 Laura M. Holson, "Power, Policy And Glory Dimmed: PG&E Finds No Sympathy Among Customers or Once-Docile State Legislators," *The New York Times*, February 22, 2001.
48 Masry quoted in Holson, "Power, Policy And Glory Dimmed.".
49 Lazarus, "PG&E Took Hard Line" (including Rosenfield quote).
50 Fax from PG&E pursuant to a phone call by Dan Richard to Davis Advisor David Rosenberg, March 2, 2001, Archive Box 144/12, GGDR/CSA; Tim Reason, "Ring Around the Subsidiary," *CFO Magazine*, October 1, 2001. NEG would declare bankruptcy in 2003. See Rebecca Smith, "PG&E Seeks Court Protection For Its Wholesale Energy Unit," *The Wall Street Journal*, July 9, 2003.
51 Reason, "Ring around the Subsidiary."
52 Governor Davis, "Governor Gray Davis Comments On PG&E Filing For Bankruptcy," Press Release, April 6, 2001.
53 Peter Behr, "California Utilities Took Different Lines," *The Washington Post*, April 17, 2001.
54 Lazarus, "PG&E Took Hard Line."
55 David Lazarus, "Power Play: PG&E Timed Bankruptcy to Blame Davis, Insiders Say," *San Francisco Chronicle*, April 8, 2001.
56 Karen Breslau, "As The Megawatts Turn," *Newsweek*, April 6, 2001.

57 Governor Gray Davis Press Conference transcript, April 9, 2001.
58 Loretta Lynch fax to the Office of Gov. Gray Davis, "Transmission Company/Power Authority Options," December 26, 2000, Archive Box 144/12, GGDR/CSA.
59 Angelides and Duke spokesperson quoted in Nancy Vogel, "$10-Billion Plan for Power Authority Would Reverse State Deregulation," *Los Angeles Times*, January 6, 2001.
60 Bryson quoted in Vogel, "$10-Billion Plan for Power Authority Would Reverse State Deregulation."
61 See, for example, Michael J. Aguirre, "Use Eminent Domain as a Power Tool," *Los Angeles Times*, April 9, 2001.
62 Linda Gledhill, "State Treasurer Urges Davis to Take Over Power Plants," *San Francisco Chronicle*, May 12, 2001. John Burton's Senate Resolution 1, which the Senate approved on a partisan vote on July 12, urged the governor to "commandeer power plants" to protect "the health and welfare of the citizens of California."
63 Susan Kennedy, "Needed From Legislature," Energy Files, Archive Box 140/7, GGDR/CSA.
64 Tina Daunt and Rone Tempest, "Freeman to Head New State Power Authority," *Los Angeles Times*, April 17, 2001.
65 All quotes from "Governor Gray Davis Bill Signing" transcript, May 16, 2001.
66 Mitchell Benson, "Angry Californians Don't Blame Davis for Power Crisis, Poll Finds, *The Wall Street Journal*, May 21, 2001.

4 Going It Alone

California Gets a Cold Shoulder from the White House and the FERC

On August 14, 2000, Governor Davis grabbed the national spotlight when he welcomed party delegates to the Democratic National Convention in Los Angeles. With all the trappings of a Hollywood production, he also welcomed "America to a state that—for 150 years—has captivated the world's imagination, from the gold rush to the silver screen to the silicon chip." After lauding Bill Clinton, Al Gore and the "new moderate direction in American politics," he jabbed at George Bush and Dick Cheney by joking that "here in the home of the film industry we've seen the previews of the Republicans' movie: 'George and Dick's Excellent Adventure.' I don't think it's going to make it."[1] However, just over five months later, the roar of approval from that convention crowd became a distant memory of what might have been, as George and Dick's adventure premiered in Washington D.C. with California as the leading and seemingly hapless foil of the petrol-powered protagonists.

On the same day that George W. Bush became the 43rd President of the United States, *Los Angeles Times* reporters Ronald Brownstein and Richard Simon noted that top California Republicans, "fearful of a backlash," had urged Bush to "aggressively intervene in the state's deepening energy crisis." Fanning the flames of this fear, Bob Mulholland, a sharp-tongued state Democratic Party consultant, warned that "every Republican candidate in 2002 may be running like cockroaches caught in the kitchen lights" if Bush let the crisis fester. However, Brownstein and Simon also insightfully observed that "as governor in Texas, Bush was ruthless in focusing on his own agenda" and avoided entanglement in other issues.[2] In fact, that focus, along with his free-market faith, fostered a rather laissez-faire approach to the crisis that fixated on California's electricity "supply" problem and the state's responsibility to fix it.

Shortly before taking office, Bush unsurprisingly made clear his opposition to price caps in California and elsewhere in the West, claiming that they would be a deterrent to the construction of power plants. Bush further maintained that California needed to "relax" its environmental rules and regulations, not only to get power facilities built, but to increase oil and gas production as well.[3] That wasn't necessarily a surprise either given his and the Bush family's oil industry ties, and that Vice President Cheney had

DOI: 10.4324/9781003518150-5

been CEO of Halliburton Corporation, the largest oil and gas-drilling services company in the nation, prior to becoming Bush's running mate and chief energy advisor. Far from offering even a guardedly cooperative hand for resolving the crisis, Bush and Cheney—with prominent support and input from Ken Lay—essentially attacked California's environmental brand and cemented the California versus Texas socio-political tilt that became emblematic of the growing divide between the "red" Republican and "blue" Democratic states in the 21st century.

***

During the first weeks of the Bush administration, pundits and energy experts took stock of California's crisis and the Texas dynamic shaping the president's perspective on it. Robert Stein, a political scientist at Rice University in Houston, noted that, in contrast to California, in the Lone Star State "energy is like a religion, and you believe in it and support it" for the economy, employment, and general well-being.[4] The Bush family certainly understood that and the transformative role that the multitude of independent oil prospectors—known as "wildcatters"—had played in making Texas the energy capital of America. That independent streak also led to the creation of a unique intrastate electricity grid in 1935 which Texas politicians established to avoid the reach of the federal government after President Franklin Roosevelt signed the Federal Power Act.[5] That self-sufficient grid, which became the Energy Reliability Council of Texas in 1970, differed from the 11-state Western grid that included California and functioned interdependently. As economist Paul Joskow noted, claims by Bush and his advisors that California could fix its own problems ignored the interconnected way that electricity markets worked in the West and the federal government's responsibilities in the energy sector outside of Texas.[6]

In the early 20th-century California led the nation in oil production, but Texas soon surged past it, and by the time of the electricity crisis, production in New Mexico and the Gulf of Mexico surpassed California's as well. Oil production remained an important part of the state's economy, but views of the industry had changed after a huge offshore oil spill in the Pacific Ocean in 1969 fouled the beaches of scenic Santa Barbara and devastated marine life and wildlife. This incident proved to be a catalyst for the emergence of the national environmental movement in the 1970s, and that movement took hold in California more than any other state and became a critical part of its ethos, much like oil and gas production did in Texas (as popularized by the hit TV show, *Dallas*).

Bush initially contended that California's stringent smog rules were a prime culprit in limiting electricity supply, and he suggested that the state should ease those rules to help prevent rolling blackouts. He seemed unaware that, pursuant to amendments to the Clean Air Act approved in 1990 by his father, President George H.W. Bush, California could not roll back its smog rules without approval from the U.S. EPA. As such, on February 15, 2001, the younger Bush ordered the EPA to accommodate California's needs for power with secondary regard for potential air pollution, and the EPA did not undertake enforcement actions during the crisis.[7] Nevertheless, even merchant generators scoffed at Bush's assertion about the impact of smog rules. Richard Wheatly, a spokesperson for Houston-based Reliant Energy, which bought and operated four divested plants in California, maintained that claims about environmental regulations holding back output at those plants were "absolutely false. We're making every megawatt available on request. We factor the air quality regulations into our daily operating basis, and they are not causing us to withhold power."[8] While we appreciated such candor in the governor's office, it did not mean the generators were not withholding power to maximize profits; it just meant, as Wheatly indicated, if the generators had to purchase expensive air pollution credits in the southern California smog market known as RECLAIM, or pay fines, they generally would and then just pass those costs on. It appears that certain generation units in the region also used the high cost of the emission credits to enhance their exercise of market power and increase the cost of wholesale electricity, especially in the summer and fall of 2000.[9] Some plants did go offline then to avoid exceeding their emissions limits. But later, at the height of the crisis when Bush took office, no essential electricity production was curtailed because the Southern California Air Quality Management District had eased pollution control rules for dirtier plants in Glendale and elsewhere in greater Los Angeles.[10]

Regardless, Bush, Cheney, and energy executives continued to seize on the state's crisis to call for rollbacks of environmental laws and regulations and blame them for the power-plant shortage. Refuting that claim, the *Los Angeles Times* contended that the "administration's attitude seems to be that California must pay a price for its environmental zeal" while it ignores the "regulatory uncertainty and economic decisions by utilities and private generating companies that caused the lack of new plants in the 1990s." The Sierra Club, founded in 1892 by the legendary environmentalist and California wilderness devotee, John Muir, issued a lengthy statement under the heading "Myth vs. Fact" and made clear that the club "has not blocked or delayed any new power plants in California over the last 10 years." In addition, the statement noted that, according to the California Energy Commission, "no electric power plant in California has been rejected over air pollution issues." *The Sacramento Bee* also rejected the environmentalism run-amok claims by highlighting that "of the 21 power plants proposed for licensing since 1997, competing companies have intervened in 12 proposals," which slowed the process "in at least four situations."[11]

Out of operational necessity, the governor on February 8 issued a series of executive orders "to comprehensively address power generation," including "increased output at existing facilities," and to "remove barriers to summertime operation."[12] On March 22, in a hearing of the House Subcommittee on Energy and Air Quality, the chair of the California Air Resources Board (CARB), Dr. Alan Lloyd, testified that the executive orders "ensure that where statutory and regulatory impediments exist—whether related to operation of an existing plant" or building a new one—"they will be swiftly addressed and resolved."[13] I worked with Lloyd, California EPA Secretary Winston Hickox, and the CARB's executive director Michael P. Kenny to "swiftly" address and resolve issues, though CARB staff occasionally pushed back on those efforts.

CARB Senior Advisor Catherine Witherspoon, who would succeed Kenny as the Board's executive director in 2003, did not hesitate to privately voice her concerns about reducing emission control requirements, and a few times proved particularly resistant to such efforts. She was smart and as well versed in air quality issues as anyone I dealt with, and I understood her consternation and that of other CARB staff; but we had to keep the lights on. The biggest concern involved the expanded use, during high electricity demand periods in the spring and summer, of small "peaker" plants that ran on natural gas but with dirtier emissions than the bigger and more efficient natural gas-fired plants with emission reduction technology. But those peakers ran considerably cleaner than diesel generators, which McKinsey consultants hired by the administration had recommended using on a considerable scale to mitigate the merchant generators' market power. That recommendation did not prevail.[14] With the virtue of going with the lesser of two air-quality evils, Witherspoon told reporters at a spring CARB news conference that "if we don't get every last megawatt we can" from the peakers and other natural gas generation, "we will see people turning to diesel more frequently." Therefore, under the circumstances, the administration argued that the peakers would provide a net air-quality benefit by avoiding the use of diesel generation, though David Freeman had a contingency plan to utilize that generation as a last resort.[15] We all had our fingers crossed that this utilization would never be needed and publicly maintained that it wouldn't be after news of Freeman's plan created concern among environmental groups.

***

While the stark difference of opinions between the Bush and Davis administrations on price caps and environmental regulations generated much finger-pointing and media coverage even before Bush took office, the frustration of the governor and Michael Kahn on caps with top Clinton administration officials was publicly limited and tempered, but privately seething. In a 2003 interview, Kahn recalled the last-ditch "summit" meeting on January 13 convened and led by Larry Summers and National Economic Advisor Gene Sperling in Washington, DC, who spoke with Davis and state legislative leaders in Los Angeles by video conference. Kahn maintained that Summers and Sperling seemed oblivious to the ample evidence and legal arguments he, Davis, and others had presented on the market's egregious dysfunction.

The two Clinton officials argued that the crisis boiled down to "a credit problem"—that "all the world will be fine, [and] prices will go down if there is sanity and solvency in the market," Kahn recalled. After hearing that and a patronizing litany of blame for all the state's electricity restructuring mistakes from Summers, Sperling, and Ken Lay, who also participated in the meeting, Kahn felt like "it was Alice in Wonderland."[16]

The fact that Kahn, two years after this meeting, still harbored such deep anger and dismay about it illuminates how critical it was beyond initiating the legislation for DWR's pivotal procurement role. To be clear, there *was* a credit problem that had to be addressed, but Kahn thought that Summers and Sperling were more concerned about getting the generators paid than bringing down wholesale prices.[17] Indeed, wholesalers charged exorbitant wholesale prices in the spring and summer of 2000, well before the credit problem emerged. It's hard to believe that Summers and Sperling, two very smart guys, didn't know that—and that whatever credit "risk premium" existed in spot market prices, having the state of California take over as the primary creditworthy buyer would not likely result in just and reasonable wholesale costs. Speculation swirled in some quarters of the capitol that, because energy company stocks had soared after the bear market and electricity crisis began in spring 2000, the Clinton administration did not want to throw cold water on the few hot performers on Wall Street.

Whatever the case, Summers and Sperling did not agree with Davis, Burton, and Hertzberg on the urgent need for price caps. Three months after the meeting, former Energy Secretary Richardson said, "I think those power marketers didn't cheat, but they took advantage of the price situation." Despite growing evidence of "cheating," he blamed the CAISO's unilateral "wholesale price caps" in 2000—his support of region-wide price caps in the West notwithstanding—and the "very botched, market-destroying" AB 1890 for the "huge price increases."[18] Summers and Sperling did not view generators and marketers taking "advantage of the price situation" as evidence of market power that required the Federal Energy Regulatory Commission (FERC) to impose just and reasonable rates in California or, unlike Richardson, throughout the Western grid. That proved to be the final word on price caps from the Clinton administration, and on January 17 Richardson carried out the administration's last act on the crisis by extending his emergency order requiring generators to continue supplying energy to the IOUs for another week.

On the heels of the hugely disappointing summit meeting, the legislature, with strong backing from the governor, passed Fred Keeley's AB X5 that required the replacement of CAISO's 26-member governing board, which included power industry representatives, with only five members appointed by the governor. As Kahn recalled, the governor was "apoplectic" over Terry Winter's removal of the wholesale price caps in early December, after which the CAISO, as the FERC's in-state proxy, clearly became an "enemy." Shortly after Winter's decision, Davis had called on Congress to investigate the FERC for approving it and warned that the state might take over the CAISO Board, though he did not issue any immediate directives. However, after the January

13 meeting, "the one thing" Davis was "going to do for sure," Kahn recalled, "is take over the CAISO" to remove the FERC's control,[19] notwithstanding the likely battle with the FERC over that action that was foreshadowed by a similar legislative showdown in 1999.

Spearheading that 1999 state effort, Senator Steve Peace, one of the strongest critics of the FERC and the CAISO, had introduced legislation to loosen the FERC's control over the CAISO and the PX. But that legislation, which was less politically charged than AB X5, fizzled after state lawyers eventually conceded that the FERC had jurisdiction under the Supremacy Clause of the U.S. Constitution because, pursuant to AB 1890, the CAISO and PX were public benefit corporations engaged in interstate commerce, and not state agencies despite being established by state law.[20] Though a "compromise" bill passed, it essentially confirmed the commission's dominant position. The FERC sought to "exercise jurisdiction over not only the interstate operations of the ISO and the PX," the Senate Rules Committee analysis observed, "but also over the framework of the institutions themselves."[21]

After the enactment of AB X5, outgoing FERC Chairman James Hoecker, a Democrat, called the bill "an unacceptable intrusion into federally regulated power markets,"[22] and most everyone expected the commission to mount a major legal challenge to reestablish control of the CAISO. Surprisingly, a pitched battle for control did not ensue as the matter did not appear to be a priority for the Bush administration, and the creation of the new board withstood more modest FERC legal challenges. The governor appointed Kahn as chair, and he was joined by California's Secretary for Business, Transportation and Housing, Maria Contreras-Sweet, Davis policy advisor Tal Finney, and Carl Guardino, the head of the Silicon Valley Leadership Group. Consumer advocate Mike Florio, an attorney for The Utility Reform Network, and the only holdover from the original board, filled the final seat. On the one hand, the new board brought a whiff of victory and empowerment to the governor's office and the legislature; on the other, we knew that the actions of the new board might well have significant impact in the long run, but in the shorter term it could do very little to address the wholesale market problems at the core of the crisis which remained firmly in the FERC's purview.

***

While Bush's ardent free-market philosophy did not bode well for FERC intervention in California's energy meltdown, the fact that he lost California by a double-digit margin in the election didn't help either. As one Republican advisor close to the new president noted, the Bush campaign "put $22 million into the state and Gore spent zero. And they lost by 13 points."[23] Republicans had hoped to win back California, which had voted decidedly Republican in post-World War II presidential elections until 1992, but the political tide in 2000 continued to flow in the Democrats' direction. In addition to Gore's resounding victory, Democrats bolstered their majorities in the state legislature and won four new seats in Congress. As southern California political analyst

Sherry Bebitch Jeffe observed, "the Republican Party is on life-support" in California.[24]

Rejecting bipartisan requests from Californians for federal intervention to help fix the electricity market, Bush press secretary Ari Fleisher steadfastly maintained that "the President believes that this is a problem that can be and should be addressed by Californians." Moreover, he contended that the "federal arsenal is not well-equipped to get California out of this problem," and "California understands that and so does Governor Davis."[25] On the contrary, the governor knew that the FERC was "well-equipped" under the Federal Power Act to impose price caps. Therefore, he and other prominent Democrats picked up that argument from where they had left off with Clinton officials, with whom there had at least been an engaged dialogue. Initial communication with the Bush administration was all but confined to preachy and perfunctory interaction with Energy Secretary Spencer Abraham and FERC officials. Senator Feinstein requested a meeting with the president to discuss the crisis, but the White House rejected her request with a form letter that misspelled her name.[26]

Ironically, Abraham, as a U.S. Senator from Michigan in 1999, had introduced a bill to abolish the Department of Energy, as noted by New Mexico Senator and former colleague, Democrat Jeff Bingham, during Abraham's confirmation hearing in the Senate Energy and Natural Resources Committee. However, Bingham claimed that Abraham "has since seen the light" and understood the great importance of the department and its work. In an equally collegial manner, Feinstein announced her support for Abraham but also that she would "introduce legislation that will give this secretary—he may not want it—the right to set" wholesale electricity rates "if FERC is going to sit by and allow...Western States to self-destruct."[27]

While Feinstein took advantage of an opportune moment to announce this new legislation, it had no realistic chance of becoming law. In addition to opposition by Bush, Republicans controlled both the house and the senate for the first time since 1953 and therefore controlled the legislative process. Feinstein's proposal soon became a draft bill to order the FERC to impose wholesale price caps in the West until March 2003 or until the commission found rates to be just and reasonable. In a legislative hearing on that bill in the same senate committee that approved his nomination two months earlier, Abraham maintained that its price caps would "make the summer's shortages even worse." And Fleischer did not mince words on the proposal: The president "thinks price controls have not worked, will not work, and do not work."[28]

On February 3, Abraham and the new chair of the FERC, Republican Curt Hébert, met with Davis and other Western state governors in Portland, Oregon, for an "Energy Policy Roundtable." The dialogue between the Bush administration and Davis—now joined by price cap allies John Kitzhaber and Gary Locke, the governors of Oregon and Washington, respectively—was now well-rehearsed and predictable and carried over to the two other West

Coast governors. "I'm very disappointed with the secretary's statement," Locke declared, "that the administration does not support even temporary, quick price caps,"[29] and Davis echoed that disappointment out of continuing and genuine frustration, but also in accordance with his administration's "Energy Independence Plan" crafted in November: "Continue to hammer on FERC to rein in wholesale prices and provide refunds, understanding that neither will likely happen."[30] Until it finally did, we hoped. In this war of attrition, time was not on our side, but the evidence of manipulation slowly increased in our favor.

At the meeting in Portland, Davis, Kitzhaber, and Locke tried to make the request by Western governors for price caps unanimous, but the Republican governors of Arizona and Idaho objected, as did Democrat Tony Knowles, the governor of Alaska. Arizona and Idaho were net power exporters, and industry representatives there staunchly opposed caps, which bolstered the ideological rejection of them by the two Republican governors. However, Oregon and Washington were net exporters as well, and, during Abraham's confirmation hearing, considerable concern had been voiced by Democratic senators Ron Wyden of Oregon and Washington's Maria Cantwell about Richardson's emergency orders to keep providing lower cost power to California. Wyden had noted that while Oregon and the northwest had been "good neighbors" by providing power to California under those orders, their continuation could potentially be to the detriment of the Pacific Northwest's economy and its electricity ratepayers. Just as Abraham had assuaged the "great urgency" of the concerns of Wyden and Cantwell on that matter during his confirmation hearing,[31] Davis did the same in Portland with Kitzhaber and Locke, who harbored similar, if more muted, concerns. He promised that California would move at "warp speed" to build power plants and trim demand through extraordinary conservation measures, and the three governors pledged to work together to ease and ultimately end the crisis.[32]

In late February, Davis made another trip to Washington, DC, during which, among other things, he briefed Abraham on the state's plan to purchase the IOUs' transmission infrastructure. He expressed confidence that Abraham would support the acquisition, but the formal approval rested with the FERC. Hébert had already disapprovingly suggested that the state's ownership would be similar to "nationalization" and perhaps not be in the best interest of the public.[33] On March 15, Abraham informed Davis that "while the actions you propose might not be the course the Administration would choose, we recognize and respect" the state's "prerogative to determine how to restore the financial health of your utilities." As such, "the Administration would not oppose the concept" of the state making the purchase, provided that the state ensured "open access" to the transmission lines pursuant to current federal regulations and received the FERC's approval.[34] Davis and legislative leaders expected and accepted that all existing regulations would apply; but the question remained whether the FERC would ultimately vote to approve the sale and relinquish its direct oversight to a state led by government officials who viewed the commission as California's archnemesis.

***

Although a steady torrent of criticism directed at Davis and state energy "bureaucrats" in 2001 targeted the purported shortage of new power plants, a much smaller number of critics derided him and other officials for scrambling to build new natural gas-fired facilities. Claiming that the power shortage was "imaginary" and that more aggressive conservation measures would bridge any actual shortfall, environmental journalist Seth Zuckerman argued that the oil crisis of the 1970s had shown that "efficiency really was cheaper than new supply. And it can arrive faster, making [more] power plants unnecessary." Similarly, journalist and renewable energy advocate Harvey Wasserman maintained that California might have avoided the worst of the crisis with bolder conservation measures prior to it, and that California needed more renewable energy, which had been shunned by the IOUs. "A year ago, natural gas would have seemed the logical choice for new generating capacity," Wasserman maintained. "But prices have soared and aren't likely to come back down soon."[35]

While these arguments proved to be clarion calls for California's energy future, the near-term dilemma, and even longer term considerations, necessitated more natural gas plants. Citing UC environmental studies professor Tim Duane, Zuckerman noted that merchant generators in California "have taken their plants offline at a rate five times greater than the historical average." As such, Zuckerman observed, the state's power woes were largely "a fabricated shortage." The governor and notable economists had of course been maintaining for months that the generators were withholding power to raise prices. Nevertheless, the IOUs imported up to one-third of their energy from other states, and many of the plants sold to the merchant generators were old. Moreover, at the end of the 20th century, California had not added any new big power plants in 11 years, mainly because the glut and low price of electricity disincentivized investment in new facilities, but also due to the regulatory uncertainty after the CPUC initiated the restructuring process. However, as much as the state needed additional plants, the need to get the FERC to do its job proved to be the most urgent of all. In that regard, a bit of light began to appear in the FERC's seemingly endless tunnel.

On March 9, the FERC ordered 13 power generators to refund $69 million to California for wholesale power charges that exceeded just and reasonable rates for the month of January unless those generators could show that the charges, which were above the commission's "soft" price cap, were justified. (The soft cap level was set by a formula pegged to the cost of electricity production for the least efficient—and presumably, highest cost—generating plant. Unlike the rigid "hard" caps that had been in place until December 2000, soft caps allowed prices above the cap with cost justification by the generator.) The FERC's action came in response to a CAISO request for a refund of $550 million for overcharges during the months of December and January, but the FERC decided to review December charges later in a separate order.[36] A few days after the initial refund order, the FERC announced another refund directive for $10.8 million from Williams Energy and AES Southland for making so-called reliability must-run (RMR) generating units in Orange County unavailable to the CAISO despite being under contract to keep those units in service.[37] The RMR contracts were developed to deal with the potential market power problems associated with localized generation, and without those contracts, CAISO's market surveillants noted, "CAISO has no means to compel generators to provide power when it is needed for [regional] reliability purposes."[38] While these initial FERC refund orders were paltry compared to what the CAISO and the state were owed, the fact that FERC did anything at all in this regard proved surprising, though the reimposition of lower hard price caps still seemed like a California pipe dream.

Meanwhile, several new big power plants were nearing completion and expected to come online by summer, but concerns grew about the high cost and tight supply of natural gas, and whether the FERC would act on evidence of manipulation in that market as well. On March 5, the Assembly Republican Caucus sent a letter to Davis requesting him to call a special legislative session to deal with the state's "pending natural gas crisis," noting that "every attempt should be made to insure that the current [electricity] problems do not expand into the natural gas sector."[39] But they already had.

Less than six months earlier there had been about a $1 per million British Thermal Units (the metric for natural gas sales) difference between natural gas prices in California and the benchmark price at Henry Hub in Louisiana; it now hovered around $10 or more. California Republicans knew that as well as Democrats. But Republicans had a key political problem in districts with colder high-altitude towns, which they represented almost exclusively, such as Big Bear in the San Bernardino Mountains. Unlike the vast majority of Californians living in more moderate climates, they "are currently facing natural gas rate-shock" due to sky-high heating bills, the caucus letter noted.[40] I worked with some of the letter's signatories along with mountain town residents and officials to address the gas supply and bill problems, with modest success at best. We didn't need a special session just for natural gas, as the governor pointed out, because the extraordinary session that began in January included natural gas issues. However, similar to the state's limited authority over merchant generators, not much could be done in the state capitol to rein in natural gas prices or increase gas supply. While Republican legislators generally proved much more restrained in their criticism of energy companies and markets than Democrats, most of the ones I engaged with agreed with their GOP colleague, Escondido's Mark Wyland, who stated that natural gas "price gouging" could be a factor, "and we have to address that."[41]

An investigation of El Paso Natural Gas for market manipulation had been initiated by the CPUC a year earlier, well before the gas price spikes that began in November. In an April 2001 interview with investigative reporter Lowell Bergman for PBS Frontline, CPUC President Loretta Lynch recalled that in March 2000, Harvey Morris, a CPUC attorney who specialized in natural gas litigation, told her that he wanted to file a case against El Paso Natural Gas before the FERC, which had jurisdiction over the transportation of gas through interstate pipelines. Lynch deemed the evidence of anti-competitive behavior with an affiliate, El Paso Merchant Energy, that Morris presented her to be "a dead-bang, absolute case of price manipulation," and the CPUC voted in late March to authorize the filing of the case. One year later, Lynch observed in the interview, the FERC had "done absolutely nothing...while all of California has suffered from higher natural gas prices."[42]

Described by the *Los Angeles Times* as "the closest thing yet to a public trial in the California energy crisis," the FERC finally commenced its proceeding in the El Paso case in Washington, D.C., on May 4th. While many lawsuits pertaining to the crisis had been filed by a myriad of stakeholders after the price spikes began, the CPUC action preceded the crisis, and Morris did a good job preparing the case. Presiding over it, Chief Administrative Law Judge Curtis L. Wagner Jr. noted that "it's sort of a bellwether—a first on this market power issue." Word had it that Wagner was a reasonable jurist; but whatever his decision, the commission could accept, reject, or amend it, which hardly elevated expectations of a favorable outcome for California in the governor's office and the CPUC, or among executives at PG&E and Edison, which had joined the CPUC as plaintiffs in the case. "The most important issue in this case is public confidence," Paul Joskow maintained. The "FERC has to restore the confidence of the states, the public and the market participants that it has rules and regulations in place to ensure that both the natural gas and wholesale electricity markets perform competitively."[43]

***

On March 16, I attended the UC Energy Institute's annual POWER Conference in Berkeley, along with other Sacramento-based attendees from the California Manufacturers Association and California Chamber of Commerce, key backers of the CPUC's restructuring proceeding and AB 1890. Notable panel participants in this academic gathering included deregulation experts Joskow and William Hogan, Borenstein, Wolak, and economists from Britain, Spain, and the Netherlands. Several of the highly analytical presentations made clear empirical arguments which further confirmed that deregulated markets could be highly susceptible to market power, and that long-term contracts hedged risk and provided market stability. While none of these studies focused on California, the state's woes were nevertheless front and center in discussions of the implications of the findings. Presenting a paper that did focus in good part on California, Tim Duane and UC graduate researcher Jolanka V. Fisher provided an analysis of recent trends in electricity consumption and generating capacity in the 11-state Western grid. They found that while the construction of utility-scale power plants in the state lagged other states in the grid from 1977 to 1998, California "added new generating capacity relative to increases in its consumption at a higher rate than all but two states" given the addition of "another 10,000 megawatts of non-utility capacity" from Qualifying Facilities (QFs).[44]

PG&E and SCE purchased the QF power through contracts but ceased paying for that energy beginning in late 2000 due to their depleted financial conditions, and the challenge to keep the QFs providing critical power for California shifted to the state. The QF portfolio held a wide range of renewable resources with significant capacity, including more than 1000 megawatts of geothermal power spread over both PG&E and SCE territories, and at least 350 megawatts of solar in the Mojave Desert. A somewhat smaller amount of wind generation came from projects around San Gorgonio Mountain Pass outside of Palm Springs, and in northern California at Altamont Pass east of San Francisco Bay. Biomass facilities (mainly using wood chip combustion) and small hydroelectric projects also provided a modicum of power.[45] Despite being owed money by the IOUs, the vast majority the QF renewable generators remained online pursuant to the terms of their contracts into 2001 when the DWR took over procurement; but a few generators, such as the geothermal firm Cal Energy, obtained court approval to sell their power into other markets despite having contracts with Edison, which reportedly owed Cal Energy $100 million.[46]

The natural gas-fired cogenerators, which provided about half of the QF power, posed the biggest challenge to keep online because of the volatility of both the cost and supply of gas. Moreover, many of these QFs were small and felt the pinch of the past-due payments from the IOUs more than the renewable QFs, and some ceased operation for financial reasons and demanded payment from the IOUs before they would come back online. State officials, led by David Freeman and another Davis energy advisor, former assemblymember Richard Katz, urged the QFs to stay online and in the DWR/CAISO market, and to provide their power at an "affordable price, possibly less than the contract price [but] on a longer-term basis." In return, the administration promised the QFs to help get the IOUs to cover their back debt, to secure reliable gas at the best price, and to work with the CPUC to resolve some long-standing technical issues.[47]

Initiated by the federal Public Utility Regulatory Policies Act of 1978, the QF contracts had proved controversial from their beginning in the 1980s due to the complicated formulas that determined their "avoided-cost" value to an IOU compared to the cost of building a large new power plant. In addition, as the price of oil and natural gas dropped in the early to mid-1980s, the IOUs eventually initiated litigation contending that the avoided-cost formula permitted QF power costs to rise well above the average electricity wholesale price from larger generation units.[48] Indeed, the cost of the QF contracts mounted and contributed to the IOUs' stranded costs and to the energy glut of the early to mid-1990s that helped stall new generation investment—including, it seems, critical QF projects that the CPUC approved but the FERC ultimately rejected in 1995 that might have blunted the crisis that began five years later.

As noted in Chapter 2, the FERC nixed a deal in 1995 that alternative energy firms and advocates had been working on with the IOUs for more than five years in the CPUC's Biennial Resource Plan Update for QF contracts. The CPUC approved the contract awards, which would have provided 1,400 megawatts of new generating capacity from 1997 through 2003, but SCE and SDG&E appealed that ruling to the FERC on the grounds that they didn't need this capacity until 2005. While a key part of the FERC's decision to block the contracts was based on its determination that the CPUC bidding process wrongfully disallowed the lowest possible bids to prevail, the FERC also expressed "grave concerns about the need for this capacity."[49]

After the FERC decision, Edison Vice President Vikram Budhraja—who later worked with Freeman to negotiate the DWR contracts with merchant generators—declared that it "removes the possibility of imposing billions of dollars in costs on California consumers."[50] It is possible that this decision resulted in just the opposite. It cannot be readily concluded that had the 1400 megawatts of additional power been added pursuant to the contract awards that the FERC blocked, the price spikes that began in May 2000 and grew after that would've been significantly blunted. But, at the very least, it makes clear that Edison, SDG&E, and the FERC had seriously miscalculated their longer term energy supply and demand assessments. Accordingly, the Sierra Club, which, along with numerous other environmental groups, had supported the QF contracts in 1995, highlighted a January 2001 article on the collapse of the QF deal that ran in the *Los Angeles Daily News* with the headline: "By Killing Plan, SoCal Edison Helped Create Power Crisis." Michael Shames, a San Diego advocate for utility ratepayers, observed that "the FERC decision froze renewable development in the state, and it is only now that it is beginning to defrost."[51]

The FERC could not stop that "defrost" process which Davis and legislators initiated in 2000 in response to the wholesale price spikes, but the state was still under the commission's thumb on price caps in spring 2001. Testifying at a congressional hearing in San Jose on April 12, FERC Chair Hébert maintained his adamant opposition to caps and contended that the state needed to "unleash market forces" and "start putting shovels in the ground" to build new plants, even though seven new plants were under construction, and four of them were scheduled to come online during the summer.[52] However, Commissioner Linda Key Breathitt, a Democrat, expressed a willingness to consider short-term caps. Democratic Commissioner William Massey, who had long supported imposing caps, said he looked "forward to working with her to assure just and reasonable rates" but also noted the need to launch a formal investigation of the wholesale market across the West and for Hébert to allow a vote to approve it. Hébert, in turn, touted a draft FERC plan to stabilize prices and stated that the commission would finalize and vote on it by the end of the month.[53]

Approved by the FERC on April 25, the plan imposed a lower "soft" cap on wholesale electricity prices in California but only during emergencies when the reserve power supply dropped below a seven percent margin. Generators could still charge more than the cap if they could justify the cost. The response in California proved unenthusiastic, and Davis tersely dismissed the plan as inadequate. The "FERC had a chance to bring meaningful relief to California's outrageous wholesale prices and they blew it," he declared.[54] Indeed, the plan paradoxically created a disincentive for the state to avoid power emergencies because it did not impose any price cap on sales during non-emergency periods. Moreover, consumer advocates pointed out that the soft cap only applied to power sales from generators and warned that those generators would just sell their electricity to brokers to share in exorbitant spot market profits. The only plainly positive provision in the decision provided more control to the CAISO for power plant maintenance scheduling.[55]

On the heels of the feckless FERC plan, Republican Representative Joe Barton of Texas introduced the Electricity Emergency Relief Act in the House of Representatives, and it was immediately assailed by Democrats and environmentalists as being an energy industry wish list. Representative Henry Waxman, a Los Angeles Democrat, contended that the bill "fails to address runaway electricity wholesale prices" and "creates massive loopholes in the nation's landmark environmental laws."[56] An attorney for the environmental group Earthjustice, Sandra Schubert, asserted that "Barton is using California's energy problems as a Trojan Horse for weakening vital public health and environmental protections" and called the bill "a gift package for polluters." In a letter to Waxman, Davis stated that the Barton bill "falls short in virtually every way" and would "create extensive new opportunities for gaming."[57]

However, three FERC commissioners endorsed the bill, calling it "welcome" and "reasonable," while Massey remained the lone commissioner holding out for hard price caps, fearful "for the health of the Western economy as high prices ripple through the region." On a two-day trip to the halls of Congress to raise support for price caps, Assembly Speaker Hertzberg—paraphrasing Texas businessman and quirky former presidential candidate, Ross Perot—told the National Press Club that "the giant sucking sound you hear is all our cash going to Texas."[58] A phalanx of energy industry lobbyists, led by Enron, continued to fervently oppose caps and fault California for not building enough power plants.

Echoing this energy industry incantation, Cheney, in a May 4 interview with the *Los Angeles Times*, repeated his steadfast opposition to price controls even if it threatened the country's economy. "The way you address these issues is you either have to reduce demand or increase supply," Cheney contended. He wryly claimed he had been "traumatized in my youth by being part of the Nixon [administration's] wage and price controls" which had distorted markets and disincentivized domestic oil and gas production.[59] While the impact of wage and price controls in the 1970s proved to be a mixed bag at best, Cheney skirted the fact that Nixon mainly sought to lower inflation and unemployment, and that his chief advisors believed that inflation at that time was "artificial," driven more by expectations than real shortages in labor or goods.[60] In 2001, many economists outside of Cheney's conservative cadre believed that, in the short term, hard price caps in the West could help stabilize the dysfunctional market that lacked "real" competition, a deficiency that even the FERC had generally acknowledged.

But Cheney's experience during the Nixon administration (and in the succeeding Gerald Ford administration) forged, tempered, and entrenched his steely resolve in opposition to price controls and support of laissez-faire capitalism. As historian Meg Jacobs has noted, Cheney was among the young free-market hawks at that time for whom "economic deregulation was at the heart of their conservatism," and who believed (with some justification) that there would have been no energy crisis in the 1970s, the Arab oil embargo notwithstanding, "if the government got out of the way and let the market work."[61] This credo formed the ideological bedrock for the deregulation movement that continued into the 1990s. The provenance of Cheney's economic conservatism, combined with his Texas-sized energy industry embrace and success, made him the Bush administration's most implacable and influential foe of price controls, no matter the near-term cost and hardship for Californians and other Western state residents. Market dynamics alone, Cheney believed, would ultimately provide the best economic corrective and growth.

***

Despite the Bush Administration's obdurate rejection of firm price caps, generators and marketers, beginning with Duke Energy in March, began informal discussions with the governor's office on resolving the crisis hoping to ward off growing investigations and to help salvage the longer term prospects for electricity deregulation nationwide. After the media reported on leaked elements of a Duke proposal, in early May the company released it in the form of a "global settlement template" which included stipulations for the "prompt suspension of state investigations, lowering of rhetoric and stay of litigation" by Attorney General Lockyer. In addition, Davis would publicly describe the crisis as "an aberration due to flawed legislation by Gov. Wilson...and will not advocate scrapping deregulation in wholesale power markets." In return, Duke would agree to reduce the $110 million it maintained it was owed by the IOUs, build more power plants in the state, and help with "the governor's political and public relations needs." Legislators, consumer advocates, and others expressed their dismay at Duke's temerity, and Davis's press secretary, Steve Maviglio, dismissed the Duke draft as a "wish list." He made clear that Davis had not even seen the document until shortly before it was publicly released, and that the governor had no conversations with Duke officials. Maviglio said that top aides, including Lynn Schenk and Barry Goode, had talked with Duke representatives, but that the governor had no intention of pulling the plug on state investigations and litigation.[62]

On May 9 Davis hosted a long-planned meeting with energy industry executives to secure their support for the Edison MOU, reinforce the need for reliable energy during the summer and for these firms to take a "haircut" on the amount of money they claimed the IOUs owed them.[63] At a press conference after the meeting, the governor said he told the executives they should "be part of the solution and not part of the problem" and accept 70 cents on the dollar, but he noted there was "no response" to that request. When asked whether he supported a state windfall profits tax bill that had been introduced for companies' profiting from California's crisis, Davis joked that "as the son of two Republicans it was not in my nature to seek" such a tax, but that he "was not ruling it out." The executives observed that the meeting had been "constructive" and facilitated further dialogue. However, a spokesperson for Reliant noted that the governor's continued refusal to halt state investigations of alleged market manipulation in return for concessions by the generators and marketers remained a sticking point in negotiations.[64]

A week later, and one day after a "constructive conversation" with Enron Chief of Staff Steve Kean, Barry Goode wrote him a letter "to repeat one thing": "The Governor's office will not be party to any effort to settle or otherwise interfere in any investigation (or litigation) being conducted (or brought) by the Attorney General...or anyone else regarding those who sell power in California." IOU ratepayers, Goode pointedly observed, "are bearing the burden of extraordinarily high power prices. Governor Davis believes that any unlawful activity must be identified and pursued to the fullest extent of the law." Goode informed Kean that "I am sending a copy of this letter to all the power sellers" to make clear that this "subject must be taken off the agenda of any discussions we may have in the future."[65] There would be no *quid pro* quo in this regard in exchange for an energy-seller haircut.

On May 17, as Goode's letter began to circulate, Ken Lay hosted a small "secret" meeting at the Peninsula Hotel in Beverly Hills during which he gave the attendees, which included actor Arnold Schwarzenegger and Los Angeles Mayor Richard Riordan, a four-page memo titled "Comprehensive Solution for California." According to reporter Jason Leopold, the document "called for an end to federal and state investigations into Enron's role in the California energy crisis and said consumers should pay for the state's disastrous experiment with deregulation through multibillion-dollar rate increases." A bullet point trumpeted the need to "Get deregulation right this time." In his epic Enron tome, *Conspiracy of Fools*, author Kurt Eichenwald stated that Lay maintained in the meeting that "Enron and Southern California Edison were working together on devising a solution that would require some action by the legislature." Lay reportedly claimed that "we're beginning to get support on both sides of the aisle," and that if "we can get something passed," he thought "the governor will sign it."[66]

On that same day, Senator Richard Polanco, a Democrat representing Los Angeles, introduced the SCE MOU bill, which sought to restore the utility's financial stability. I, along with Goode, Richard Katz, and senior advisor Nancy McFadden, assumed the responsibility for moving the bill through the legislative process on the governor's behalf. Of the four of us, I interacted the most with legislative staff working on the bill and other energy issues, and I never heard of any proposal remotely close to what Lay contended was beginning to get bipartisan traction. Moreover, nothing of this sort ever came up in the meetings I had with Goode, Katz, and McFadden, who engaged more with Edison officials. We all met with a legion of Sacramento lobbyists, including Enron's, and none of them ever floated taking another legislative shot at deregulation, and for good reason: That proposal, and Lay's other "solutions," would have been dead on arrival. That should've been clear to Greg Whalley, who ran Enron's wholesale trading unit and represented the company at the May 9 meeting with Davis. And Lay himself should've known that; but, as we later learned, the increasingly desperate Enron founder seemed to tune out ominous political realities as serious financial problems emerged for Enron in 2001 and soon engulfed the company in scandal and then ruin.

***

On May 23, a week after the release of the overwhelmingly fossil-fuel-friendly Bush Energy Plan that had been drafted largely by Lay and other energy company executives, Davis invited President Bush to meet with him in California for a discussion on the crisis and the plan, which provided no immediate help for the state. Bush accepted the invitation the next day, and the meeting was scheduled for May 29 in Los Angeles.

Around the time of this invitation, the governor's chief political strategist, Garry South, provided him an 80-minute video of two focus-group discussions showing that while Californians were not happy with Davis's handling of the energy crisis, they were quick to blame Republicans for causing it by enacting electricity market deregulation.[67] In addition, a recent poll showed that 38 percent of Californians rated Davis's responses to the crisis as poor or very poor, but that compared favorably to Bush's 54 percent rating. Most importantly, 74 percent supported temporary price caps to bring the calamitous costs under control.[68] Accordingly, Davis ratcheted up his attacks on Bush for doing nothing while electric "cowboys" from Texas profited immensely at California's expense.

On the day of the meeting, the public pronouncements from the president were limited and stayed on script: "Price caps do nothing to reduce demand, and they do nothing to increase supply," Bush stiffly affirmed. A "stone-faced" Davis maintained that Californians were getting a "raw deal" with a "massive transfer of wealth from California to Houston," and that he would "pursue every recourse" to stop it, including suing the FERC.[69] The governor also presented a letter to Bush from "ten top economists who have expressed 'deep concern'" over the FERC's failure to "'act effectively to enforce the provisions of the Federal Power Act that require it to set just and reasonable wholesale prices for electricity in California.'" Californians "are not pleading for relief," Davis declared in a press release highlighting the letter, "we're entitled to it."[70]

No one expected Bush to change his mind at the meeting, but as reporters for *The Wall Street Journal* later noted, "analysts from both parties agree, Mr. Davis scored public relations points at the president's expense when the two met."[71] The governor had more spring in his step after the meeting, and in early June he called *Los Angeles Times* columnist George Skelton and told him "we're turning the corner" on the crisis. "Bush handed Davis a microphone to shout his message," Skelton wrote. "He's building plants and conserving electricity—but only federal regulators can order price relief, and they've refused. The word finally got through to people, the governor thinks."[72] It did, especially to Republicans.

As CNN reporter Major Garrett detailed, congressional GOP leaders issued "dire" warnings to energy industry representatives "that they may not be able to block legislation imposing price caps" and that the White House didn't understand the "political pressure on Republicans" regarding the issue. According to Garrett, "the final straw for many House and Senate Republicans was Mr. Bush's trip to California," which one top GOP advisor labeled "a total disaster" because it spotlighted Bush's opposition to controlling costs that the public increasingly viewed as price gouging. Nevertheless, the White House signed off on a multi-million-dollar energy company ad campaign to fight price caps. "Leading congressional Republicans have urged the entire energy industry to spend up to $50 million on the ads," Garrett reported, and he cited a source "intimately involved" in the campaign stating that "every penny right now will be spent in the Golden State."[73]

However, by the time this effort took shape, the battle against hard electricity price caps had already been lost. A prominent poll found that 79 percent of Americans favored them, and Republican leaders in the house pulled the Barton bill from the legislative docket out of concern that they would not be able to block a Democratic attempt to add caps to the bill. In the senate, the GOP had lost its majority in early June when Vermont Senator James Jeffords left the Republican Party and became an independent member, but he chose to caucus with Democrats, which allowed them to control the chamber. Democrats, at Feinstein's behest, quickly initiated and led hearings on the electricity crisis in the West, with a focus on California. One Republican senator conceded there "wasn't five votes" among his GOP colleagues to block caps in California. Lobbyists and congressional aides predicted that the likely outcome of the issue's now-favorable dynamics was that the FERC would finally impose caps.[74] Sure enough, that day came on June 18th.

With the support of all five commissioners, including two new Republican Bush appointees, the FERC approved an order requiring hard caps on wholesale electricity prices from all sellers at all hours in California and the other ten states in the Western grid. The caps were tied to plant heat rates and fuel costs and were set at the highest accepted bid (likely from the least efficient generator). The order also eliminated market practices such as "megawatt laundering," in which generators in California that were subject to caps for in-state sales would sell their power to out-of-state buyers who would then sell that power back to the state at prices above the cap.[75] Finally, the commission ordered all public utility sellers and buyers in the CAISO's market to reach a refund settlement agreement for overcharges in 15 days, an exceedingly daunting task given the immense differences between the parties on the amount of those overcharges. Outgoing FERC chairman Curt Hébert declared that, with the passage of the plan, it was "time to stop blaming and start solving the problem."[76]

Hébert acknowledged that "FERC probably made a mistake… Not probably; FERC did make a mistake in giving too much deference to the state of California in waiting too long to intervene and step in. We hate for government to intrude at any time that they don't need to, but clearly we had a dysfunctional market."[77] That "mistake" had cost California billions of dollars. While the FERC order had largely stopped the state from bleeding more cash in the spot market, the scope of the remedies needed to recover from the damage done loomed larger than any other challenge in the state's history.

Notes

1 Governor Gray Davis speech, *PBS Newshour with Jim Lehrer* transcript. https://www.pbs.org/newshour/spc/election2000/demconvention/davis.htm.

2 Ronald Brownstein and Richard Simon (and Mulholland quoted in), "GOP Leaders Warn Bush of Backlash From Power Crisis, *Los Angeles Times*, January 20, 2001.

3 Ronald Brownstein and Richard Simon (and Mulholland quoted in), "GOP Leaders Warn Bush of Backlash From Power Crisis, *Los Angeles Times*, January 20, 2001.

4 Stein quoted in Paul Van Slambrouck, "President vs. governor over California's power," *The Christian Science Monitor*, January 31, 2001.

5 Kate Galbraith, "Texplainer: Why does Texas have its own power grid?" *The Texas Tribune*, February 8, 2011.

6 Van Slambrouck, "President vs. governor over California's power."

7 Steven Ferry, "Soft Paths, Hard Choices: Environmental Lessons in the Aftermath of California's Electric Deregulation Debacle," *Virginia Environmental Law Journal*, Vol. 23 (2004): 270.

8 Wheatly quoted in Marla Cone and Gary Palakovic, "Bush's Idea of Easing Smog Rules Won't Help, Experts Say," *Los Angeles Times*, January 25, 2001. Nitrogen oxide emissions more than doubled during the first three months of 2001 compared to the same period in 2000.

9 In a 2003 paper, Jonathan T. Kolstadt and Frank Wolak found evidence that "Nox emission permit prices during 2000 and 2001were primarily used by [certain] generation unit owners to cost-justify higher bids into the California electricity market that would set higher prices for *all* the electricity they produced." (Emphasis added.) Kolstadt and Wolak, "Using Environmental Emission Permit Prices to Raise Electricity Prices: Evidence from the California Electricity Market," May 28, 2003. https://users.nber.org/~confer/2003/si2003/papers/ee/wolak.pdf.
10 The Glendale facility and other dirtier plants in the Los Angeles Basin that produced emissions exceeding exceeded their limits to help supply power in most cases agreed to use profits to install equipment to reduce future emissions if they hadn't done so already. See Jean Guccione, "Pollution Is Price of Power Crisis," *Los Angeles Times*, April 25, 2001.
11 Editorial, "Arctic Oil a Sham Answer," *Los Angeles Times*, January 31, 2001; The Sierra Club, "Myth vs. Fact." http://fbaum.unc.edu/lobby/_107th/126_CAFE_Standards_2/Organizational_Statements/SC/SC_San_Diego_Chapter_Myth_Vs_Fact.htm; Editorial, "Power Plant Delays," *The Sacramento Bee*, January 28, 2001.
12 Winston Hickox to Diane Feinstein, March 28, 2001, Congressional Record (Bound Edition), Senate, Volume 147 (2001): Part 5, 6218–6222.
13 Testimony of Dr. Alan Lloyd, March 22, 2001, Congressional Record (Bound Edition), Senate, Volume 147 (2001): Part 5, 6218–6222. For more on the executive orders and emissions concerns, see Ferry, "Soft Paths, Hard Choices," 266–75.
14 Interview with Winston Hickox, October 16, 2022.
15 Witherspoon quoted in Dan Morain, "Davis Eases Power Plant Pollution Rules," *Los Angeles Times*, June 12, 2001; Chris Bowman, "Davis loosens limits on older plants," *The Sacramento Bee*, June 12, 2001.
16 O'Donnell interview with Kahn.
17 O'Donnell interview with Kahn.
18 Richardson interview by *PBS Frontline*, April 10, 2001, for "Blackout." Appointed by Davis to be one is his legal advisors in April 2002, attorney William Kissinger had previously served as Senior Advisor for International Economic Policy in the Clinton administration and reported directly to Sperling. While Kissinger did not work on energy policy, he recalled that the prevailing opinion within Sperling's office was that California was culpable for the crisis due to the poor design of the market and therefore the state had to resolve it. Interview with William Kissinger, April 9, 2022.
19 O'Donnell interview with Kahn.
20 *NGI* staff, "CA Fights FERC For Control of ISO and PX," *Natural Gas Intelligence*, March 15, 1999.
21 Office of Senate Floor Analyses, "Unfinished Business," Senate Bill 96, August 30, 1999.
22 Hoecker quoted in O'Donnell, *Soul of the Grid*, 170.
23 Consultant quoted in Richard L. Berke, "Bush is Devoting Scanty Attention to California," *The New York Times*, April 15, 2001.
24 Bebitch Jeffe quoted in Carter M. Yang, "Energy Crisis Poses Political Quandary for Bush," *ABC News*, January 26, 2001. https://abcnews.go.com/Politics/story?id=121967&page=1
25 Fleischer quoted in Yang, "Energy Crisis Poses Political Quandary for Bush."
26 Robert Bryce, "Pipe Dreams: George W. Bush to the rescue, part 1," *The Austin Chronicle*, October 4, 2002.
27 Spencer Abraham Nomination, Hearing before the Committee on Energy and Natural Resources, U.S. Senate, 107th Congress, First Session, January 18, 2001.

28 Abraham and Fleischer quoted in Tom Detzel and Jim Barnett, "Smith Pursues Cap on West's Power Prices," *The Oregonian*, March 16, 2001.
29 Locke quoted in Sam Howe Verhovek, "Energy Secretary Rejects Request to Cap Electricity Price," *The New York Times*, February 3, 2001.
30 "Energy Independence Plan" memorandum, November 10, 2000, Archive Box 146/14, GGDR, CSA.
31 Abraham Nomination Hearing.
32 Verhovek, "Energy Secretary Rejects Request to Cap Electricity Price."
33 Dan Morain and Nancy Vogel, "Governor Renews Criticism of Regulators," *Los Angeles Times*, February 28, 2001.
34 Spencer Abraham to Governor Davis, March 15, 2001, Archive Box 146/12, GGDR/CSA.
35 Seth Zuckerman, "California: Don't Forget History," *The Christian Science Monitor*, March 8, 2001; and Harvey Wasserman, "California's Deregulation Disaster," *The Nation*, January 26, 2001.
36 Jennifer Coleman, "FERC orders refunds to utilities," *Stockton Record*, March 9, 2001.
37 Joseph Kahn, "U.S. Suggests Electric Firms Inflated Prices in California," *The New York Times*, March 15, 2001. Williams and AES used a common tactic for generators with RMR contracts in California: Each company would tell the CAISO that the RMR unit CAISO wanted to "dispatch" (that is, order into operation) was offline for repairs and thereby essentially forced the CAISO to buy power from each of the generator's other units at a market-bid price that greatly exceeded – by as much as a factor of 10 – what that generator would have earned through its fixed-price RMR contract. See Jeremy Mullman, "Contract Killings: How the State's Contracts with Crucial Electric Power Providers Actually Encourage them to Gouge Us," *SF Weekly*, May 30, 2001.
38 Frank Wolak and James Bushnell, "Reliability Must-Run Contracts for the California Electricity Market," April 2, 1999, 2–3. http://web.stanford.edu/group/fwolak/cgi-bin/sites/default/files/RMR_Report_Bushnell.pdf. While the concept behind the utilization of RMR units was theoretically sound, Wolak and Bushnell noted that the "'must-run' status of certain generation units endows them with a special form of local market power," and that the CAISO's flawed RMR contracts facilitated the exercise of that power by certain RMR generators.
39 Letter quoted by Mitchell Benson and Rebecca Smith, "California Republican's Request Session on Pending Gas 'Crisis'," *The Wall Street Journal*, March 5, 2001.
40 Letter quoted by Mitchell Benson and Rebecca Smith, "California Republican's Request Session on Pending Gas 'Crisis'."
41 Wyland quoted in Dan McSwain, "Davis signs 10-year power deals," *The San Diego Union-Tribune*, March 6, 2001.
42 Lynch interviewed by PBS *Frontline* and *The New York Times*, April 11, 2001, for "Blackout."
43 Wagner and Joskow quoted in Ricardo Alonzo-Zaldivar, "Natural Gas Firm's Tactics Focus of Trial," *Los Angeles Times,* May 4, 2001.
44 Jolanka V. Fisher and Timothy P. Duane, "Trends in Electricity Consumption, Peak Demand, and Generating Capacity in California and the Western Grid, 1977-1998," Power Working Paper-085, UC Energy Institute, September 2001.
45 Interview with Jan Smutny-Jones; interview with John White; Michael R. Peevey and Diane O. Wittenberg, *California Goes Green: A Roadmap to Climate Leadership* (North Charleston, SC: CreateSpace, 2017), 83.

46 *NGI* Staff Reports, "CA Gears Up for Implementation of Edison Agreement," *Natural Gas Intelligence*, April 17, 2001.
47 Kellan Fluckiger to Lynn Schenk and Susan Kennedy, "QF Meeting Today," May 3, 2001, Archive Box 140/7, GGDR/CSA.
48 See Timothy P. Duane, "Greening the Grid: Implementing Climate Change Policy Through Energy Efficiency, Renewable Portfolio Standards, and Strategic Transmission System Investments," *Vermont Law Review*, Vol. 34, No. 4 (Summer 2010): 755–59; interview with Ralph Cavanagh.
49 John Marshall, "U.S. Tells Utilities to Buy Cheaper Power," https://www.ctinsider.com/business/article/U-S-Tells-Utilities-to-Buy-Cheaper-Power-3043986.php
50 Budhraja quoted in Marshall, "U.S. Tells Utilities to Buy Cheaper Power."
51 The Sierra Club, "Myth vs. Fact;" Shames quoted in Susan Sward, "A Lost Opportunity That Worsened Crisis," *San Francisco Chronicle*, February 12, 2001.
52 Hébert quoted in Marshall Wilson and Zachary Coile, "Start Digging, Energy Chief Tells State," *San Francisco Chronicle*, April 12, 2001.
53 Massey quoted in Nancy Vogel, "Price Caps Excluded in FERC Plan," *Los Angeles Times*, April 12, 2001.
54 Davis quoted in Hil Anderson, "Davis blasts FERC power cap plan," UPI, April 26, 2001. https://www.upi.com/Archives/2001/04/26/Davis-blasts-FERC-power-cap-plan/5866988257600/.
55 Davis quoted in Hil Anderson, "Davis blasts FERC power cap plan."
56 Waxman quoted in Ricardo Alonso-Zaldivar and Richard Simon, "FERC Backs GOP Energy Relief Bill," *Los Angeles Times*, May 2, 2001.
57 Earthjustice, "House Bill Introduced Yesterday Takes Aim at Clean Air & Water, Species and More," May 2, 2001. https://earthjustice.org/news/press/2001/house-bill-introduced-yesterday-takes-aim-at-clean-air-water-species-and-more-a-polluter-gift-package; Davis to Waxman letter, May 3, 2001, Archive Box 140/7, GGDR/CSA.
58 All quotes in the Davis Daily Energy Action Agenda, http://gray-davis.com/ViewLibraryItem.aspx?ID=5942.
59 Cheney quoted in Doyle McManus and Richard Simon, "Cheney Rejects Price Caps," *Los Angeles Times*, May 5, 2001.
60 Steve Mufson, "Price Controls: Past as Healthcare Prologue," *The Washington Post*, March 14, 1993.
61 Meg Jacobs, *Panic at the Pump: The Energy Crisis and the Transformation of American Politics in the 1970s* (New York: Hill and Wang, 2016), 21, 9.
62 All quotes in Dan Morain, "Power Firm's Offer to Davis Denounced," *Los Angeles Times*, May 3, 2001.
63 Barry Goode, "List of Generators, May 2, 2001 Meeting," Archive Box 146/12, GGDR/CSA.
64 Davis quoted in Generator Meeting Press Conference Transcript, May 9, 2001, http://gray-davis.com/ViewLibraryItem.aspx?ID=9611; Reliant comment in NGI Staff Reports, "CA Governor, Generators Meeting 'Cordial'," *Natural Gas intelligence*, May 11, 2001.
65 Barry Goode to Steve Kean, May 16, 2001, Archive Box 146/12, GGDR/CSA.
66 Jason Leopold and Utne.com, "Arnold's Enron Connection," *Utne Reader*, August 1, 2003, https://www.utne.com/community/arnolds-enron-connection/; Kurt Eichenwald, *Conspiracy of Fools: A True Story* (New York: Broadway Books, 2005), 454.
67 John Harwood and Mitchel Benson, "Power Politics: Strategist for Gov. Davis Toughens Energy Policy," *The Wall Street Journal*, June 19, 2001.
68 Frank Pellegrini, "Bush Turns on the Megawatt Charm for California," *Time*, May 29, 2001.

69 All quotes in Pellegrini, "Bush Turns on the Megawatt Charm for California."
70 Governor Davis, "Economists Express 'Deep Concern' Over Failure of Federal Government to Temper Wholesale Electricity Prices," Press Release, May 29, 2001.
71 Harwood and Benson, "Power Politics."
72 George Skelton, "Gov. Davis Feisty About Gaining Leverage Over the 'Cowboys'," *Los Angeles Times*, June 11, 2001.
73 Major Garrett, "Power of advertising fights energy rate caps," CNN, June 10, 2001.
74 Public support for price caps cited in Jeff Gerth, "U.S. Agency Widens Its Curbs on Price of Power in the West," *The New York Times*, June 19, 2001; Republican senator quoted in Garrett, "Power of advertising fights energy rate caps;" lobbyists and aides cited in Richard Simon, "Senate Will Weigh Price Control Issue," *Los Angeles Times*, June 1, 2001.
75 Blumstein, et al., "The History of Electricity Restructuring in California," 29.
76 Hébert quoted in Gerth, "U.S. Agency Widens Its Curbs on Price of Power in the West."
77 Hébert quoted in Ray Suarez interview, "Wholesale Electricity Price Limits," *PBS Newshour*, June 18, 2001.

5 Cleaning Up and Looking Ahead

The Renewable Energy "Hedge" Takes Shape

The region-wide price caps at long last ensured market price stability, but when the Federal Energy Regulatory Commission (FERC) imposed them in June, spot market costs had already dropped under $100 per MWh due mainly to the impact of the Department of Water Resources (DWR) contracts and increased conservation, which the Davis administration touted.[1] However, as the spot-market price for electricity dropped, the criticism of the relatively high-priced DWR contracts increased along with barbs about those contracts being almost exclusively with merchant generators utilizing natural gas and not with renewable energy providers. In addition, the threat of numerous rolling blackouts due to supply shortfalls during peak summer demand hours remained, and the governor's call for $8.9 billion in refunds from electricity sellers dwarfed the roughly $1 billion that FERC Judge Curtis Wagner put forth as the maximum amount owed in cash or in kind. While the acute cost crisis had passed, the recovery from it and the future course of California's energy policy faced a very rocky road.

***

Though the high temperature in often sweltry Sacramento in June rose only to 101 (°F) for one day, July 2001 began with a short heat wave, with temperatures reaching 106 on two consecutive days. The state had not experienced a blackout since May 8, and these two days were the first real test of whether the grid could handle an electricity demand surge during a summer heat event. To everyone's relief, it did—as it would for the rest of the summer for a variety of reasons: The weather was somewhat milder than usual, with no long heat waves, and early indicators showed that Californians rose to the conservation challenge voluntarily and in response to electricity bill and energy-efficient appliance purchase rebates. The DWR contracts greatly reduced the need for spot-market power, and the June FERC order explicitly barred generators from withholding available electricity in that market.

California Republicans had established a website for political purposes to disseminate presumably grim news on what almost everyone—including me and others in the governor's office—had once thought would be a bevy of

DOI: 10.4324/9781003518150-6

blackouts. One long-time lobbyist told *The Washington Post* reporter David Broder that Davis was "just one blackout away from drawing a serious primary opponent" in his 2002 reelection campaign.[2] The governor ultimately escaped putting that assertion to the test.

As summer progressed, avoiding even one rolling blackout proved to be a feather in Davis's cap, but, as more information emerged on the DWR contracts, the paucity of renewable energy agreements in that portfolio drew increasing criticism for its "green blackout." The DWR had either agreed to or was negotiating contracts for nearly 3400 MW of electricity from solar, wind, geothermal, and biomass providers in early July,[3] but almost all the initial DWR contracts that had been signed in the spring, which met the vast majority of the state's long-term contract power goals, had been agreed to with merchant generators utilizing natural gas-fired plants. In response to the criticism of those contracts, the administration highlighted the renewable energy legislation the governor had supported and signed in 2000 and early 2001, in addition to the $110 million for clean energy in the new state budget Davis would sign at the end of July. Nevertheless, the criticism continued.

The green blackout proved more apparent than real for the DWR contract portfolio because most of the readily available renewable energy was already under Investor Owned Utility (IOU) contracts with qualifying facilities that either continued to operate through the crisis or came back online pursuant to a mid-June deal negotiated by Davis advisor Richard Katz.[4] That effort was separate from the DWR contract negotiations with the merchant generators led by David Freeman, in which, as he often noted, the state had to accept terms "with a gun to our head." Administration officials maintained that the DWR accepted most of the renewable energy bids that had been offered early on, but numerous providers strongly disputed that assertion. While there likely were more bids—and perhaps many more—beyond what the DWR accepted, they were mostly for projects under development and not for power that would be available by June or July,[5] a critical criterion. Still, a green blackout did exist to a notable degree, but the primary culprit for that was the FERC and its 1995 decision, at the behest of Southern California Edison (SCE) and San Diego Gas & Electric (SDG&E), to block the 1400 MW of alternative energy agreements that the CPUC had approved.

The ongoing flap over the green blackout did highlight the hard truth that the DWR's power portfolio overwhelmingly tapped natural gas-fired facilities—and from the same companies that Davis and other prominent state officials had derided as "energy pirates." Understandably uncomfortable with that reality, the governor expressed a desire to increase his profile on green energy and the need for greater resource diversity. In a May memo to him from me and Policy Director Kari Dohn, we suggested that "your renewed commitment to alternative energy in California, particularly to solar," would "allow the state to remain the undisputed leader in alternative energy in the U.S."[6] With the governor's sign off, in early July I enlisted renewable energy advocates John White and NRDC's Ralph Cavanagh to help set up an event for Davis at PowerLight Corporation's solar manufacturing plant in Berkeley where he would make a major announcement on the state's renewable energy policy and goals.

At the event on July 30, which featured a 100-kW solar panel "power plant" on PowerLight's rooftop, Davis announced his support for a plan by the state Energy Commission to increase California's use of renewable energy from the current 12 to 17 percent by 2006. "For decades, California has been a leader in the development of renewable energy supplies," he noted. "This plan will help ensure that we continue to set the standard for decades to come."[7] A week earlier, Senator Byron Sher had gutted and amended one of his bills, SB 532, with a proposal that would establish the California Renewables Portfolio Standard Program, which required statewide use of renewable energy to increase to 20 percent by 2010. While Sher's bill largely aligned with the Energy Commission's plan, there were some differences, and I began having discussions with Sher's chief advisor, Kip Lipper, about reconciling those differences with the CEC plan and possibly using SB 532 to establish the renewable energy increase in state law.

Three weeks after the governor's announcement, the *Los Angeles Times* ran a commentary by Freeman in which he laid out the largely green goals for the new California Power Authority that he now chaired. Using his folksy wit, Freeman joked that with the launch of the Authority, "Californians may wonder how many state agencies it takes to keep the lights on." He pledged to "keep the 'big boys'—the power generators and suppliers—honest" by restoring the "15 percent rule" for the state's energy reserves that "the disaster of deregulation" drove to "extinction." Emphasizing the paramount importance of this reserve as a "hedge against uncertainty," he promised that the Authority would diversify "California's power portfolio with all types of renewable technologies" and "find a way to answer Governor Davis's call to meet 17% of the state's energy supply" with that power.[8]

***

Reconvening on August 20 after a month-long summer recess, the legislature still faced major energy crisis challenges due primarily to the inability of the state and the merchant generators to reach a refund agreement by the July deadline set by the FERC. Representing the state, Michael Kahn made clear that he would reject any refund offer less than \$8.9 billion and would seek much more than that if the venue shifted from FERC mediation to a courtroom. In response, the generators collectively made a "very substantial global settlement offer" of only \$716.1 million and also sought protection from future legal action by the state.[9] After the negotiations concluded in a stalemate in mid-July, FERC Judge Wagner reported to the commissioners that while "very large refunds are due," perhaps in excess of \$1 billion, the state did not present evidence showing that the refunds should be exponentially more than that. He ordered a new round of hearings to consider further evidence presented by the California Independent System Operator (CAISO), and expectations mounted that the matter would ultimately end up in a protracted court battle.[10]

Though expected, the refund stalemate meant that, in the final month before the adjournment of the 2001 legislative session, the Edison Memorandum of Understanding (MOU) bill would be front and center due to its multi-billion-dollar cost to restore the utility's financial footing. Edison's share of an $8.9 billion settlement—or even a sum approaching that amount—would've provided substantial funds to "rescue" the utility without raising customer costs significantly, if at all, for that purpose. To the extent it would still have been needed, the legislation would not be a brazen "bailout bill" and therefore would be a much easier vote for legislators. But "what might have been" had predictably come and gone, and the stakeholders were now geared up for a showdown over the bill in the capitol.

To further prepare for that battle and other energy crisis flack, Davis decided to hire the political communications duo of Chris Lehane and Mark Fabiani, who were known as the "masters of disaster" for their "rapid response" efforts against Clinton White House critics, especially during several scandals. The governor's chief political advisor, Garry South, was based in Los Angeles and had his hands full going after a wide range of Davis detractors, and he had other clients. Davis wanted some heavy communications hitters in the governor's office itself and brought Lehane and Fabiani on to the office's payroll in July after Clinton recommended them.[11] Their $30,000 monthly salary ignited controversy, which quickly grew after it became known that they also had a consulting contract with Edison. Lehane threw another log on that fire after he told reporters that "the governor and Edison have the same energy policy; there's no conflict in working for both." By the end of July, Fabiani and Lehane terminated their state employment with Davis without pay pursuant to a settlement of a conflict-of-interest lawsuit filed by a taxpayer group.[12] The enlistment of Lehane and Fabiani proved to be a distraction and setback to the effort to get the MOU bill passed as it provided more fodder for its many opponents.

Authored by Senators Richard Polanco, who represented Los Angeles, and Byron Sher, the bill, which had been drafted primarily by Barry Goode and Edison representatives, was amended significantly in the senate before it passed on July 20 prior to the recess. The amendments proved so significant that Edison now opposed the bill, and Davis directed Goode and others—mainly me, Richard Katz, and Nancy McFadden—to figure out a way to amend the legislation in the assembly to the point that Edison could once again support it. That would not be an easy task given that the often surly and implacable John Burton strongly backed the amendments to the bill the senate passed and warned that he would not support a bill with assembly amendments adding to its cost. The bill would then have to go back to the senate where Burton could oppose concurrence. Nevertheless, according to Edison executives, the bill needed to be substantially amended to add funding to cross back into the utility's financial survival threshold. It had been 15 months since the crisis had begun, and though the worst of it clearly had passed, it felt like the wear and tear of it all was now snowballing toward a final bout between Davis and Burton, two exasperated yet fatigued heavyweight fighters and erstwhile allies.

***

As part of the governor's team on this legislation, my main task was to help with the "Christmas tree" bill provisions—that is, amendments that didn't pertain directly to Edison's needs but were deemed necessary to win the support of enough lawmakers to get the legislation passed. To that end, in August, I began discussions mainly with Sher and Lipper to add a Renewables Portfolio Standard Program to the bill, and with other legislators and staff to draft amendments allowing the resumption of direct access for IOU customers that, upon departure from IOU service, would agree to pay an "exit fee" to cover their share of the DWR power costs.

Many of the large energy consumers that had returned to IOU service when electricity costs soared in late 2000 and early 2001—when the DWR began signing long-term contracts—wanted to go back to direct access service in the summer when spot-market retail prices plunged to near pre-crisis levels. However, those customers could not just come and go as they pleased (though some thought they could) given that they had earlier been the beneficiaries of low frozen IOU rates when their direct access providers abandoned them and the DWR began procuring their electricity in place of the IOUs. The idea for the exit fee arose in spring when Hollywood's Universal Studios theme park, a Southern California Edison customer, wanted to buy cheaper power from the Los Angeles Department of Water and Power and proposed paying a fee to cover any stranded costs that would be created by this arrangement for SCE customers paying for the higher priced DWR power. I didn't think this exit-fee proposition would pencil out for Universal, but its supporters disagreed. One of the administration's consultants, Navigant's Ron Nichols, advised me that calculating the exit fee would be tricky and contentious, and he shared my skepticism about it being worthwhile for direct access customers wanting to leave IOU service. But that was their decision. If this provision could help secure support for the MOU bill and keep IOU customers whole, then it met the Christmas tree litmus test.

Barry Goode worked once again with Edison attorneys under the direction of senior Vice President Robert Foster to amend the financial provisions in the version of the MOU bill approved by the senate. Goode—who joined the administration after his nomination by Clinton to a seat on the U.S. Ninth Circuit Court of Appeal had been blocked by senate Republicans—possessed a nimble legal mind and keen focus, while Foster, a former California Senate and Energy Commission staffer, functioned as the avuncular tactician of this effort. Davis remained adamant about keeping SCE from going bankrupt and conferred often with Edison CEO John Bryson, a co-founder of the Natural Resources Defense Council (NRDC) whom former Governor Jerry Brown had appointed to chair the State Water Resources Control Board and later to be president of the CPUC before he joined Edison. Davis, who had served as Brown's chief of staff, knew Bryson, and began working closely with him on the Edison MOU framework after Pacific Gas & Electric (PG&E) declared bankruptcy.[13]

In the assembly, the Edison bill's first and foremost hurdle was getting enough votes to pass in the Committee on Energy Costs and Availability, in which the amendments would be made during a number of marathon committee proceedings due in good part to the myriad stakeholders seeking to express their wide-ranging views. In addition to the amendments to add the Renewables Portfolio Standard and to allow new direct access options with the exit fee, the amount of the state-backed bonds Edison could issue was increased from $2.5 billion in the version approved by the senate to $2.9 billion, and the amount the state could pay to purchase Edison's transmission lines—during a five-year window at the state's option—doubled to $2.4 billion.[14]

None of the Republicans on the committee supported the bill, mainly, it seemed, to spite the governor and throw a potential wrench into his 2002 reelection quest. However, we didn't need their votes and could even afford to lose one Democrat, but we lost two due mainly to controversy over a MOU provision giving the state control of thousands of acres of Sierra Nevada land around SCE's hydroelectric facilities in Fresno County. Fortunately, Foster cajoled Republican committee member Bill Leonard to support the bill, and it eventually passed by that one vote.[15] Four days later, with Speaker Hertzberg helping Katz and McFadden secure votes for the bill on the assembly floor, it narrowly passed and headed back to the senate for final approval. Or so we hoped. The low-key celebratory mood in the governor's office reflected the fact that Burton would have to be appeased, and there was no indication that this would happen easily, if at all.

***

On the verge of a standoff, head-butting discussions on the MOU bill between the governor's office and senators and key staff—and fleetingly with Davis and Burton—continued into the final week of the legislative session, and September 11 was set to be yet another dwindling day in that grind. That it proved to be a harrowingly dark day for the nation suspended that process briefly and cast gloom over the exhausting and unproductive endeavor. Nevertheless, in the final three days of session, we had several positive discussions with Sher and Senate Energy Committee chair Debra Bowen, capped by a late-night meeting on the second-last day of session in which the two senators thought they could convince Burton to accept the assembly version of the MOU bill with a few "modest" amendments. As we quickly learned the next morning, he did not.

Known for his often profane and blunt demeanor, Burton brusquely dismissed the proposal by Bowen and Sher and vehemently cemented his opposition to the bill. Katz and McFadden scrambled to resuscitate senate support for the legislation, though we knew that Burton himself was the only one who could do that in sufficient numbers. In the early evening, with only hours left until the session ended, Burton met briefly with Davis in the governor's private office. When the two emerged into the anteroom, Burton cordially told Davis to give his regards to his wife as he made his exit. I knew then and there that no agreement had been reached. Then again, no one else waiting with me in the anteroom had figured they would reach an agreement either. As Burton left, I thought about one of his adages regarding exceedingly unlikely outcomes: "The chances are slim to none, and slim just left town."[16]

Shortly after meeting with Burton and learning that he would not even allow the MOU bill to be taken up for a vote, the governor issued a statement: "I am proud of the work done by the Assembly to get the state out of the business of buying electricity by restoring Edison to creditworthiness. Unfortunately, however, the Senate has not gotten the job done." Incensed by Davis's comments, Burton fired back on the senate floor well after midnight: "I didn't want to embarrass the governor and bring it up and have it get only seven votes. It would have been a rip-off of residential people to help big business and bail out a corporation." He then expressed regret about *not* bringing the bill up so the senate could have "killed this baby once and for all."[17] But Burton and like-minded others were in for a rude surprise.

Less than three weeks after the bill's rather ignominious demise, CPUC President Loretta Lynch, reportedly concerned that Edison could prevail in its $5.5 billion lawsuit to raise rates to fully recover its losses, announced that she had reached an agreement with the company on a $3.3 billion plan to restore the utility's finances.[18] The plan would cost ratepayers $400 million more than the assembly version of the MOU bill that Burton and most consumer groups loathed and buried. In an editorial, the *San Francisco Chronicle* observed that Lynch's "bailout deal...never would have stood a chance" in the legislature and "comes at a stiff price for average ratepayers," whom legislators such as Burton sought to protect. Consumer activist Harvey Rosenfield called Lynch's announcement "a bad day for democracy" and bristled at having "to pay off Edison's losses to protect its shareholders."[19] Ironically, Lynch had locked arms with Burton in opposition to the MOU bill, and, right after the bill died, he championed her as "fighting for the homeowners and small ratepayers against big business."[20] Lynch's deal with Edison was a necessary and arguably pragmatic move, but it came with more than a little hypocrisy and self-aggrandizement.

***

Davis "applauded" the CPUC's agreement with Edison and accordingly rescinded his request for another special legislative session to revisit the MOU, but he called the commission's denial of a revenue allocation from rates for a multi-billion-dollar bond sale the state needed to recover DWR's power costs "an irresponsible act."[21] Over the summer, the administration and state Treasurer Phil Angelides had issued dire warnings about the consequences for the state's General Fund of further delaying the bond sale, but the commission refused to take necessary actions to ensure that the bondholders would be repaid through IOU ratepayer revenues.

The DWR borrowed money from the state's General Fund when it began buying about one-third of the power for IOU customers pursuant to Keeley's AB X1 enacted on February 1, but the rate revenue paid by those customers went to the IOUs to cover their own power production costs. Keeley's bill authorized the state to sell bonds to recover the DWR purchases, but because the bonds would be repaid by IOU ratepayers instead of taxpayers, the CPUC had to approve a dedicated rate component on customer bills for that purpose. The commissioners, led by Lynch, proved reluctant to do so because their regulatory authority did not extend to DWR power transactions, so the commission essentially would have to acquiesce to the revenue requirement determined by the DWR. In late April 2001, with tax revenues plummeting due to the tech-bubble burst and anticipating that the DWR could be paying sky-high prices for power into the summer, Tim Gage, the director of the California Department of Finance, had provided a grave fiscal update to the governor: "In the absence of the authority to sell the power purchase bonds, we could find ourselves not only with no funds to continue purchasing power, but with no General Fund cash, period," by the end of September.[22]

While the bond-sale stalemate continued through the summer, the FERC price caps, consumer conservation, the DWR contracts, and a CPUC decision to allow the DWR "to recover its revenue requirements on a timely basis"[23] helped mitigate the shorter term fiscal crisis and enabled the state to borrow $4.3 billion to bridge cash flow problems. By early October, when the commission voted to approve the Edison agreement but not the bond sale, Lynch argued that doing so would prevent the state from renegotiating the increasingly maligned DWR contacts, which totaled close to $43 billion. She backed a different bond repayment plan in a Burton bill that had been passed but was not sent to the governor after he threatened to veto it. Angelides maintained that both the bond proposal he and Davis backed and the Burton plan could subject the state to viable lawsuits, but that the risk proved greater with the Burton plan.[24]

The feud between Lynch and the governor attracted the media spotlight given its duration and huge fiscal stakes for the state budget. In a feature article on the Edison deal and bond standoff, two *Los Angeles Times* reporters labeled Lynch "perhaps Davis' least favorite appointee" and quoted an anonymous "top aide" who described the governor's relationship with Lynch as "nonexistent."[25]

Davis had appointed Lynch to be director of the Governor's Office of Planning and Research (OPR) at the beginning of his administration, prior to which she had been a politically active partner at a San Francisco law firm. She had helped raise funds for Davis's 1998 campaign and had worked for President Clinton as a private attorney. OPR was not located in the governor's office, but Lynch often interjected in deliberations there by the governor's inner circle. By the end of Davis's first year, the welcome mat for Lynch in the governor's office had frayed, and she expressed an interest in leaving OPR and joining New Jersey Senator Bill Bradley's campaign for the Democratic presidential nomination. That ultimately prompted the governor—a prominent and staunch Al Gore ally—to offer her a seat on the CPUC and, as his first appointee to the commission, to be its president, a decision he would later greatly regret. Though he could demote her from president of the CPUC, her five-year term on the commission had been approved by the senate, so he could not remove her altogether.

The governor's "nonexistent" relationship with Lynch meant that communication between the two of them in the effort to work out a bond deal was done through intermediaries, and such "discussions" continued after the commission rejected the administration's proposal in October. Lynch's contention that the Davis-Angelides bond proposal would somehow prevent the state from renegotiating the DWR contracts was not shared by legal counsel for the two men. Davis supported contract renegotiations and, in accordance with that, by fall his lead renegotiation attorney reached an agreement with his counterpart in Attorney General Lockyer's office to seek "universal relief" from the merchant generators, which combined overcharge refund deliberations with contract renegotiations.[26] The biggest issue for Lynch, it appeared, was the principal of not acceding to any terms that would, as the CPUC's general counsel stated, "limit or restrict the commission's regulatory authority." Yet, when the commission finally reached an agreement with the administration in February to sell as much as $13.4 billion in bonds, DWR was empowered to compel the CPUC to raise or adjust rates accordingly to service the bond debt and to cover other electricity costs the department incurred pursuant to its duties in AB X1.[27] At long last, the commission approved the rate allocation decision on February 22, and that helped stabilize the General Fund and allowed the treasurer to finalize the details of the massive bond sale with investment banks and eventually proceed to the market.

***

While few merchant generators expressed interest in renegotiating their DWR contracts in the summer and early fall of 2001, that began to change when Enron—after its already-declining stock price plunged from $50 a share in July to $1 by the end of November—declared bankruptcy on December 2nd. By spring 2001, it had become clear that the company, once a darling of Wall Street, was experiencing significant financial problems, and an investigative exposé in *The Wall Street Journal* in October revealed that Enron's business model and finances appeared to rest on a house of cards. With a mix of schadenfreude and dismay, we watched Enron begin to "implode in a wave of accounting scandals"—the apt and now-infamous prediction of Enron's fate in an executive's in-house August 2001 memo to the captain of the sinking ship, Ken Lay.[28]

Unlike Enron, the merchant generators were not besieged by accounting scams, but their stock prices had dropped precipitously along with the spot price of electricity in California and elsewhere in the West, and Enron's demise added to those woes. During a January 23, 2002, press event, Davis noted that markets continued to "punish" the generators "for the problems associated with Enron," and that some of them saw "the wisdom in renegotiating their contract" to mitigate investor "uncertainty" about company revenues from those agreements. However, the governor made clear that while renegotiation discussions had taken place, no deals had been reached.[29]

Taking matters a step further, on February 24, Davis announced he would petition the FERC to overturn the contracts or compel their renegotiation because, he maintained, the contractors had manipulated the market to bring about unreasonable and unjustifiable high prices that factored heavily into the cost and terms of those agreements. Adding to the pressure on the governor regarding the contracts, prospective Republican gubernatorial opponents joined the chorus of critics who maintained that Davis bought too much power at high prices for too many years.

While Enron's collapse provided a springboard for his request, the odds that the FERC would act seemed slim. "I don't think the state has a long shot of getting what they're seeking here," the head of the trade association representing many of the generators contended. Indeed, the FERC showed no indication that it would take such action, and a "gun-to-the-head" clause in the DWR contracts stipulated that the state must pay for them even if the FERC found them to be unjust and unreasonable. Nevertheless, Davis expressed confidence that the FERC "will be sympathetic to our complaint."[30]

Though that optimism appeared to be more wishful thinking than a likely outcome, that changed remarkably in early May after the FERC released damning Enron memos obtained during an investigation by the commission that revealed market manipulation not only by the now-bankrupt firm but implicated other power sellers as well. Enron had used manipulative strategies, such as phantom transmission congestion, to spike wholesale electricity prices in California and gave some of these strategies code names such as "Fat Boy" and "Death Star." Moreover, Enron and other industry manipulators took cavalier delight in their ill-gotten gains and the misfortune of Californians, as shown in this Enron email[31]:

From: Jeffrey.Fawcett@enron.com

Date: 2001-04-30

Subject: California Sing-Along

And to start off the week.....
California's new State Song!
The Rolling Blackout Theme Song
(To the theme music from the TV western *"Rawhide"*)
Rollin', rollin', rollin',
Though the state is golden,
Keep them blackouts rollin', statewide.
A little colder weather,
And we all freeze together,
Wishin' more plants were on the line.
All the things I'm missin',
Like lights and television,
Are waiting 'til we can pay the price.

(Chorus)
Turn 'em on, turn 'em off,
Shut 'em down, block 'em out,
Turn 'em on, turn 'em off, statewide!
Brown 'em out, black 'em out,
Charge 'em more, give 'em less,
Let the pols fix the mess, statewide!

Keep movin', movin', movin',
Though they're disapprovin',
Keep them rates a-movin', statewide.
Don't try to understand 'em,
Just raise, charge, and collect 'em.
Soon we'll be livin' high and wide.
My heart's calculatin',
Nuclear plants will be waitin',
Be waitin' at the end of my ride.

(Chorus)
Turn 'em on, turn 'em off,
Shut 'em down, block 'em out,
Turn 'em on, turn 'em off, statewide!
Brown 'em out, black 'em out,
Charge 'em more, give 'em less,
Let the pols fix the mess, statewide!

STATEWIDE! Hyaah!

In a May 7 letter to FERC Chair Pat Wood, the governor declared, "it is past time for FERC to investigate the extent to which others, in addition to Enron, engaged in the manipulative practices described in Enron's confession."[32] (Davis used "confession" as a figure of speech; there was no formal confession but an abundance of incriminating evidence.) Wood tacitly agreed, and in the coming months, more sellers were shown to have used such tactics. The revelations proved to be a godsend for Davis politically and added significant leverage to the administration's contract renegotiation effort.

The Washington Post columnist Steve Pearlstein observed in mid-May that Davis "clearly took delight last week in turning the tables on a Republican administration that had blamed his incompetence for the [energy] fiasco." And Pearlstein keenly noted the ominous implications for electricity deregulation devotees: "The fresh evidence of how easily electric markets can be manipulated by a handful of wholesale suppliers is almost certain to set back even further the already stalled pace of electric deregulation in other states."[33]

***

In his January 2002 state of the state address, Davis solemnly noted at considerable length how September 11 had "changed our world forever," and that "more than 100 Californians" had perished on the four hijacked planes, all of which were heading to the Golden State. After describing the state's preparation to guard against potential terrorist attacks, the governor pivoted to the improvements attained during his administration in education, health care, and other policy areas. He then spoke relatively briefly about the energy crisis, mainly to commend Californians for their conservation efforts and to note the addition of new generation built "in record time." Looking ahead, he touted the establishment of the Power Authority "to help ensure our energy future," in which "we must continue to build cleaner" and "more efficient plants to replace our aging facilities."[34]

Several weeks after Davis's speech, the Authority issued its draft state power plan titled "Clean Growth: Clean Energy for California's Future." The cornerstone of the plan was "aggressive investment in energy efficiency and renewable energy resources," which would be "implemented in phases, and it will involve actions by other public and private-sector entities." As he had promised, Freeman focused on building up the state's power reserves and enhancing reliability, especially in "transmission constrained areas."[35] The "Clean Growth" plan did not lack ambition and clear purpose, but it did lack solid data to support the extraordinary economic benefits it projected that included tens of billions of dollars in new economic development and savings from major reductions in natural gas purchases as the nascent "green" power economy grew.

Some people harbored great expectations for the Authority, including John Burton, who authored the bill that established it and declared that it would allow the state to "control its own destiny against the energy pirates." Freeman, in his inimitable way, described how the Authority could give the middle finger to merchant generators by giving "us the ability, in California, to say 'If you don't like our prices, if you don't like our environmental laws, you can go back to Texas. We'll just build these facilities ourselves.'"[36] That notion provided a nimble catharsis for our energy cost trauma and, at the same time, a bulwark against being gamed again. But the reality proved far more complicated.

Burton's bill allowed the Authority to issue up to $5 billion in bonds for power projects, but, like the DWR bonds, they would not be backed by California taxpayers through the state's General Fund. Instead, these "revenue bonds" would be issued only after the Authority secured a clear and reliable revenue stream from a public or private partner to service the bond debt. Unlike Keeley's AB 1X, which authorized the DWR to recover its costs through revenue bonds serviced by an IOU ratepayer surcharge, Burton's bill had no similar provision; and the power companies that could potentially partner with the Authority were now struggling financially in the wake of the collapse of both wholesale prices and Enron. They could not be creditworthy project partners with the Authority without having long-term contracts with a third party for that project's power output, and those contracts proved scarce given the DWR's large portfolio of agreements that

Freeman, ironically, had negotiated in 2001. By the end of 2002, the Authority's board considered asking the CPUC for an IOU ratepayer surcharge to back its bonds,[37] but an effort to add yet another debt-service charge to IOU bills would have gone nowhere. As such, the Authority's *raison d'être* withered, but Freeman pressed on.

I had many interesting discussions with Freeman while he chaired the Authority, and energy efficiency and conservation pioneer Art Rosenfeld participated in a number of them. Rosenfeld, a physicist at UC's Lawrence Berkeley National Laboratory, began developing energy efficiency methods and standards there in the 1970s and convinced then-governor Jerry Brown, and many others from then on, of the wisdom of his adage that "the cheapest energy is what you don't use." Freeman and Rosenfeld were kindred spirits in some ways, and, for a time, they consulted frequently given that Davis had appointed Rosenfeld in 2000 to serve as a member of the Energy Commission. Freeman wanted Rosenfeld, who came to be known as the "godfather of energy efficiency," to help the Authority become a multi-faceted power bazaar—"a Walmart for energy," as he declared at the outset of his chairpersonship.[38] But it was not meant to be.

The Energy Commission, along with a CPUC partnership with the IOUs, managed and funded the state's efficiency and conservation programs, and there was no clear need for an additional state entity to get integrally involved. That compounded Freeman's frustration with the inability to fund large power projects, particularly for renewable energy. He floated a few rather quixotic ideas for big solar panel ventures, during which his determination to do *something* got the better of him. The Authority did fund some power peaker projects to enhance reliability and energy reserves, but these efforts were small and far short of Freeman's expansive vision and bond funding capacity. In 2003, he perfunctorily noted that "we've got a small, lean, capable organization that is sitting there like a backup generator."[39] Indeed, the Authority ended up being a quite capable yet second-tier team waiting for the curtain to rise to meet a great need that once seemed almost certain to materialize. It did not, and that turned out to be another curious twist in California's energy saga.

Though Freeman's time as a state official in the vanguard of the green renaissance proved fleeting and minimally productive, his and Rosenfeld's embrace and promotion of a new power paradigm, with energy efficiency and renewable resources at the forefront, nurtured the green zeitgeist that flourished in the wake of the energy crisis. A July 2001 survey conducted by the Public Policy Institute of California found almost "two in three Californians say they would favor the development of more solar and wind power, even if it meant higher electricity prices," but support was considerably higher among "non-Hispanic whites." In a February 2002 Public Policy Institute of California (PPIC) survey, "nearly seven in 10" Californians favored more renewable energy even if it raised rates, and that "support is high across all demographic groups." By June of 2002, state residents expressed "overwhelming support (85%) for a state policy" requiring the doubling of renewable energy use to "account for 20 percent of all state power in the next 10 years." Support proved so strong that even among those who prioritized the "development of energy supplies" over possible environmental degradation, "only 21 percent are opposed to this renewable energy policy."[40] Green power, long a popular but boutique resource, had emerged as a top preference for the state's energy future, along with even more rigorous efficiency and conservation efforts.

* * *

Since then, solar energy has become as emblematic of sun-soaked California as the Golden Gate Bridge, Half Dome and surfing, but that may not have happened if not for actions taken during the great environmental awakening of the 1970s, which included the passage of an initiative establishing the California Coastal Commission in 1972. Galvanized by the disastrous oil spill off (and on) the Santa Barbara coast in 1969, this effort was bolstered by growing opposition to building more nuclear power plants along the coast, highlighted by PG&E's unsuccessful attempt to site one aside an earthquake fault near Bodega Bay in Sonoma County.[41] In 1976, the legislature passed and Governor Brown signed legislation that placed a moratorium on the licensing and construction of new nuclear plants until the federal government established a safe radioactive waste disposal process and permanent main site (which is still pending as of the publication of this book).

The genesis of the state's renewable energy commitment came from the enactment of the Private Power Producers Act of 1976, which promoted the development of "non-conventional" power sources and allowed them to "feed-in" to the state's power grid. Two years later, at the behest of President Jimmy Carter, Congress passed the Public Utilities Regulatory Policies Act (PURPA), which gave another big boost to wind, solar, biomass, and geothermal energy producers under 80 MW known as "Qualifying Facilities."[42] Congress also approved the Energy Tax Act of 1978, which offered a 30 percent tax credit to residential consumers for the purchase of solar and wind equipment and a 10 percent credit to businesses that purchased these technologies.[43]

Brown jumped at the opportunity to use PURPA to bolster the state's commitment to renewable energy and established the SolarCal Council in 1978 to further assist in promoting and subsidizing solar projects. Brown named Sim Van der Ryn, his appointee as state architect, to head the SolarCal Council. A professor of architecture at UC Berkeley, Van der Ryn, like his Berkeley colleague Rosenfeld, was a catalyst of the green building movement of the 1970s and established the Energy Efficient Office Building Program as a state architect. His building designs incorporated unique air duct systems and "solar architecture," maximizing shade with trellises and decks, and many designs included solar panels. Brown and the state legislature added a state incentive that gave a 55 percent tax credit to Californians purchasing solar panels to help offset their high cost. In addition to expanding the use of solar in the near term, the long-term goal was to back more research and development for innovations that would lead to economies of scale for solar technology manufacturing and reduced costs.[44]

However, by 1983, cheap oil and natural gas began to dim renewable energy's allure, and Brown's successor as governor, Republican George Deukmejian, eliminated funding for the SolarCal Council and cut other alternative power programs at the Energy Commission as he dealt with a state budget deficit resulting from a recession.[45] Though Deukmejian also sought to eliminate both the solar energy and the energy conservation tax credit programs, legislators reached a compromise with him and preserved them but reduced their benefits. In 1985, the benefits of these and other green energy programs were further trimmed, and a few were eliminated altogether.[46] Those actions corresponded with the dismantling of most Carter-era sustainable energy programs during the administration of President Ronald Reagan, which issued a clarion call for deregulation and opposed and then rolled back fuel economy standards for new internal-combustion engine vehicles. By the late 1980s, the green American zeitgeist that had burgeoned in the 1970s had largely given way to a laissez faire spirit through which Reagan arguably achieved his goal to "reawaken this industrial giant."[47]

Support for environmental causes in California, however, remained fairly strong compared to the rest of the U.S., and environmental groups there decided to mount a major campaign in 1990 for a ballot initiative that came to be known as "Big Green." Running 39 pages, the initiative offered sweepingly tougher changes to the state's environmental laws, including a phased-in ban on the use of many pesticides (even on imported produce) and a commitment to reduce emissions of "any gases which may contribute, directly or indirectly, to global warming" by 40 percent by 2010. Though Big Green polled well initially, support dropped as concerns grew about its cost. The state's nonpartisan Legislative Analyst's Office projected the direct cost to state and local governments to be about $2.6 billion over 20 years, but the Los Angeles Department of Water and Power claimed that it would have to spend more than $6 billion just to meet the greenhouse-gas emission reduction requirement.[48] One leery backer of the initiative observed several weeks before the election that "people get scared when they hear it's going to cost billions of dollars. Until recently I would have said it would pass easily. Now, it just might lose." Indeed, Big Green failed by a two to one margin, and similar, albeit less ambitious, efforts in other states also went down by wide margins. After the election, *Newsweek* noted that the "Green Revolution" showed "signs of a slow fizzle."[49] Down but not out, alternative energy advocates in California moved wearily in 1992 into the deregulation process at the CPUC to make the case for the renewable energy market incentives they strongly backed.

As noted in Chapter 2, the CPUC's Preferred Policy Decision on deregulation in late 1995 contained something for all the stakeholders to like and dislike, but the dislike grew for consumer advocates after the enactment of AB 1890 mainly because it allowed the IOUs to fully recover their stranded costs. Led by The Utility Reform Network (TURN) and Harvey Rosenfield's Californians Against Utility Taxes, consumer groups qualified an initiative for the 1998 state ballot that required the IOUs to cut their rates by 20 percent and eliminate the ratepayer charge for $6.3 billion in bonds that the IOUs sold to pay for their 10 percent "rate reduction" in AB 1890. It also barred the IOUs from passing on the stranded costs of their nuclear facilities to ratepayers. While the initiative, known as Proposition 9, received support from the League of Women Voters, Consumers Union, and Ralph Nader's Public Citizen, the only prominent environmental group to support it was the Sierra Club, which opposed California ratepayers "subsidizing nuclear power."[50] The measure, which never polled well, drew major opposition from a wide range of stakeholders, including the NRDC and Environmental Defense Fund, the International Brotherhood of Electrical Workers, and virtually every notable business group in the state. The provision to eliminate the ratepayer bond-charge proved particularly problematic as it raised numerous legal questions about "whether the measure would have any impact on the repayment of these bonds or, if it did, what that impact would be," according to the Legislative Analyst.[51] Averse to uncertainty and overreach, voters overwhelmingly rejected the proposition seven months into deregulation's seemingly smooth launch.

***

In May of 2000, Senator Sher gutted and amended one of his bills to add provisions extending the "system benefit charge" for all ratepayers established in AB 1890 to fund energy efficiency, conservation, research, and "existing, new and emerging renewable energy resources." Set to expire on March 31, 2002, the statutory authority to collect the charge in Sher's bill was extended to January 1, 2012, and another provision directed the Energy Commission to evaluate and report on "the appropriateness and structure of a mandatory state purchase of renewable energy."[52] While opposition to the extension of the charge was modest, Sher's incremental approach to the Renewable Portfolio Standard (RPS) that required only a study of its viability was as far as he could go at that time given that the IOUs and other business interests were no more interested in an RPS in 2000 than they had been in 1996. When the bill passed easily in the senate on August 31 and then went to the governor's desk, high wholesale electricity costs—though nowhere near their apex—had been vexing politicians in the capitol for three months. While the governor and Democratic legislators voiced support for increasing the use of renewable energy and passed several bills to do so, the RPS remained a more ambitious concept in need of a bigger catalyst to become a reality.

That catalyst jarringly emerged three months later when wholesale prices soared so high that PG&E and SCE went into financial tailspins and

Californians plunged into a full-fledged energy crisis and quandary. The din of the dialogue on the disaster then contained many policy prescriptions, including one from the leading utility-rate consumer group, TURN. As part of a comprehensive and complicated plan, TURN urged state officials to "specify a minimum percentage of renewable resources" for utility power portfolios to increase "resource diversity and serve as a hedge against fluctuations in fuel and emissions credit prices."[53] To be sure, this specific proposal hardly popped out at me or others in the governor's office when the plan came out in mid-December as we scrambled like never before to keep the lights on, but it was important for several reasons. Consumer groups generally supported renewable energy but were somewhat conflicted due to its higher cost, which hindered their mission to minimize rates, and some energy environmentalists had criticized the consumer groups' Proposition 9 for not including an increase in renewable incentives beyond programs funded by the system benefits charge in AB 1890.[54] At the height of the crisis, with natural gas-based electricity costs greatly exceeding the cost of most renewable power, the latter grew far more attractive as a hedge against being gamed by "out-of-state" generators, traders, and natural gas companies as we headed into 2001.

However, the epic energy challenges during the first half of that year, and the heated debates through the end of the legislative session in September, crowded out the nascent RPS and relatively moderate renewable energy increases that would provide little help to stabilize the state's energy market in the near term. Moreover, the intermittent output of solar and wind power—the two renewable resources with the highest profile and potential—made these power sources less reliable, and opponents seized on that and their high cost compared to falling electricity spot-market prices in the summer. Despite these challenges, the RPS would have become law if the Edison MOU bill that had passed in the assembly had been approved by the senate. Sher also tried to move his "stand-alone" RPS bill, SB 532, which had passed in the senate, to the assembly floor for a vote, but it failed to get out of the Utilities and Commerce Committee and could not be taken up again until the next legislative session. These failures notwithstanding, by 2002 the bill appeared to be ready for prime time on a less crowded stage as support grew while more information on the market manipulation by Enron and others came to light.

On March 18, 2002, Davis endorsed SB 532 in San Francisco at the Potrero Hill Neighborhood House, a community center that utilized rooftop solar panels. Though the Silicon Valley Leadership Group supported the bill, the IOUs continued to oppose it, as did almost all the other big business groups, including political powerhouses such as the state Chamber of Commerce and the California Manufacturers and Technology Association. I and others working to get the bill to the assembly floor knew we needed a break, and we got one when SCE offered to support the RPS if the purchase requirement could be structured with regulatory cost "guardrails." While some renewable energy producers grumbled about this request, *Windpower*

Monthly rightly noted that, like "many of the RPS variations" in other states, "achieving the goal is subject to reasonable cost limitations."[55]

After Tommy Ross, Edison's vice president for public affairs, and his colleague, regulatory policy expert Catherine Hackney, briefed me on the details of the company's RPS proposal, we met with Sher and Kip Lipper, and we all agreed to move ahead with the proposal as the template for negotiation. The discussions that ensued were mainly with clean power advocate John White, Julia Levin with the Union of Concerned Scientists, TURN's Matt Freedman, Nancy Rader with the California Wind Energy Association, and lobbyists for PG&E and SDG&E, who were still lukewarm at best to an RPS.

Edison's legislative proposal included two key amendments to Sher's SB 532: The mandatory monetary penalty for IOU noncompliance with RPS procurement targets was removed, and a "benchmark price," to be established by the CPUC, was added for renewable energy procured pursuant to the RPS. The benchmark price would serve as a market-based wholesale price ceiling for renewable energy, and any cost above that ceiling would be covered only by funds from the systems benefit charge established in AB 1890, now known as the Public Goods Charge (PGC). This arrangement reflected Edison's insistence that the IOUs should not be put in a position in which they had to pay above-market prices for renewables, even if they could pass those higher costs on to consumers. Given the exorbitant costs Californians had experienced during the crisis (and after to a lesser extent with the DWR contracts), that seemed eminently reasonable. Legitimate concerns were raised by some renewable power providers and environmentalists about the possibility of the CPUC setting the benchmark price too low, which could potentially drain the funds from the PGC, perhaps entirely, and hobble RPS compliance. As a result, Sher introduced, and Davis sponsored, a separate RPS "companion" bill, SB 1038, that increased the amount of PGC funds dedicated to renewable facilities and technologies.

The San Francisco-based Energy Foundation contributed a million dollars for a media campaign supporting the RPS, and the list of backers grew to include numerous environmental, consumer, public health, labor, and religious groups along with dozens of government officials led by California's two U.S. senators. The state's three most-circulated newspapers, the *Los Angeles Times*, *San Francisco Chronicle*, and San Jose's *The Mercury News*, also strongly endorsed the RPS.[56] Touting the benefits of energy resource diversity, the *Chronicle*'s endorsement declared that "if nothing else, our energy crisis should have underscored the risk of relying on a single energy source that can be easily disrupted, manipulated and priced beyond reason."[57]

The benchmark price and the use of PGC funds continued to be controversial as the legislative session reached its final stretch, and Sher refrained from adding the SCE amendments to the RPS bill. That prompted Tommy Ross to send Sher a letter on August 14, noting that while Edison representatives had "participated constructively in negotiations" with him and other stakeholders, "we have been unable to come to closure to date" and therefore "remain opposed [to the bill] unless amended."[58] The next day Sher gutted and amended a new RPS bill, SB 1078, to add Edison's changes, but it still contained language that Edison and PG&E, which had decided to support the proposal, opposed. After further negotiations that included Rod Wright, the Democratic chair of the Utilities and Commerce Committee, additional amendments were made to delete that language and to exempt municipal utilities such as the LADWP from the RPS requirement given that, unlike the IOUs, they were not under the state's jurisdiction. The IOUs were not happy about the exemption, nor were other RPS backers. However, the "Munis," as they were known, had the clout to kill the bill and had to be placated. With that and other amendments done, SB 1078—which required 20 percent of the electricity from the state's energy service providers under the CPUC's jurisdiction to come from renewable sources by 2017—passed on the assembly floor on August 29 with 55 votes, including four Republicans.

Like the ill-fated Edison MOU bill the previous year, the senate needed to concur in the assembly's RPS bill amendments to send the legislation to Davis. Unlike the MOU bill experience, I, along with Sher and Lipper, were not expecting problems in securing the vote for that concurrence. However, on the last night of the session, Senate Energy Committee chair Debra Bowen strenuously objected to a provision in SB 1078 that exempted PG&E from RPS compliance until it became "creditworthy," which she believed meant until the utility emerged from bankruptcy. She threatened to pull the bill from the senate floor and hold it in her committee, which she had procedural authority to do. Sher, Lipper, and I tried to mollify her, and we appealed to Burton to intervene, but, after a few profane blurts and glaring at Bowen, he walked away. Before she headed back into the senate chamber, and at wit's end, I reiterated my commitment to work with her to address her concerns in the next session.[59] A short while later, Lipper informed me that, after a brief heart-to-heart chat, Bowen had told Sher she would not pull the bill back to her committee, and about an hour before the end of the session, the senate concurred in the assembly amendments to both SB 1078 and SB 1038.

Though many crisis "cleanup" items remained, passage of the RPS bill brought another cathartic element of closure to the crisis for many Californians as it helped mark the beginning of a new, green energy commitment by the state. During the governor's second term, his administration would help meet and perhaps even increase that commitment, but first, Davis had to be reelected.

Notes

1 Jeff Gerth, "U.S. Agency Widens Its Curbs on Price of Power in the West," *The New York Times*, June 19, 2001.
2 Lobbyist quoted in David S. Broder, "Daylight for Gray Davis," *The Washington Post*, September 5, 2001.
3 Information in a July 2001 draft press release by and in possession of the author.

4 *NGI* Staff, "California Hammers Out a Deal with QFs," *Natural Gas Intelligence*, June 18, 2001.
5 Bill Bradley, "Light and Darkness," *LA Weekly*, September 6, 2001; interview with Smutny-Jones. In addition, according to *Windpower* Monthly, of the 1300 MW of new renewables projects awarded funding from the AB 1890 incentive programs since 1998, only 200 MW had come on-line as of spring 2002. Staff, "California Considers Renewable Mandate," *Windpower Monthly*, May 31, 2002. https://www.windpowermonthly.com/article/953620/california-considers-renewables-mandate
6 Kari Dohn and Kurt Schuparra to File (i.e., Davis), "Solar Energy Programs," May 17, 2001, Archive Box 975, GGDR/CSA.
7 Clarion Energy Content Directors, "Gov. Davis announces plan to increase state's renewable energy generation," *Power Engineering*, July 31, 2001.
8 S. David Freeman, "One Way to Keep the 'Big Boys' Honest," *Los Angeles Times*, August 24, 2001.
9 Charles Pope, "Utilities Demand Refunds," *Seattle Post-Intelligencer*, July 9, 2001.
10 Wagner quoted in Carolyn Lochhead, "Regulators Say $1 Billion Power Refund Is Fair," *San Francisco Chronicle*, July 26, 2001.
11 Interview with South.
12 Lehane quoted in (no author listed) "Gray Davis' Edison Problem," *Salon*, July 31, 2001. https://www.salon.com/2001/07/31/edison_2/; Walter Kelley, Jeffrey L. Rabin and Daryl Kelley, "Davis' Energy Advisors Draw SEC Attention," *Los Angeles Times*, July 31, 2001.
13 Nancy Cleeland, "For CEO, Life in 'Foxhole' Means Little Sleep, Peace," *Los Angeles Times*, May 8, 2001.
14 Assembly Committee on Energy Costs and Availability analysis of SB 78 (second extraordinary session), August 23, 2001.
15 Goode, Katz, McFadden, and I conferred with Foster on this effort and encouraged it.
16 The accounts in this and the preceding paragraph are from the author's first-hand experience.
17 All quotes are from Staff Reporters, "Legislature in California Gives No Aid to a Utility," *The New York Times*, September 17, 2001.
18 Dan Morain and Tim Reiterman, "PUC Chief's Iron Resolve Evident in Edison Deal," *Los Angeles Times*, October 8, 2001.
19 Editorial (including Rosenfield quote), "Through the Back Door," *San Francisco Chronicle*, October 5, 2001.
20 Burton quoted in Dan Morain, "Davis Concedes Edison Rescue Is 'Uphill' Battle," *Los Angeles Times*, September 19, 2001.
21 Governor Davis, "Governor Makes Statement on Public Utilities Commission Actions," Press Release, October 2, 2001.
22 Tim Gage to File, "Selling the Power Bonds Is Critical to General Fund Cash Flow," April 23, 2001, Archive Box 144/12, GGDR/CSA. Gage explained in the memo that because the state needed to borrow money for cash flow purposes through "revenue anticipation notes," the state might not be able to secure those notes without the bond sale "because the General Fund would be perceived as too risky a credit."
23 Decision quoted in Tim Reiterman and Nancy Vogel, "PUC Ensures State Covers Cost, Even If Rates Must Go Up," *Los Angeles Times*, March 8, 2001; interview with Kevin Civale, August 26, 2022.
24 Bernadette Tansey and Robert Salladay, "PUC Czar Warns of 'price crisis' in Power Pacts," *San Francisco Chronicle*, October 2, 2001.
25 Morain and Reiterman, "PUC Chief's Iron Resolve Evident in Edison Deal."

26 Interview with Ken Alex, March, 8, 2022.
27 Counsel quoted in Morain and Reiterman, "PUC Chief's Iron Resolve Evident in Edison Deal"; Nancy Vogel, "Impasse Ends on Energy Bonds," *Los Angeles Times*, February 1, 2002.
28 The series of articles on Enron in *The Wall Street Journal*, by Rebecca Smith and John Emshwiller, began on October 17, 2001; quote from Enron executive Sherron Watkins in https://www.pbs.org/newshour/economy/business-jan-june02-enron_01-15
29 Governor Davis, Sacramento Press Club comments, January 23, 2002, transcript: http://gray-davis.com/ViewLibraryItem.aspx?ID=9413
30 Trade association representative and Davis quoted in Times Staff and Wire Reports, "Davis Seeks Cuts in Power Deals," *Los Angeles Times*, February 26, 2002.
31 Lockyer, "Attorney General's Energy White Paper," 21–22.
32 Letter to Wood in "Governor Davis Continues Fight against Enron and Other Energy Profiteers," May 7, 2002. http://gray-davis.com/ViewLibraryItem.aspx?ID=7402
33 Steve Pearlstein, "How Enron Gave California a Power Bust," *The Washington Post*, May 12, 2002.
34 Governor Davis, State of the State Address, January 8, 2002.
35 Draft plan excerpts quoted in *NGI* Staff Reports, "CA Power Authority Releases Draft Plan for Future Energy Projects," *Natural Gas Intelligence*, January 28, 2002.
36 Burton quoted in "Governor Gray Davis Bill Signing" transcript, May 16, 2001. http://gray-davis.com/ViewLibraryItem.aspx?ID=9622; Freeman quoted in "Energy, Conservation, and the Public Interest," Institute of International Studies, UC Berkeley, September 29, 2003. http://globetrotter.berkeley.edu/people3/Freeman/freeman-con4.html
37 *NGI* Staff Reports, "CA Power Authority Focuses on State Reserve Levels," *Natural Gas Intelligence*, December 2, 2002.
38 Freeman quoted in Lynda Gledhill, "Davis Energy Expert Resigns before New Governor Forces Him Out," *San Francisco Chronicle*, October 24, 2003.
39 Freeman quoted in Nancy Rivera Brooks, "Hydrogen Fuels Energy Broker's New Adventure," *Los Angeles Times*, October 24, 2003.
40 PPIC Press Release, "Californians Galvanized By Energy Crisis," July 19, 2001; Mark Baldassare, "PPIC Statewide Survey: Californians and Their Government," February 18, 2002; Baldassare, "PPIC Statewide Survey: Special Survey on Californians and the Environment," June 2002, 15.
41 Peevey and Wittenberg, *California Goes Green*, 38.
42 Peevey and Wittenberg, *California Goes Green*, 44.
43 Geoffrey Jones, *Varieties of Green Business: Industries, Nations and Time* (Cheltenham, UK: Edward Elgar Publishing Limited, 2018), 79.
44 Jones, *Varieties of Green Business*, 79; http://solarhousehistory.com/blog/2014/11/23/revisiting-the-bateson-building
45 Leon Lindsay, "Anti-Tax Sentiment Still Shapes Deukmejian Budget," *The Christian Science Monitor*, July 26, 1983; and Legislative Analyst, "Summary of Legislative Action on the Budget Bill 1983–84 Fiscal Year," August 1983, 39–41.
46 Terrence M. Green, "California Continues Energy Tax Credits," *Los Angeles Times*, August 4, 1985; for more details on these actions see *Regulatory Choices: A Perspective on Developments in Energy Policy*, edited by Richard J. Gilbert (Berkeley, CA: University of California Press, 1991). http://ark.cdlib.org/ark:/13030/ft838nb559/
47 Reagan noted and quoted in Joseph Romm, "Reagan Helped Save the Ozone Layer but Ruined America's Leadership in Clean Energy," *Grist*, February 8,

2011. After 1982, both U.S. labor productivity and GDP growth accelerated, though real wages continued to decline.

48 Robert Reinhold, "Once Considered a Sure Thing, California's Environmental Package Falters," *The New York Times*, September 16, 1990.

49 Leery backer quoted in Robert Reinhold, "Once Considered a Sure Thing, California's Environmental Package Falters;" *Newsweek* Staff, "It's Not Easy Being Green," *Newsweek*, November 18, 1990.

50 Kenneth Howe, "State Propositions/Proposition 9," *San Francisco Chronicle*, October 25, 1998; and Sierra Club quoted in "Sierra Club condemns use of name against Prop. 9, demands retraction," https://consumerwatchdog.org/newsrelease/sierra-club-condemns-use-name-against-prop-9-demands-retraction

51 Analyst quoted in Douglas P. Shuit, "Prop. 9 Anxiety Goes All the Way to Wall Street," *Los Angeles Times*, October 23, 1998.

52 SB 1194, Chapter 1050, September 30, 2000.

53 See "California Group Argues for Mandatory Renewable Energy," December 12, 2000. https://www.renewableenergyworld.com/solar/california-group-argues-for-mandatory-renewable-energy-5046/

54 Interview with Mike Florio, July 1, 2021; Ralph Cavanagh letter to Friends and Colleagues, "Why NRDC Opposes California's Proposition 9," September 22, 1998 (copy in possession of the author).

55 Quoted in Staff, "California Considers Renewable Mandate."

56 Staff, "California Considers Renewable Mandate."

57 Editorial, "A Promising Energy Plan," *San Francisco Chronicle*, April 27, 2002.

58 Ross to Sher, RE: SB 1078, "Oppose unless amended," Southern California Edison, August 14, 2002. Archive Box 975, GGDR/CSA.

59 Bowen's concerns were addressed the following year in her bill, SB 67, which, with the governor's signature, became Chapter 731 of 2003. It authorized the CPUC to require PG&E to procure renewable electricity pursuant to the state's RPS for "reasonable" costs, with financing if necessary, provided that "the procurement will not impair the restoration of an electrical corporation's creditworthiness."

6 Davis's Demise and Arnold's Rise

Schwarzenegger Touts Deregulation *and* Green Energy

While the 2002 legislative session proved to be a banner year for bills that provided pivot points to a greener energy future, the energy crisis, the key catalyst for this transition, had clearly become a political albatross for Davis as he pursued reelection. In addition, the halcyon first two years of his administration, highlighted by unprecedented state budget surpluses, gave way to a $23 billion deficit due mainly to the collapse of the "Tech Bubble" and the precipitous drop in capital gains revenue from taxpayers exercising stock options and selling other assets. Even though many Republican legislators had voted for the big, surplus-laden budgets in 1999 and 2000, they now hammered Davis for his "reckless" spending. In early 2002 I mentioned to Susan Kennedy that state spending growth (adjusted for inflation) during the governor's first term was notably less than during either of the two terms of former Governor Reagan—who, as president, became the patron saint of fiscal conservatives—and that quickly became a staple of Davis's talking points to counter criticisms of his budget management.[1] Fortunately, Davis was not running against a candidate of Reagan's ilk, and another politically inclined actor, Arnold Schwarzenegger, once the biggest box office star in the world, had declined to run after making comments that he might do so. Though hobbled, Davis seemed destined for another four years in office.

* * *

Of the Republican gubernatorial candidates in the GOP primary race, former Los Angeles Mayor Richard Riordan emerged with a strong early lead in the polls given his name recognition and political pragmatism that enabled him to be elected in 1993 as the city's first Republican mayor in 30 years and reelected in 1997. However, Riordan's pragmatism made him a moderate, and while that was an asset in heavily Democratic Los Angeles, that didn't necessarily hold true for winning a statewide Republican primary. Davis did not want to face Riordan in the general election, and Garry South seized an opportunity to undermine the former mayor's chances of winning the primary. In a shrewd and unconventional move, South spent $10 million from Davis's ample campaign war chest on political ads against Riordan claiming,

DOI: 10.4324/9781003518150-7

for example, that he was a "closet pro-lifer" on abortion, which goaded Riordan into reiterating that he was pro-choice, like most Californians—but not Republicans.[2] His two opponents, Secretary of State Bill Jones and wealthy businessman Bill Simon, pounced on him for being pro-life and shirking other core conservative positions, and for having made campaign donations to Democrats. Simon, who quickly pulled away from Jones as the chief challenger to the former mayor, maintained in a campaign ad that "unlike Dick Riordan, I'm not ashamed to be a Republican."[3] Simon's sallies, fueled by Davis's campaign ads, put Riordan in freefall while Simon, with the support of "America's Mayor," Rudy Giuliani of 9/11-ravaged New York City, overtook Riordan in the polls and won the primary in early March.

Despite Davis's relentless attacks on Simon in the general election campaign for being a "far right" ideologue and having a number of legal and ethical matters besetting his business ventures, including being sued for fraud, the governor struggled to pull away from him in polls. In Public Policy Institute of California surveys from September and October, Davis led Simon by 8 and 10 percent, respectively, though other polls showed a closer race. The PPIC polls indicated that Davis had a huge advantage over Simon in terms of who could best handle education—the top issue for voters—and a slight advantage over Simon in terms of dealing with the economy and state budget. However, of the other issues that most concerned voters, Simon led Davis by 6–7 percent on electricity and energy policy.[4] As Bill Carrick, Senator Feinstein's chief political advisor, noted, "voters have a snapshot of [Davis] in their mind from the time of the energy crisis, and they don't like what they see. They see a governor who did very little to prepare them or warn them of what was coming, and they were left saying, 'How the hell did this happen?'"[5]

This broad-brush perspective and similar ones critical of Davis's handling of the energy crisis were facile and often flat-out wrong. For example, the governor did not "warn" Californians "of what was coming" because even energy experts did not foresee the exorbitant wholesale prices during the summer of 2000, let alone those prices more than doubling by late November. But the bottom line is that these spikes and eventual blackouts happened on Davis's watch, and that meant he was going to pay a political price, but how steep? He clearly benefitted in the summer and fall of 2002 from the growing media accounts of market manipulation, and in April he had announced that his negotiators had trimmed $3.5 billion from the cost of eight Department of Water Resources (DWR) contracts and threatened legal action against generators who refused to renegotiate their agreements.[6] Still, significant damage had been done to Davis's image as a decisive leader. Three years earlier, *Time* magazine had hailed him as the "most fearless governor in America."[7] The energy crisis now eclipsed that depiction, and that, combined with California's economic downturn and steep state budget deficit, could not help but make Davis appear rather hapless.

Garry South, along with Davis's pollster, Paul Maslin, found out first-hand how tough it was to convince California voters that the governor had responded even somewhat effectively to the crisis. As South later recalled, "we produced a lot of beautiful campaign ads about building power plants, taking on the out-of-state generators, and standing up to Bush." However, when they tested the ads with focus groups, they fell flat, even those with positive messages. "One of the points we pushed in these groups," South noted, "was that Davis had cut red tape and built more power plants than had been built under any previous governor—even those who had served two terms. People just wouldn't accept that." He and Maslin became so frustrated with this response that they decided to distribute a fact sheet from the California Energy Commission to the group, with detailed information corroborating the power plant information, "and people would read it and still say they didn't believe it." They maintained that "'governors don't build power plants, the private sector does,'" and that the governor just had the benefit of being in office when these plants came on-line. South, Maslin, and ultimately Davis, decided not to run any campaign ads dealing with electricity and to instead escalate their attacks on Simon.[8]

***

On the campaign trail, Davis continued his diatribes against the merchant generators and the ties that Bush and Cheney had to them and Enron, but, to the extent that he highlighted energy topics, the focus was on building plants and his green accomplishments, especially the RPS and the most controversial bill of 2002, Assemblymember Fran Pavley's AB 1493. Pavley's landmark bill, which required the California Air Resources Board (CARB) to develop and approve regulations reducing GHG emissions from motor vehicles beginning with model-year 2009, drew staunch opposition from the automotive industry, Chamber of Commerce, and other major business interests.

Unlike the Renewable Portfolio Standard (RPS), AB 1493 was not a direct response to the energy crisis, but it did benefit from the green wave the crisis helped generate.[9] The roots of the bill tapped into the decades-old efforts to curtail severe air pollution in the Los Angeles Basin, which had produced the first tailpipe-emission standard in the nation in 1966 and the use of catalytic converters on internal combustion engines beginning in the 1970s to further reduce emissions contributing to smog. In the 1990s, the CARB passed seminal regulations requiring auto manufacturers to increase the number of zero-and-low-emission vehicles for the California market, though these regulations experienced many bumps on the road to implementation. The Pavley bill would help smooth that road but faced its own challenges from opponents who argued that only the federal government could establish and enforce vehicle fuel and emission standards under the Clean Air Act of 1970. However, supporters countered that assertion, noting that California was the only state empowered under the Act to establish air pollution regulations more stringent than federal requirements.[10]

Introduced in 2001 and sponsored by the Bluewater Network and the Coalition for Clean Air, Pavley's bill soon gained support from the Sierra Club, Natural Resources Defense Council (NRDC), and other bigger and better known environmental organizations. By spring 2002 the bill had initiated the most contentious debate in the legislature, particularly in the Assembly, where its fate hung in the balance. Davis had been leery of the bill given its numerous powerful opponents; but, after a meeting with a group of environmental backers of the bill and a supportive nudge from Winston Hickox, his environmental protection secretary, Davis was open to potentially signing it provided that numerous amendments were added to prohibit additional fees and taxes on vehicles or fuels or restrictions on vehicle type, miles traveled or weight. Chief Deputy Legislative Secretary Linda Adams worked closely on the amendments with Anne Baker in Pavley's office, but Davis took no public position on the bill.[11]

Aided by parliamentary maneuvers orchestrated by Democratic legislative leaders to fast-track the bill, AB 1493 passed narrowly in the senate on June 29 and by one vote in the assembly two days later. Shortly after that, Davis stated that he was "strongly inclined" to sign the bill because most Californians "believe that we can have the choice of the auto or truck we want and still do a better job" of "cleaning up" the environment. Simon, echoing the main argument of the bill's opponents, had criticized the legislation in May as "a thinly veiled attempt to regulate the types of vehicles Californians are allowed to drive." However, after its passage, he said that "reducing global warming, if indeed there is such a thing as global warming, is always a good idea" but disparaged the CARB's competence and ability to implement the bill.[12] On July 22, at high-profile ceremonies in San Francisco and then Los Angeles, Davis signed AB 1493 and dismissed "opponents of this bill [who] say the sky is falling." On the contrary, he noted, "it's just getting a whole lot cleaner."[13]

Most big business interests outside of Silicon Valley opposed the bill, and they also weren't particularly happy with the status of direct access, which had been the primary reason for their strong support of the state's deregulation effort. The CPUC had suspended new direct access contracts on September 20, 2001, after many large electricity customers left IOU (and DWR) service and returned to direct access when spot-market prices plunged during the latter half of summer. The CPUC decision included the possibility that the commission could later decide to disallow even those "new" contracts that had been signed between July 1 and September 20th. This matter generated much contentious debate, with consumer groups fighting for the contract rollback to July 1 while the providers and customers pushed for September 20th. Direct access supporters reluctantly acceded to the imposition of exit fees, which had initially been proposed in the Edison Memorandum of Understanding bill, to cover their share of the DWR contract costs.

Figure 6.1 With the Golden Gate Bridge as a backdrop, Governor Davis and Assemblymember Pavley pose at the AB 1493 signing ceremony in San Francisco.

Source: Photo courtesy of Gray-Davis.com.

Despite the objections of California Public Utilities Commission (CPUC) President Loretta Lynch, in late March of 2002 the commission voted 3-2 to accept direct access contracts signed by September 20 and to initiate the formal and complicated procedure for determining the exit fee. That process had informally begun during the previous month after Navigant Consulting informed me that direct access "markets may be viable in the presence of exit fees," but that depended on market prices remaining relatively low. Navigant outlined the basis for its calculations, and, as expected, when I shared that information with representatives of the large energy consumers, they pushed back and asked for more details.[14] With the commission's March decision, however, my intermediary role mostly came to an end. From the administration's perspective, the CPUC's exit-fee decision had to be secured to assure Wall Street that there would be sufficient revenue to service the DWR bond debt. Though we accomplished that, acrimonious debates over the future of direct access would continue.

Bill Simon skirted this debate, but in the closing weeks of the campaign he ramped up his charge that Davis had ignored "the early signs of power shortages" and added that the governor had "left us vulnerable to manipulation."[15] This attack marked a bit of a shift in Simon's blame game for the crisis. While he had chastised Davis for his handling of it from the outset of his candidacy, Simon initially cited California's flawed restructured market design as the main crisis culprit and, like the vast majority of conservative deregulation backers, downplayed market manipulation.[16] However, after the release of the damning Enron and merchant generator information, even Simon had to acknowledge the role of manipulation, but the main target of his blame for it was Davis's purported inaction, not the FERC's, and not the flawed market design or corporate misdeeds. In turn, Davis continued to depict Simon as an unrepentant deregulation booster who ran shady businesses and had ties to Enron.[17]

On election night, Simon held a surprising, albeit narrow, early lead, and Davis did not move ahead of him until the large Democratic vote from Los Angeles was added to the tally later that evening. Voter turnout proved to be the lowest in the history of the state's gubernatorial elections, and Davis ended up with a remarkably underwhelming and humbling five percentage point victory. As *Los Angeles Times* columnist Mark Z. Barabak aptly observed, "in a sense, Davis and Simon were battling not just one another but a mood—a combination of apathy and antipathy—that hung over the election like a dank fog."[18] Nevertheless, the governor had prevailed. A Davis staff celebration party shortly after the election featured karaoke, and the highlight of that evening was Susan Kennedy's rousing rendition of Gloria Gaynor's "I will Survive," a cathartic moment for us all as we looked ahead to the next four years.

***

Looking ahead to the out years of the second term held the prospect of better times because everyone knew the near-term budget deficit would be ugly once again, but it proved to be worse than anyone had thought during the campaign. In August of 2002, the governor had directed all state departments in the executive branch to freeze expenditures by the maximum amount allowable by law and plan to reduce their budgets by a hefty 20 percent. In a press conference one month after the election, he announced that he would call for a special session of the legislature to deal with "budget reductions [that] are severe by any measure...totaling 10 billion dollars over the current year and [next] budget year combined."[19] On December 18, Davis decided to provide another fiscal update three weeks before the formal release of the new state budget proposal "so people understand the magnitude of the problem we're facing. The shortfall is 34.8 billion dollars, far more than any expert predicted," he gravely disclosed. He also announced that Steve Peace, who Davis had known since serving with him in the assembly in the mid-1980s, would replace Tim Gage as director of the Department of Finance.[20]

Prevented by term limits from running for reelection to the senate in 2002, Peace had set his sights on running for secretary of state, but his reputation for being a sharp and able politician took a big hit from being the driving force behind AB 1890. In 2001 he had tried to counter that image by posting a 12-minute video on his senate website highlighting earlier claims by him that he had always opposed deregulation. He also publicly criticized UC economist Severin Borenstein, an acquaintance, for promoting the flawed restructured market design (and, privately, for not defending him in the media).[21] However, as the *Los Angeles Times* observed in January 2001, Borenstein and a colleague had reported to the Energy Commission in 1997 that electricity prices could "soar" in the restructured market if too few merchant generators bought the divested IOU plants to ensure competition. If that occurred, the report presciently stated, those "firms might have an incentive to restrict output" to raise prices four or five times, or more, above the frozen retail rate of 65 cents per kWh.[22]

In what amounted to a Peace apologia, the Senate Office of Research had noted in a 2001 publication that "Peace described his role [in AB 1890] as realizing he and fellow Democrats lacked the votes to defeat the deregulation bill, whereupon he set out to make it 'friendly to consumers, workers and environmentalists.'"[23] There is some truth to that. With the Republicans controlling the Assembly in 1996 and broad agreement on the need for regulatory reform, it is quite likely that AB 1890 could not have been stopped in the legislature; but when the bill passed, Peace crowed about it as a huge and transformative accomplishment. Of course, he was far from alone in doing so. However, after that legislative capstone of California's deregulation effort, it was often whimsically described as the "Steve Peace Death March." Unfortunately for him, that also applied to his political career.

Peace had been chair of the Senate Budget and Fiscal Committee and had a good command of the budget process and keenly understood the ebb and flow of state revenues and program funding. Though he described Davis's selection of Peace as a "potentially brilliant move," *Los Angeles Times* columnist George Skelton declared that the governor had nevertheless taken a "gamble on Wild Man Steve Peace." Skelton hailed him as a "visionary" who, "unlike most Davis aides, won't be afraid to speak up and say what he thinks"; yet he also was an "incessant talker and frequent pain in the backside who never stops thinking, analyzing, visualizing." Skelton maintained that Peace had gotten a "bad rap" for AB 1890 and echoed the former senator's own defense for it, contending that he had "negotiated a better bill for consumers than what Wilson and his Public Utilities Commission had wanted."[24] While both Davis and Peace could not shake their negative association with the energy crisis, their overwhelming concern in 2003 was the budget crunch which loomed like a giant wrecking ball for a swath of state programs and operations. "Health care," Peace bluntly noted as he began his new job, "is going to get hammered."[25] Though many of its impacts and challenges remained, the energy crisis receded in California's rear-view mirror as the state headed into its fiscal abyss.

***

The exceedingly grim budget numbers notwithstanding, the governor in his inaugural address touted the "true greatness of this Golden State" as the "national standard bearer" on health care research, "clean air, clean water, renewable energy and individual privacy. In short, California is leading again," Davis proclaimed. "It has regained its rightful place as the premier state in America and the envy of much of the world."[26] Most Californians, however, did not buy into that restoration narrative.

Describing the findings of the PPIC's February 2003 survey of "Californians and Their Government," Research Director Mark Baldassare observed that "the new year finds Californians in a dark mood—deeply bearish about the state's economic prospects and acutely resentful of their elected representatives." He noted that in early 2002, 56 percent of Californians said the state was heading in the right direction; one year later, that number had fallen to 28 percent. Moreover, disapproval ratings for Davis had hit an all-time high of 60 percent of registered voters compared to 43 percent in October of 2002; and "more Californians blame Davis (23%) for the budget crisis than any other cause," including the energy crisis, which was near the bottom of the blame scale at 13 percent.[27] That dour public mood was palpable in the governor's office as we looked back at Davis's first four years and came to terms with having gone from the best of times to the worst of times. And soon it would get even worse.

When a quirky 62-year-old conservative political activist named Ted Costa began DavisRecall.com in February 2003, no one paid much attention to it. After all, since 1911, when Californians amended the state's constitution to allow the collection of voter signatures to place initiatives, referenda, and recalls on local and state ballots, no effort to recall a statewide constitutional officer had ever received enough signatures to be placed on the ballot. Moreover, beginning with Governor Pat Brown in 1960, every one of Davis's predecessors had been subject to a recall petition and a total of 31 had been approved for circulation by the secretary of state. [28] Costa's effort initially appeared to be just another ill-fated venture in that process, Davis's dismal poll numbers notwithstanding. However, Costa and his ragtag group of supporters persisted, and their recall endeavor gained some momentum in April when Davis significantly increased the annual motor vehicle license fee—which had been reduced during the budget-surplus years—to help close the budget gap, but the effort still seemed unlikely to succeed. That changed in May when Republican Darrell Issa, a multi-millionaire car-alarm business owner and member of congress from San Diego, began writing big checks to bankroll legions of signature gatherers.[29]

Issa started a new organization called Rescue California and hired political campaign operatives to bolster the voluntary process that Costa had spearheaded, and he made clear his interest in running for governor if the recall qualified for the ballot. By July Issa had spent $1.7 million and recall activists had submitted more than 1.3 million signatures to Secretary of State Kevin Shelley. On July 23, Shelley announced that 82 percent of the signatures had been deemed valid and that the recall had qualified for the ballot.[30] A day later Lt. Governor Cruz Bustamante, in accordance with his state constitutional duties in the recall process, selected October 7 as the date voters would decide whether to keep Davis in office and pick a candidate to succeed him if he was ousted. Davis blasted the recall as a "hostile takeover by the right" and promised to "fight like a Bengal tiger" to keep his job.[31]

* * *

In April 2003, the governor appointed me to be Deputy Secretary for Policy and Intergovernmental Relations at the California Environmental Protection Agency (CalEPA). I had worked closely with Secretary Winston Hickox during the energy crisis, and he asked me to join his team when Davis appointed my CalEPA predecessor, Nancy Sutley, to the State Water Resources Control Board. After more than four years in the narrow and demanding confines of the governor's office, I enjoyed moving into a much bigger office on the top floor of the first building in the nation to be certified "Platinum" by the U.S. Green Building Council in its Leadership in Energy and Environmental Design program. I also enjoyed having an office window—which I and numerous others in the governor's office did not have—and with a sweeping view, no less. And I very much looked forward to working on renewable energy, climate change, and other environmental issues at a more measured pace, though many of my "new" tasks still posed considerable challenges.

As much as I appreciated being out of the executive corridors in the capitol, by June the anxiety over the increasingly likely recall unsettled the entire administration which had been struggling from day one of the second term to find firm footing on the crumbling slopes of the budget disaster. I worked with the governor's office to fine-tune and update energy crisis fact sheets and narratives, and that included adding details about the landmark $1.625 billion settlement with El Paso Corporation on June 26 that provided $1.45 billion in relief to IOU electricity and gas ratepayers. "This is more evidence that the energy crisis was not a California-created problem," Davis averred, "but rather market manipulation by the energy pirates that FERC is trying to sweep under the rug." After thanking Attorney General Lockyer for his pivotal role in the settlement, Davis also announced that more of the DWR contracts had been renegotiated and that the total savings had grown to $6.3 billion.[32] To a certain extent, the energy crisis had morphed into a vindication platform for the governor, but nothing could undo all the damage to his reputation that had been done during the crisis.

The governor had, however, burnished his environmental reputation in 2002 when he signed the RPS bill and Pavley's AB 1493, and he touted these achievements as evidence of his leadership and to counter arguments for his recall in the summer of 2003. Highlighting these accomplishments amplified

Davis's criticism of President Bush's decision to end U.S. participation in the UN's 1997 Kyoto Protocol agreement in which the U.S. and other industrialized countries committed to GHG emissions reduction targets. I began working with NRDC's Ralph Cavanagh and Eric Heitz, the CEO and co-founder of the Energy Foundation, to establish a partnership with Davis and his counterparts in Washington and Oregon to curb climate change. The NRDC and the San Francisco-based Foundation had long worked together on energy efficiency programs in the Pacific Northwest, and both were also part of a broad environmental group effort to establish the Regional Greenhouse Gas Initiative in northeastern states to reduce power plant GHG emissions.[33] I soon linked up on conference calls with staff from the offices of Oregon Governor Ted Kulongoski and Governor Gary Locke of Washington, and Mary Nichols, secretary of the California Resources Agency, joined me in these conversations.

On August 6, as I waited at Sacramento International Airport to board a flight to Portland for the first in-person meeting of our tri-state group, I returned a missed call from my colleague, Nancy McFadden. I knew she wanted to talk about a draft report by the California Commission on Tax Policy in the New Economy, which had been established pursuant to legislation the governor had signed in 2000. "How's it going?" I asked when I reached her. "All hell is breaking loose," she responded and proceeded to inform me that Arnold Schwarzenegger had just declared his candidacy for governor during the taping of *The Tonight Show with Jay Leno*. The speculation that he would do so had run rampant in the weeks leading up to his announcement. Now that the speculation had ended, the reality set in: Davis would be up against the brawny mega-star of the blockbuster *Terminator* film franchise that would kick Muscle Beach sand in the face of the incumbent "weakling." As a formal candidate, Schwarzenegger's new moniker was "The Governator," and he would milk that tough, transformative image for all it was worth.

***

Prior to Schwarzenegger's candidacy, the recall had already turned into a three-ring circus with a throng of candidates seeking to replace Davis, including *Hustler* magazine publisher Larry Flynt, the watermelon-smashing comedian, Gallagher, and Gary Coleman, the "pint-sized star" of ABC's 1980s sitcom *Diff'rent Strokes*.[34] Issa, who had been expected to formally file papers to run, instead broke into tears outside the San Diego Registrar of Voters office the day after Schwarzenegger's announcement and stated that he would continue to financially support the recall but would not be a candidate. He insisted that Schwarzenegger's candidacy had no impact on his decision. Michael Riordan had been mentioned as a possible candidate, but he instead urged Schwarzenegger to run and quickly endorsed "Arnold for governor of California." When he filed his candidacy papers surrounded by fans and news cameras, Schwarzenegger pledged that as governor he would "overhaul our economic engine" and prioritize the public interest over "special interests and politicians."[35]

Ably aided by former Governor Pete Wilson's campaign team, Schwarzenegger ran largely as a populist badass and invoked cinematic pyrotechnics by vowing to "blow up the boxes" of state government, though his destructive agenda was not matched by an equally constructive one. Regarding the latter, his overarching argument was that less government and more capitalism would boost the state's economy and the ingenuity and well-being of Californians. He did not talk frequently about the energy crisis, but when he did he largely circumvented the ample evidence of market manipulation and instead blamed Davis for a "lack of leadership." In a lengthy interview with CNN's Larry King, Schwarzenegger bemoaned the lack of private investment in power plants and maintained that "of all the energy plants that were proposed to be built, only a quarter of them were."[36] Though the governor could cogently refute that exaggeration, voters, as Garry South and Paul Maslin had discovered the previous summer, proved averse to giving Davis much credit for energy crisis accomplishments. But they did strongly support the RPS and AB 1493,[37] and I worked with others to make the most of that for Davis's benefit.

On September 22, Davis and Governor Locke ascended a hill at a recreation area overlooking smoggy downtown Los Angeles and announced a new partnership between California, Oregon, and Washington to address "global warming" challenges.[38] "The governors of the West Coast states," Locke declared, "have concluded that in the absence of meaningful federal action, we must act individually and regionally to address the sources of global warming." He read a statement in strong support from Governor Kulongoski, and Davis said that the three governors would "use current technology" and innovations "in the near future" in this endeavor.[39] Though this event was not directly part of Davis's campaign against the recall, he used it as an opportunity to jab at Schwarzenegger's spotty participation as a voter in California elections and suggested that in addition to not voting much, "Arnold...obviously hasn't been reading the papers [either], or he'd be aware that we've been providing [environmental] leadership on a global basis right here in California."[40]

Environmental activists lauded both the tri-state partnership announcement and Davis, who had signed a slew of controversial environmental bills in 2003 to help firm up his green credentials, but they were generally more unsure than afraid of what Schwarzenegger might do on environmental policy as governor. Though he was an unabashed supporter of free markets and deregulation, his wife's cousin, NRDC attorney Robert F. Kennedy Jr., had connected him with Terry Tamminen, a self-described "tree-hugger" who headed the Santa Monica-based foundation Environment Now.[41] The principal author of Schwarzenegger's "Action Plan for California's Environment," Tamminen got him to pledge to retrofit one of his gas-guzzling Hummer

SUVs to run on hydrogen and to back building a network of "hydrogen highways" to help decrease dependence on fossil fuels.[42] The Plan also touted solar panels and proposed increasing the RPS from 20 percent renewable energy by 2010 instead of 2017, as enacted in the Sher bill the previous year. And when Davis announced several days before the election that California and nine other states were suing the U.S. EPA over its decision that the state lacked the authority to regulate tailpipe emissions under the Clean Air Act, Schwarzenegger supported the action on his campaign website: "California's landmark legislation to cut greenhouse gases is now law. I will work to implement it and to win the expected challenges in court along the way."[43]

As the final week of the campaign began, polls showed that a majority of voters—with percentages ranging from the mid to upper fifties—wanted to remove Davis from office, and that, among the 135 candidates running to replace him, Schwarzenegger had a double-digit lead on his closest challenger. (Davis needed a straight majority of voters to vote "no" on the recall to remain in office; his name could not appear on the ballot to replace him in which the winner would be the candidate with the most votes.) However, Schwarzenegger's final campaign bus tour dubbed the "California Comeback Express," encountered a rough stretch after the *Los Angeles Times* reported that he had repeatedly groped and sexually harassed women on movie sets and, before that, as a world champion bodybuilder.[44] No one knew if these charges in the waning days of the race would impact his front runner status, but I and other Davis staff viewed them as a glimmer of hope that the governor just might survive the recall.

Schwarzenegger, who had cultivated a macho image throughout his career, stated that the allegations were exaggerated but acknowledged that "I have behaved badly at times" and that he was "deeply sorry" about this behavior. Measured in his response, Davis said "it is a matter voters will take into account" when they cast their ballots, but he also cast subtle aspersions on Schwarzenegger's character and veracity by noting, for example, that his "story seems to constantly change." To the extent that these improprieties may have hurt the actor's election prospects, his wife, TV personality, and family member of the Kennedy political dynasty, Maria Shriver, came to his defense and seemingly minimized the damage. "It takes great courage to stand before anybody and apologize," she said, and that's "what Arnold did today."[45] By election eve, what had been a glimmer of hope for the governor's chances had been reduced to a dying ember.

On election day, 55 percent of California voters chose to remove Davis from office and 49 percent selected Schwarzenegger to replace him, well ahead of the runner-up, Cruz Bustamante. The shock of Davis being only the second governor of *any* state to be recalled persisted for some time, but the results surprised no one. During the campaign Schwarzenegger had attacked Davis for his "photo ops" in front of new power plants, claiming they sought to obscure his "lack of leadership" during the energy crisis.[46] But on the campaign trail, the actor showed his Hollywood mastery of photo ops by staging events in which he wielded a broom on the capitol steps and pledged to "sweep" out special interests and their crony politicians. In addition, as *Los Angeles Times* columnist Michael Hiltzik observed, Schwarzenegger "staged some crowd-pleasing agitprop…by dropping a wrecking ball on an Oldsmobile spray painted with the words 'Davis Car Tax,'" and he vowed to sign an order repealing that highly unpopular auto license fee increase. "People love a show and he was a showman," veteran Democratic political consultant Richie Ross noted years later. "It was the Superbowl halftime show of politics."[47]

***

The transition period between the recall election and Schwarzenegger taking office was two weeks shorter than for a regular election, and that hastened the scramble for Davis appointees to find other jobs, though some had left even before the election in anticipation of Davis losing. The governor's Appointments Office offered me a lower profile position with the California Waste Management Board, one of the six departments under the CalEPA. As a CalEPA executive—and as a former governor's office staffer with bylines on several newspaper commentaries in support of Davis policies—I figured I would be told to clean out my deputy secretary desk sooner rather than later, perhaps even on day one of the new administration. As such, taking a position at the Waste Management Board would likely provide an opportunity for me to "hide" for a while and buy time to find more secure employment. As I mulled my prospects prior to Schwarzenegger being sworn in as governor on November 17, I received an unexpected phone call from Terry Tamminen. He told me that both he and the governor-elect liked the tri-state global warming partnership, and I briefed him on the status of the partnership's activities. Tamminen's name had come up frequently as a possible, and then the likely, Schwarzenegger appointee to lead the CalEPA. Acting on the assumption that he would be the next secretary, I rather sheepishly asked him if he would like me to stay on at the agency to assist with the tri-state partnership and whatever else I could be of help with. I also sensed that, as a newcomer to state government, he appreciated my institutional knowledge of the governor's office and legislature. Affable, smart, and self-assured, Tamminen said he looked forward to working with me. After that, I contacted the appointments office and appreciatively declined the position at the Waste Management Board.

Schwarzenegger announced Tamminen's appointment several days before being sworn in as governor, and the new secretary and I picked up seamlessly on our earlier discussions after the inauguration which included the hydrogen highways endeavor. It was my understanding that this chemical energy resource—which, when consumed through a fuel cell, produces only water as a byproduct—was an emerging technology in need of much more innovation and infrastructure before we could possibly get to a hydrogen network on the scale that Tamminen envisioned. But he had convinced the governor to steadfastly commit to the undertaking after several lengthy discussions with him on environmental issues at the outset of the recall campaign. And they had a noteworthy ally in this cause. Schwarzenegger had targeted the California Power Authority for elimination during his campaign, and, as such, David Freeman had resigned as head of the Authority's board in October and announced he would be joining two partners in a start-up called the Hydrogen Car Company. Vowing to hold Schwarzenegger to his commitment to retrofit one of his Hummers to run on this new "clean" fuel, Freeman, who would soon call himself the "green cowboy," said "let the SOBs have their SUVs as long as they run on hydrogen."[48]

In the grand scheme of California's energy issues, the governor's interest in hydrogen was a curiosity compared to the much bigger issues of reducing electricity rates and building more power plants, both of which he had pledged to accomplish during his campaign, mainly by incentivizing private investment. However, while he shared the prevailing view of free market advocates that deregulation failed in California primarily due to state government missteps, as a candidate he had not specifically endorsed giving deregulation another try under his administration. But less than a week after Schwarzenegger's October 7 victory, Joe Rodota, a former top Wilson advisor now serving in the same capacity for the former actor, said the governor-elect "is very adamant that he wants to develop a structure that would provide some competition and would encourage private investment, but would be resistant to gaming."[49] Regarding the latter, Rodota neglected to note that the FERC had been asleep at the wheel during the energy crisis and that the efficacy of increased competition would depend in good part on the FERC's willingness to enforce the Federal Power Act. Two weeks later the Associated Press reported that "Schwarzenegger hopes to sell the state on the virtues of electricity deregulation for a second time, despite the expensive legacy of the first attempt," though Schwarzenegger was not quoted directly in that regard. His advisors, the AP article noted, maintained that it was unfair to compare this new attempt to the AB 1890 reforms that were "mismanaged" by the Davis administration. "Deregulation would work," they contended, "under a decisive governor."[50]

I had several engaging chats with Tamminen about the perils of another deregulation attempt, both politically and structurally, and emphasized that the "decisive governor" tenet gave short shrift to the complexity of the endeavor and the limitations of both the state's and the governor's authority. However, while Tamminen had a wide range of interests—including Shakespeare and a life-long dedication to preserving ocean ecosystems—delving into energy market dynamics, as I expected, was not among them. He already had plenty of responsibilities as CalEPA secretary. He just needed to ensure that, whatever energy restructuring plan emerged, there would be room for the governor's green agenda. He knew some of Schwarzenegger's energy advisors were less than enthusiastic about that agenda, but he also knew that the governor would not back away from it.

***

In his State of the State Address in early January, Schwarzenegger focused on California's dire economic circumstances, and especially, as he contended, the state's profligate "spending." He made clear he would be a man of action during this "time of crisis" by making necessary state budget cuts. "The good news," he maintained, "is that the spending crisis forces us to bring badly needed reform to government." Among those reforms, he vowed to make changes to both the wholesale and retail electricity markets "to attract new energy investment" and "so that large energy customers can get competitive prices." He also reiterated his pledge to establish "a hydrogen highway to take us to the environmental future" and an ambitious new program for solar-powered homes, and to increase energy efficiency efforts. He concluded this part of his speech by proclaiming that "I intend to show that economic growth and the environment can coexist."[51] This credo served as a driving force for the administration's commitment to sustainability and economic development, but it also constrained the governor's capacity to accept calculations and other evidence that didn't support the preferred environmental and economic equilibrium.

As in 2003, the state's huge fiscal challenges took center stage in the new year, but the salience of the debate over the future of California's electricity market grew due to the administration's interest in revisiting market restructuring and the equally determined skepticism of that effort by most Democratic legislators and staunch resistance from consumer groups. The hybrid market created by AB 1890, with the deregulated wholesale market glued to the regulated retail one, continued to function well enough to avoid the need for emergency action by government officials, but the complexity and large scope of numerous challenges remained. The CAISO had started to work on a "market redesign" (known as MD02) in 2002 pursuant to a FERC order to ensure that the California Independent System Operator (CAISO) "has the tools it needs to reliably operate the transmission grid," and this highly technical and interactive process had made some progress as of early 2004.[52] But that proved to be a plodding effort with a highly uncertain outcome. Meeting the state's broader energy resource needs—that is, ensuring that the IOUs and other energy service providers had enough power to reliably meet customer demand—loomed as a more immediate challenge. The merchant generators that had made hundreds of millions of dollars during the crisis and built plants had mostly fallen on hard times, and none of them—or other investors, for that matter—were willing or able to invest in a new generation facility without a long-term contract for the sale of the power from that plant. Adding to this challenge, direct access energy service providers continued to try to play the spot and short-term contract markets and declined to sign long-term agreements because, as one of their lobbyists explained to me, "they don't fit with our business model."

The IOUs got back into the power procurement business in January of 2003 when DWR's procurement duties ended as required by AB 1X, the emergency procurement bill enacted in February of 2001. In preparation for the IOUs resuming their power purchasing roles, the legislature had passed, and Davis signed, Assemblymember Rod Wright's AB 57 in 2002, which assured IOU cost recovery through rate increases for power procurement debt that exceeded a fixed threshold; if procurement costs fell, IOU ratepayers would receive a rate cut.[53] The Utility Reform Network (TURN) and the NRDC worked with IOU representatives to reach agreement on the bill, but its implementation at the CPUC moved slowly and carried over to 2004. Schwarzenegger urged the commissioners to "expeditiously" implement AB 57 to establish a "competitive procurement process" in which "the utilities get the least cost alternatives to meet their demand" and companies built new power plants.[54] But who would build these plants?

In February, Assembly Speaker Fabian Núñez, who represented a Los Angeles district, introduced the Reliable Electric Service Act of 2004, which was sponsored and largely drafted by Southern California Edison. The bill, AB 2006, would allow the IOUs to build power plants without soliciting bids from the merchant generators and to establish energy "resource adequacy" and reliability for "core" residential and small business customers that would ensure sufficient revenues for IOU cost recovery. The bill permitted large energy consumers—known as "noncore" customers—to receive power from private providers as of January 2006; but if those customers left IOU service, the IOUs, unlike under AB 1890, would have no "obligation to serve" them pursuant to regulated rates if they wanted to return to the utility. Under those circumstances, if a large consumer sought to return, it would have to initially cover the full cost for the IOU to procure the additional power for them and commit to long-term IOU service. There would be no "safe harbor" for these ratepayers similar to the IOUs' frozen retail rates that they returned to when the direct access market collapsed during the crisis. Another bill, AB 428, co-authored by Republican Assemblymember Keith Richman and his Democratic colleague, Joe Canciamilla, would allow large consumers, and even some smaller customers, to leave IOU service and receive private power under the core/noncore model but with more flexibility than in AB 2006. The legislation also required the IOUs to compete with the merchant generators for the lowest cost construction of plants, which, the authors and other bill supporters maintained, would help get plants built *and* revitalize the competitive retail market.[55]

Key provisions in both bills faced significant challenges from existing statutes and ongoing CPUC implementation proceedings, especially from the procurement provisions in AB 57 and SB 1078, the Renewable Portfolio Standard bill. In addition, while most everyone agreed that the potential departure of more large customers to the noncore—which was tantamount to direct access service—should not result in stranded costs for the remaining IOU customers, opinions varied widely on what those costs should include. In AB 2006, SCE wanted to ensure that it and the other IOUs would never again be in a situation in which they could not recover their procurement and other costs in customer rates, but the bill appeared to shelter the IOUs from almost any element of risk whatsoever. Moreover, consumer groups were not keen on the core/noncore model as that just seemed to be another way of expanding direct access and allowing those customers to get the "cheapest power" to the further disadvantage of the smaller core customers.[56] However, the resource adequacy and reliability provisions in the bill held considerable appeal, as did the prospect of more power plant construction—but at what cost?

The problems with AB 428 proved greater and more fundamental. Similar to AB 2006, supporters touted the bill as a vehicle that would help get plants built, but the large energy consumers' reliance on short-term commitments undermined that claim. Senate Energy Committee consultant Lawrence Lingbloom highlighted a statement by a direct access trade association from a CPUC proceeding in which it claimed that "mandatory long-term contracting would entail significant and potentially untenable risks" for its retail sellers. Lingbloom noted that in California, "to secure power plant financing, project developers have been required to secure recovery of at least 125% of their capital costs in long-term contracts," and that AB 428 didn't require providers or customers to enter into "contracts for any fixed terms." While the bill's advocates decried the "failure of the marketplace to invest in new construction in California,"[57] they essentially ignored the fact that the spot-market meltdown during the energy crisis prompted investors to demand long-term contracts for financial security. Senate Democrats on the committee clearly did not ignore that fact. Accordingly, they voted to kill the bill.

***

Bob White, who had been Governor Wilson's chief of staff and served as Schwarzenegger's campaign manager in 2003, had advised the actor to avoid any reference to wanting to revisit deregulation on the campaign trail, and he had heeded that advice. White knew that however much Californians disapproved of Governor Davis's handling of the energy crisis, they disliked deregulation much more.[58] As such, even after his victory, Schwarzenegger generally delegated statements about the need for energy reforms to his top aides, and even they referred to "deregulation" sparingly.

But in an open letter to the CPUC in April 2004 on his energy plan, the governor finally weighed in on the matter directly: "By fostering competitive wholesale and retail electricity markets that are properly monitored by regulators," he maintained, "California can begin to lower electricity bills and once again become the job creation machine." Michael Peevey, who had been appointed by Davis to be president of the CPUC in 2002, reacted favorably to Schwarzenegger's letter, noting that "having a more competitive market is in the public interest." However, Democratic legislators mostly recoiled at the prospect of revisiting deregulation. As Senator Debra Bowen, the chair of the Senate Energy Committee, observed, "the last time" the state tried deregulation, "it was the blind date from hell. I don't want another blind date from hell."[59]

The governor's letter came on the heels of the release of a thorough and decidedly damning report on electricity deregulation in California and the FERC's administrative failures by Attorney General Bill Lockyer. "Laws, rules and regulators are supposed to protect consumers and deter misconduct," Lockyer said in a statement. "But in the case of the California energy crisis, the system has sheltered wrongdoers and left ratepayers out in the cold. The enforcement defects continue to provide sellers incentives to game and gouge." A spokesperson for the governor said he had not yet reviewed the report, but that he "does agree that in a restructured market, it's important to have strict market monitors."[60] The fact that two weeks later he sent his letter to the CPUC touting what some pundits and pols were calling "deregulation light" indicates he believed that existing regulatory monitoring capabilities were sufficient. As the legislature headed into the final months of the 2004 session, the die seemed to have been cast for a stalemate on significant energy market changes: The governor clearly lacked the political muscle to help pass legislation he would sign; but the Democrats, despite controlling both legislative chambers, didn't have enough votes to override the governor's veto of legislation they sent to his desk.

Schwarzenegger's energy team worked with Núñez's staff and other stakeholders on amendments to AB 2006 in the hope of reaching a compromise that included the core/noncore market structure and competition to build the "cheapest" plants, but to no avail. Consumer advocates staunchly opposed the core/noncore model and in August persuaded Núñez and SCE to abandon it altogether and instead have the bill "reaffirm California's traditional regulatory doctrine"—that is, to essentially reregulate the state's electricity market. While the bill did not propose to end direct access for current customers or to alter the private ownership of the plants that the utilities had divested, meeting future electricity needs, including plant construction, would almost exclusively be the domain of the IOUs (outside of the municipal utilities, such as the LADWP). In a letter to Núñez, Mike Chrisman, the secretary of the California Resources Agency, telegraphed the governor's veto of the bill by criticizing its lack of "consumer choice" for energy providers and a "transparent competitive procurement process" to bolster new energy sources.[61] However, Chrisman's missive did not deter legislators from approving the bill without significant changes a few days before the session ended. On September 25, the governor, as expected, vetoed AB 2006, claiming that it would create "a redundant and burdensome energy procurement process that would steer the state back to monopoly utilities." In response, consumer advocates vowed to make their case for reregulation in a 2005 ballot initiative. In a statement, Núñez contended that "the power pirates that sided with the governor in opposition to this bill remain firmly in control of our energy future."[62]

***

Throughout the market-structure legislative battle, Schwarzenegger had maintained his commitment to green energy, but it was largely obscured by the contentious AB 2006 debates that played out in news media. Early in his administration, he invited CPUC President Mike Peevey along with fellow commissioner and 2002 Davis appointee, Susan Kennedy, to his office to discuss energy issues. He told them about the bureaucratic problems his Hollywood friend James Cameron, the director of *The Terminator* and *Titanic*, had in getting solar panels on his Los Angeles home, and asked if the commission could help hasten the process for future installations. Peevey and Kennedy were receptive to that entreaty,[63] but Schwarzenegger also took more immediate action in 2004 by backing legislation to establish his "Million Solar Roofs" initiative authored by Senator Kevin Murray, a Democrat from Los Angeles.

Murray's bill, SB 199, which would have established the Solar Homes Peak Energy Procurement Program, touted the residential solar market as a key element of "a fully competitive and self-sustaining California renewable energy supply," and it authorized significant rebates for purchases of solar panel installations on new and existing homes. It also would greatly increase the number of customers eligible to participate in the existing Net Energy Metering (NEM) program that required utilities to pay for the "surplus solar energy" that those customers do not use and send back to the electricity grid. As noted by the Assembly Utilities and Commerce Committee consultant Ed Randolph, the proposal "is based on the belief that solar power can be the most cost-effective way for the state" to provide peak power production "and replace power that would otherwise have to be purchased from heavily polluting peaker plants." However, he also noted that, under NEM, the IOUs would have to pay NEM customers the full retail rate for their "excess solar power" rather than buying cheaper wholesale power from other generators. Moreover, Randolph, who would later become the head of the CPUC's Energy Division, pointed out that NEM allowed "most solar customers to avoid paying" a ratepayer surcharge that funded low-income assistance and energy efficiency programs, creating "a cost shift to all other utility ratepayers."[64]

The prospect of this cost shift unsettled committee members, and that resulted in the bill receiving only two "aye" votes while the ten other members, Republicans and Democrats alike, voted no or abstained. The committee's chairperson, Democrat Sarah Reyes of Fresno, expressed concern that the bill's solar program would likely require rate increases for all customers except for those getting the rebates and NEM benefits. The committee did pass Senator Bowen's Solar Peak Procurement Act legislation, a similar but less ambitious and costly bill, but she chose not to have it brought up for an assembly floor vote after Schwarzenegger called it "unworkable" and threatened to veto it.[65] While the governor's opposition to Bowen's bill did not come as a surprise, his veto of a bill by Senator Sher that would have bolstered the RPS did. That bill, SB 1478, mirrored Schwarzenegger's pledge to have electric utilities obtain 20 percent of their power from renewable sources by 2010 instead of 2017 and had bipartisan support. In his veto message, the governor lauded the bill's intent but lamented "several onerous restrictions" on the use of "renewable energy credits" intended to help the IOUs, particularly SDG&E, meet the 2010 requirement. Clean energy advocate John White scolded the governor for his action, maintaining that "there's nothing in this bill that should have caused it to be vetoed."[66]

The first legislative session under Schwarzenegger in 2004 had proved rocky and yielded very little to strengthen energy policy or enhance reliability and supply, though the governor made clear he remained committed to those goals and to a greener grid. The year drew to a close on a positive note, as Schwarzenegger, along with governors Kulongoski and Locke, formally announced the West Coast Governors' Global Warming Initiative in which California, Oregon, and Washington would work together on efforts that held "the most promise for achieving greenhouse gas reductions." Those efforts included developing standards to reduce GHG emissions from vehicles; developing "a market-based carbon allowance program"; and expanding "markets for energy, efficiency, renewable resources, and alternative fuels."[67]

Building on what Davis, Kulongoski, and Locke had started 14 months earlier, the West Coast Governor's initiative helped Schwarzenegger maintain his green *bona fides* after his equivocations on sustainable energy policy. These equivocations came about as he tried to balance the political tightrope strung between business interests and more "traditional" Republicans who did not embrace his green agenda and the countervailing, and largely Democratic, interests of those who did. That was not an easy task. While filming *Terminator 3* in 2002, Schwarzenegger had told reporter Bill Bradley that he liked what Davis was doing on renewable energy and climate change "but would go bigger if he ever got the chance as governor."[68] With his 2004 energy experience behind him, Schwarzenegger had learned first-hand that going bigger with his green ambitions was not destined to proceed in accordance with his initial script.

Notes

1 See, for example, transcript from Davis's release of the May Revise, May 14, 2002, Press Conference, http://gray-davis.com/ViewLibraryItem.aspx?ID=9616.
2 Howard Fineman, "Bill Simon Jr., California Governor," *Newsweek*, February 27, 2002.
3 Jeffrey L. Rabin, Nicholas Riccardi and Doug Smith, "Simon Attack Ad Says Riordan Is Ashamed to Be a Republican," *Los Angeles Times*, February 22, 2002.

4 Mark Baldassare, "PPIC Statewide Survey: Californians and Their Government," PPIC, October 2002, 4.
5 Carrick quoted in Marc Cooper, "California's Gray Politics: Davis May Win Reelection Only because the GOP's Simon Is Such a Loser," *The Nation*, August 19, 2002.
6 Governor Davis, "State Restructures Eight Power Pacts," Press Release, April 22, 2002.
7 Steve Lopez, "Gray Davis: The Most Fearless Governor in America," *Time*, October 11, 1999.
8 Interview with South.
9 "Despite the continuing economic doldrums, 64 percent of Californians believe that stricter environmental laws are worth potential costs to the economy" compared to "June 2000 (57%)" when the electricity crisis began. Mark Baldassare, "Special Survey on Californians and the Environment," PPIC, June 2002, 13.
10 CARB History, https://ww2.arb.ca.gov/about/history; Miguel Bustillo and Carl Ingram, "Auto-Emission Bill OKd, Sent to Davis," *Los Angeles Times*, July 2, 2002.
11 Interview with Winston Hickox; interview with Linda Adams.
12 Davis and Simon quoted in Miguel Bustillo, "Davis Signals Emissions Bill Support," *Los Angeles Times*, July 4, 2002.
13 Governor Davis, "Governor Davis Signs Historic Global Warming Bill," Press Release, July 22, 2002.
14 Navigant Consulting to Schuparra, "Direct Access Exit Fees," February 14, 2002, Box 975, GGDR/CSA; Dorothy Rothrock to Schuparra, February 15, 2002, Box 975, GGDR/CSA.
15 Simon quoted in Mateo Gold, "Simon Targets Davis's Energy Plan," *Los Angeles Times*, October 19, 2002.
16 Richard, Stravos, "California: Beginning Anew," *Fortnightly Magazine*, February 15, 2002.
17 Gold, "Simon Targets Davis's Energy Plan."
18 Mark Z. Barabak, "Davis Narrowly Defeats Simon," *Los Angeles Times*, November 6, 2002.
19 Davis Introduction transcript, "Budget Update Conference Call," Press Conference, December 6, 2002.
20 Davis Update transcript, "Budget," Press Conference, December 18, 2002.
21 "12-minute video" in Russell, "Dim Bulbs"; interview with Borenstein.
22 John M. Glionna, "Energy Experts Are Talking, but Who's Plugged In?" *Los Angeles Times*, January 9, 2001; Borenstein and Bushnell, "An Empirical Analysis of the Potential for Market Power in California's Electricity Industry," *The Journal of Industrial Economics*, Vol. XXVLI, No. 3 (September 1999): 319–20.
23 Staff, "An Overview: How We Got Here," Senate Office of Research, no date. https://sor.senate.ca.gov/sites/sor.senate.ca.gov/files/ctools/How%20We%20Got%20Here%20A%20Historical%20Look%20at%20Californias%20Restructuring%20of%20Electricity%20Regulation.pdf
24 George Skelton, "Desperate Davis Takes Gamble on Wild Man Steve Peace," *Los Angeles Times*, December 19, 2002.
25 Peace quoted in George Skelton, "Desperate Davis Takes Gamble on Wild Man Steve Peace."
26 Governor Davis, Inaugural Address, January 6, 2003.
27 Mark Baldassare, "Californians and Their Government," PPIC Survey, Press Release, February 2003.
28 Recall data from the Office of the California Secretary of State: https://www.sos.ca.gov/elections/recalls/complete-list-recall-attempts
29 Carla Marinucci and Joe Garofoli, "Legacy of Gov. Gray Davis Recall Endures," *San Francisco Chronicle*, April 13, 2013.

30 Judy Woodruff, et al., "California Governor to Face Recall Vote," *CNN*, July 25, 2003.
31 Davis quoted in Judy Woodruff, et al., "California Governor to Face Recall Vote."
32 Governor Davis, "Governor Davis and Attorney General Announce El Paso Energy Settlement Finalized," Press Release, June 26, 2003.
33 Interview with Cavanagh.
34 *ABC News*, "Schwarzenegger Files Candidacy Papers," August 7, 2003. https://abcnews.go.com/Politics/story?id=120935&page=1
35 Issa and Schwarzenegger quoted in *ABC News*, "Schwarzenegger Files Candidacy Papers," August 7, 2003. https://abcnews.go.com/Politics/story?id=120935&page=1. In a three-part documentary on his life, Schwarzenegger stated that Riordan didn't have much interest in running but encouraged him to do so instead. Leslie Chilcott and Allen Hughes. *Arnold*, June 2023, Netflix.
36 *Larry King Live*, "Interview with Arnold Schwarzenegger" transcript, *CNN*, September 17, 2003.
37 Mark Baldassare, "PPIC Statewide Survey: Special Survey on Californians and the Environment," PPIC, July 2003, 11–12.
38 Gary Polakovic, "Governors Target Global Warming," *Los Angeles Times*, September 23, 2003.
39 Joint announcement, Governors Davis, Locke and Kulongoski Announce "Tri-State Strategy to Reduce Global Warming," September 22, 2003. http://gray-davis.com/ViewLibraryItem.aspx?ID=9616
40 Governor Davis, "Tri-State Strategy to Reduce Global Warming," Transcript, September 22, 2003. http://gray-davis.com/ViewLibraryItem.aspx?ID=9922
41 Michael Hanneman, "How California Came to Pass AB 32, the Global Warming Solutions Act of 2006," UC Berkeley Working Papers. https://escholarship.org/uc/item/1vb0j4d6
42 Miguel Llanos, "Green Hummer for Schwarzenegger?" *NBC News*, October 5, 2003. https://www.nbcnews.com/id/wbna3180817
43 Schwarzenegger quoted in Danny Hakim, "States Plan Suit to Prod U.S. on Global Warming," *The New York Times*, October 4, 2003.
44 Gary Cohn, Carla Hall and Robert W. Welkos, "Women Say Schwarzenegger Groped, Humiliated Them," *Los Angeles Times*, October 2, 2003.
45 All quotes in Terence Smith, "California Recall Revelations," *PBS NewsHour*, October 3, 2003. https://www.pbs.org/newshour/show/california-recall-revelations
46 *Larry King Live* Interview.
47 Michael Hiltzik, "Reversing Car Tax Pledge Is Best Course," *Los Angeles Times*, October 9, 2003; Ross quoted in Carla Marinucci and Joe Garofoli, "Legacy of Gov. Davis Recall Endures," *San Francisco Chronicle*, April 13, 2013.
48 Freeman quoted in Nancy Rivera Brooks, "Hydrogen Fuels Power Broker's New Venture," *Los Angeles Times*, October 24, 2003.
49 Rodota quoted in Nancy Rivera Brooks, "Schwarzenegger Plan Blends Energy Ideas," *Los Angeles Times*, October 13, 2003.
50 J. Scott Applewhite, "Schwarzenegger Plans to give energy deregulation another try in Golden State despite chaos the first time," Associated Press, October 29, 2003.
51 Governor Schwarzenegger, State of the State Speech, January 6, 2004.
52 FERC, "Order on Further Development of California ISO's Market Redesign and Establishing Hearing Procedures," Docket No. ER02-1656-017, et al., June 17, 2004.
53 Nancy Vogel, "Pulling Plug on State's Power Buying," *Los Angeles Times*, September 1, 2002.
54 Schwarzenegger quoted in *NGI* Staff, "CA Governor Draws Support for Initial Power Strategy," *Natural Gas Intelligence*, May 3, 2004.

55 Nancy Vogel, "Power Deregulation May Linger," *Los Angeles Times*, March 21, 2004.
56 Vogel, "Power Deregulation May Linger."
57 Lingbloom analysis of AB 428, Senate Energy, Utilities and Communications Committee, July 8, 2003; "bill advocates" quoted in Vogel, "Power Deregulation May Linger."
58 Beginning in February 2007, I worked at the consulting and advocacy firm California Strategies, LLC., which was founded and headed by White. He shared many recollections from his long political career with me, including this one.
59 Schwarzenegger and Bowen quoted in Christian Berthelsen, "Schwarzenegger Backs Energy Deregulation," *San Francisco Chronicle*, April 29, 2004; Peevey quoted in Staff Writer, "Assembly Reviews Energy Plans of Schwarzenegger," *The Stockton Record*, May 11, 2004.
60 Lockyer and the governor's spokesperson quoted in Elizabeth Douglass and Jonathan Peterson, "Lockyer Calls for Stronger Energy Laws," *Los Angeles Times*, April 14, 2004.
61 Chrisman quoted in Craig Rose, "Secretary Says Consumers Wouldn't Be Able to Choose," *The San Diego Union Tribune*, August 11, 2004.
62 Núñez quoted in Marc Lifsher, "Schwarzenegger Turns Down 2 Energy Bills," *Los Angeles Times*, September 24, 2004.
63 Peevey and Wittenberg, *California Goes Green*, 87–88.
64 Randolph analysis of SB 199, Assembly Utilities and Commerce Committee, August 25, 2004.
65 Marc Lifsher, "Governor's Solar Plan Is Rejected," *Los Angeles Times*, August 27, 2004.
66 White quoted in Lifsher, "Schwarzenegger Turns Down 2 Energy Bills."
67 James L. Olmstead, "The Global Warming Crisis: An Analytical Framework to Regional Responses," *Journal of Environmental Law and Litigation*, Vol. 23, No. 125 (2008): 145.
68 William Bradley, "Jerry Brown, Arnold Schwarzenegger, or Gray Davis? Which Governor Spearheaded California's Climate Change Program?" *Huffington Post*, July 29, 2015.

7 The Global Warming Solutions Act Puts a Capstone on a Tumultuous Ten-Year Transformation

While the political dynamic between the governor's office and the Democrat-controlled legislature was often quarrelsome in 2004, the over-arching discourse was generally diplomatic as they attempted to navigate partisan policy differences. But that would not remain the case in 2005. In his January State of the State Address, Schwarzenegger announced he would call the legislature into a special session to overhaul state government, and he attacked labor unions and other "special interests" for their purported control of state spending that had "removed our ability to make the best decisions for California." He proposed, among other things, to cut funding for public pensions and to impose spending caps on the state budget, including for social services and "safety net" programs that Democrats had long strongly supported. He concluded his speech by declaring that if the legislature wouldn't work with him on the reforms, "the people will rise up and reform it themselves." And, in a line seemingly lifted from a *Terminator* script, he vowed "I will join them. I will fight with them."

After the speech, Assemblymember Joe Canciamilla, a prominent moderate Democrat from Pittsburg, remarked, "deep down inside, at the end of the day, I don't think we're going to be able to come to agreements" with the governor.[1] Canciamilla helped lead the Moderate Democrats—the "Mods," as they were known—who had worked with Schwarzenegger on some issues in 2004. They proved instrumental in passing a workers' compensation reform bill that arguably was the governor's biggest legislative accomplishment that year. But they were still Democrats, and they weren't about to enlist in the governor's 2005 scorched earth crusade against unions and public assistance programs, as Canciamilla implied—much to my relief. In the spring of 2004, I had departed the CalEPA at the behest of the Governor's Appointments Office and shortly thereafter went to work for Canciamilla as his principal consultant. After almost five-and-a-half years of serving at the pleasure of the governor, my executive branch stint had ended, but not the policy battles that had defined that experience.[2]

DOI: 10.4324/9781003518150-8

***

Schwarzenegger's sharp partisan turn began with his high-profile endorsement of President Bush for reelection in late August of 2004 and on the heels of the release of his reform plan, pursuant to his campaign promise, to "blow up the boxes" of state government. While the governor never specifically declared that he wanted to run government more like a business, that was the general intent of his plan. He idolized free-market economist and Nobel Prize winner Milton Friedman and President Reagan, whose tax-cut fiscal policy drew extensively from the "supply-side" and business-friendly economics that Friedman championed. When Reagan died on June 6, 2004, Schwarzenegger canceled a planned trip to Las Vegas and, in a press release, noted that he didn't just "admire" Reagan, "I was fortunate enough to know him. He was a hero to me."[3]

Nevertheless, Reagan wasn't necessarily a political role model for Schwarzenegger. When Reagan berated the government, he did it in the amiable "good guy" manner of the roles he tended to play in Hollywood, which proved critical to his political success. He never could have pulled off Schwarzenegger's take-no-prisoners persona on screen, but Schwarzenegger couldn't match Reagan's sunny side or casual jocularity without seeming at least somewhat stiff. Finally, when Reagan became governor in 1967, he knew next to nothing about government policymaking and soon learned and accepted that he could not enact reforms the way he had pledged to do on the campaign trail. Schwarzenegger, a far bigger movie star than Reagan had ever been, did not accept such limitations, and he would ultimately pay a steep price for that.

In February 2005, the governor appeared before a big crowd at Sacramento's Cal Expo, the home of the California State Fair, and repeated a recall campaign stunt in which he closed a large spigot of flowing red water that symbolized "the state's autopilot spending problem." And once again, he vowed to "stand with the people to stop the red ink" if "legislators don't do their job" to cut spending.[4] However, his political theatrics were wearing thin, and his penny-pinching proposals seemed unduly harsh given that state officials projected tax revenue growth to be at least $5 billion more than in the previous budget year. In addition, in 2004 voters had approved a Schwarzenegger-backed bond measure allowing the state to borrow $15 billion through a bond sale to help cover the residual budget deficits from Davis's last two years.

Unlike governors Reagan and Wilson, who addressed budget shortfalls by raising the top tax rate on the state's wealthiest residents to 11 percent, Schwarzenegger refused to even consider raising the upper income bracket above 9.3 percent. Instead, as *Los Angeles Times* columnist Michael Hiltzik observed, the governor depicted himself as a "victim of circumstance," forced by "spending formulas embedded into law" to balance the budget "by skinning the poor, old, and sick" while "protecting the top 5% from any sacrifice at all."[5] Democrats amplified that criticism. And when the governor reneged on a deal to pay back $2 billion that he had "borrowed" in 2004 from the state's K-12 education fund, the Democratic speaker of the assembly, Fabian Núñez, declared that Schwarzenegger "needs to clear the air and reestablish a certain level of trust."[6]

The governor's budget antics and ill-conceived elements of his reorganization plan clearly hurt his popularity. In February, citing the need for "further review," he quietly withdrew his proposal to eliminate 88 state boards and commissions that he had maintained were unnecessary or duplicative. In early April he nixed his public pension reform proposal after it became clear that it would strip disability and death benefits from police officers and other public safety officials, and widows of slain officers spoke out vehemently against it.[7] An April PPIC poll showed that Schwarzenegger's approval rating had dropped from 60 percent in January to 40 percent as widespread criticism eroded his larger-than-life image and support for his plan to put many of his reforms on a special election ballot in the fall—at an estimated $70 million cost to taxpayers.[8] The stakes were high. The governor had invested a lot of political capital in promoting his ambitious reforms and proved headstrong in attacking almost anyone who opposed them as a "special interest," including the California Teachers Association when it ran ads attacking him for "breaking his promises on education." He discovered that even Hollywood action superstars couldn't ride roughshod over powerful political stakeholders in Sacramento and emerge largely unscathed.

***

While the governor's reform agenda dominated the administration's policy priorities, on February 28 Schwarzenegger touted the reintroduction of his Million Solar Roofs proposal which had died in the legislature the previous year. Unlike that bill, the new version, SB 1, became a bipartisan effort when Senator John Campbell, a Republican from Orange County, agreed to jointly author the bill with Kevin Murray. In a lengthy press release, the governor stated that, "in California where we are famous for the sun, we are going to put the positive benefits of that sun to good use" by "providing a stable source of alternative energy." He neglected to mention that the stability of that power depended exclusively on the rays from "that sun," which, even in California, did not always shine during the daytime. And Campbell's claim that the proposal would "reduce the cost of electricity for consumers"[9] omitted that the cost reductions would only be for the customers with solar panels at the expense of IOU customers without them. Nevertheless, even for those who, like me, harbored reservations about the back-up power—likely fossil-fueled—needed to cover solar intermittency, and the cost-shifting of net energy metering, that famous California sun made solar power elemental to the state's revitalized clean energy ethos.

On the flip side of that ambitious solar endeavor, a business coalition led by the California Chamber of Commerce and the Manufacturers and Technology Association began pushing in late 2004 for the construction of liquified natural gas (LNG) terminals along the state's coast. Though California had been the victim of natural gas supply manipulation by a subsidiary of El Paso Corporation during the energy crisis, the state did have gas pipeline conveyance and storage constraints that increased price volatility. Advocates promoted the LNG terminals as an effective way to mitigate this volatility by storing natural gas from Asia and Australia that would be supercooled to liquid and shipped in special tankers to offshore terminals where it would be warmed and re-gasified. Supporters trumpeted Schwarzenegger's promise in 2003 "to explore building facilities for safely importing" LNG, and in 2005 he backed having a terminal "approximately 11, 12 miles off the shore" of Oxnard,[10] between Santa Barbara and Los Angeles. Top members of his staff worked closely with the business coalition and LNG industry representatives. Pushing back on claims by environmentalists and other LNG opponents that these facilities weren't needed, administration representatives cited the California Energy Commission's determination prior to Schwarzenegger's election that the state needed one or two terminals.[11]

Environmentalists opposed any LNG infrastructure on or off the coast and correctly maintained that importing LNG would increase the state's dependence on foreign fossil fuels. However, numerous clean energy advocates erroneously claimed that increased conservation and renewable energy could meet California's growing electricity needs, ignoring the intermittency challenges and the relatively slow ramp-up of alternative energy sources despite government incentives. Politics and bureaucracy soon bogged down the terminal debate. Opponents accused Schwarzenegger of catering to a few influential businesses—including the developers behind the Oxnard proposal—that prioritized their potential large LNG profits over the environment and thwarted climate change. On the other hand, supporters highlighted that natural gas prices had doubled since the end of 2003 and maintained that LNG was safe and critical to economic growth.[12] Everyone understood that the effort to build terminals off the coast would get caught up in lengthy litigation, which had already begun due in good part to the FERC's support for LNG and attempt to secure primary jurisdiction over terminal siting.[13]

Schwarzenegger's proposal to reconfigure the state's energy bureaucracy and create a new cabinet-level Department of Energy, led solely by a secretary appointed by the governor, added to the energy debates of 2005. Introduced in May, the Governor's Energy Reorganization Plan would first be reviewed by a bipartisan citizens' panel known as the Little Hoover Commission which, after the review, would make a non-binding recommendation to the legislature to approve or reject it before the end of its session in August. The new department would include the Energy Commission, which would be chaired by the new secretary, and the Electricity Oversight Board's functions would be transferred to the department's new Office of Energy Market Oversight. Even some of the ratemaking functions of the CPUC, which was established in the state's constitution as opposed to just state law, would be subsumed by the department. Though some opponents of the proposal acknowledged that it might have streamlining benefits, most saw it as a power grab by Schwarzenegger and the business interests that supported his flagging effort to revisit deregulation.[14]

Though Schwarzenegger sided with large business interests on the need for a new energy department and LNG terminals, he frustrated almost all of them outside Silicon Valley when he signed an executive order (EO) with the goal of incrementally reducing GHG emissions in California by 80 percent by 2050. He signed the order and gave an impassioned speech on the topic before business, environmental, government, and academic representatives on June 1 at the United Nations World Environment Day conference at San Francisco's city hall. The goals were not as ambitious as those in the 1997 Kyoto Protocol that the Bush Administration had rejected, but the order nevertheless garnered much attention and praise. Nancy Ryan, a senior economist with the Environmental Defense Fund, called Schwarzenegger "a real-life climate action hero today" while San Francisco Mayor (and future governor) Gavin Newsom hailed the event as "the start of a new way of thinking about our earth."[15] With only a few exceptions, Republicans in the state legislature criticized the governor's actions. Doug LaMalfa, a rural northern California Republican, referred to global warming as a "dubious theory" while some of his liberal Democratic colleagues maintained that the governor's order didn't go far enough.[16]

During his speech, Schwarzenegger pledged his support for increasing the RPS to 20 percent by 2010—despite having vetoed Sher's 2004 bill with that requirement—and for increasing it to 33 percent by 2020. He also reiterated his commitment to prevailing in the litigation led by the auto industry against AB 1493, Pavley's GHG emissions reduction bill.[17] Responding to questions about how emissions reductions beyond those from the RPS and AB 1493 would be achieved, Terry Tamminen, now the governor's cabinet secretary, maintained that the early targets could be largely achieved through existing programs and complimentary Schwarzenegger proposals, some of which still needed to be adopted. When asked about the possibility of the state establishing a cap-and-trade emissions reduction program similar to the one launched in the European Union, Tamminen said "there's definitely potential for those kinds of market-based approaches."[18]

***

Despite the acrimony between the governor and Democrats over his reform proposals, they managed to reach a deal on the state budget without inordinate delay. Aided by a somewhat better-than-expected increase in state revenues, Schwarzenegger and legislative leaders compromised on numerous fiscal issues. Democrats abandoned their effort to raise taxes and agreed to fully fund Proposition 42, a road and transit improvement and expansion initiative passed in 2002. In turn, Schwarzenegger pulled back his request for cuts to various health and human services programs and met Democrats halfway on fixing a contribution shortfall in the state teacher retirement fund. In support of the budget agreement, Núñez called it "fiscally sound" but also "compassionate." His counterpart in the assembly, Republican Minority Leader Kevin McCarthy, remarked that while Republicans would continue to fight for more budget cuts, "I think we have come a long way." The governor expressed hope that "we can continue the bipartisan momentum for other negotiations," most notably on the initiatives his administration was preparing for the ballot in November 2005.[19] But that comradery quickly dissipated as Democrats had no appetite for significantly compromising on what they viewed as a Republican wish list.

In addition to an initiative capping state spending and another on redistricting reform, Schwarzenegger targeted public sector labor unions, and particularly the California Teachers Association (CTA), in two others. One initiative sought to lengthen the time for public school teachers to earn tenure and make it easier for school boards to dismiss even tenured faculty through poor performance evaluations. The second initiative targeted the use of union dues and fees of public employees for political purposes without each employee's written consent. Polls over the summer showed considerable support for both proposals, but that support began to wane when the CTA and other public employee unions ramped up their activism and media campaigns to defeat them.

The governor's energy policy legislation also faced opposition from labor, especially SB 1, the Million Solar Roofs bill. Murray and Campbell accepted several significant amendments to remove opposition from interest groups during summer committee hearings on the bill. However, an amendment backed by the International Brotherhood of Electrical Workers (IBEW) to require solar contractors to pay "prevailing wages" to workers on nonresidential projects prompted Republicans, led by Campbell, to pull their support for the bill. (Prevailing wages are determined by the state's Department of Industrial Relations and generally are higher—and in some cases, substantially so—than what contractors would otherwise have to pay.) Campbell lamented that the IBEW amendment, added by a party-line vote in the Assembly Appropriations Committee, constituted a "hostile union takeover" of the bill that increased "the cost of an already too expensive technology in order to line their own pockets."[20] Núñez and other assembly Democrats had sided with IBEW, but there also was a palpable sense that they didn't want to give Schwarzenegger a significant legislative victory prior to the special election in November. Therefore, the bill never came up for an assembly floor vote. Had the Democrats sent SB 1 to the governor with the prevailing wage amendment, they knew he would veto it, and they did not want to give him that satisfaction either.

The governor's energy reorganization plan faced considerable resistance as well, and opposition grew after the Little Hoover Commission recommended to the legislature that the plan should be rejected. The commission generally supported the idea of centralizing state energy policy under one entity but agreed with attorneys from the legislature and Attorney General's office that the plan's proposal to take away some ratemaking functions from the CPUC was likely unconstitutional.[21] In addition, consumer advocates and Democratic legislators bristled at the power that would be given to the new energy secretary—the so-called energy czar. TURN's Bob Finkelstein maintained that "concentrating power in an appointee serving at the governor's pleasure will exacerbate conflict-of-interest issues inherent in the governor's acceptance of political donations from energy companies." Senator Bowen and other Democrats echoed that concern.[22] Assemblymember Lloyd Levine, chair of the Utilities and Commerce Committee, added that the plan's proposed "streamlining is just code for eliminating checks and balances."[23] The senate rejected the plan during the last week of August, coinciding with the assembly adding the "hostile" prevailing wage amendment to SB 1. While SB 1 became a "two-year bill" with another chance for amendments and passage in 2006, the reorganization plan would have to be revised and reintroduced to be considered again by the Little Hoover Commission and the Legislature. The administration ultimately abandoned the plan.

Democrats faced criticism for being petty and "deliberately" blocking the Million Solar Roofs bill with the wage requirements, but they claimed that Schwarzenegger had created the hostility with his brazen initiative campaign. "He has gone out of his way to antagonize us," San Francisco Assemblymember Mark Leno declared. "This special election is just one more barrier the governor has created in any kind of positive relationship with the legislature." Moreover, Leno fumed, "he has called us 'thieves,' 'children,' 'untrustworthy,' 'evil,' and 'girlie men.'"[24] Keenly aware that the governor's job approval rating had dipped precariously low, Leno, other Democrats, and aligned interest groups focused their sights, energy, and money on defeating his special-election proposals in November.

Utilizing a campaign war chest that included $100 million from public-sector unions alone, they succeeded in defeating all four of the governor's initiatives. At an election-night celebration in Sacramento, CTA president Barbara Kerr told activists that the "governor wasted $50 million [on the election], and he does not have the courage to apologize to all of you for all the trash he talked about you. He doesn't have the courage to say he was wrong." At the Beverly Hills Hilton Hotel, with his wife, Maria, beside him, the governor declared that Californians "are sick and tired of all the fighting, and they are sick and tired of all the negative TV ads." He acknowledged the need for "more bipartisan cooperation." In a bit of a riff on his most iconic movie line—"I'll be back" (from *The Terminator*) —Schwarzenegger promised, "I will deliver that."[25]

***

Less than a week after the ignominious defeat of his initiatives, Schwarzenegger humbly joked that "if I would do another Terminator movie, I would have the Terminator go back in time and tell Arnold not to have the special election." But behind that jocularity was his anger and dismay that he, at least in popular perception, had somehow morphed from being a capacious centrist into a rigid Bush Republican, his climate change policy differences with the president notwithstanding.[26] The governor clearly accepted that no one had twisted his still-chiseled arm in pushing for the failed initiatives, but he seemed to agree with the post-election comment of the state senate leader, Democrat Don Perata, that he had received "a lot of bad advice." Though Schwarzenegger didn't publicly blame anyone in his inner circle for that advice, he disdained the conservative groupthink from his top advisors in the governor's office outside of Tamminen and attorney Bonnie Reiss, an environmental advocate and long-time confidante of the governor and his wife.[27] Rumors swirled that Chief of Staff Pat Clarey, a former high-level Wilson aide, would be replaced, but Schwarzenegger dismissed that speculation.

However, three weeks later he surprised Democrats and Republicans alike when he announced that Democrat Susan Kennedy, Governor Davis's former cabinet secretary, would be his new chief of staff. "She is an action-oriented person who gets things done," Schwarzenegger declared, and the right choice to work with him "to make California once again the golden dream by the sea." Kennedy had served on the CPUC for three years at the time of the announcement. Reporter and long-time Kennedy acquaintance Bill Bradley called her "Arnold's go-to commissioner" who had developed a clear "pro-business slant" in stark contrast to when Bradley had met her decades earlier while they both worked for Tom Hayden and Jane Fonda's left-wing Campaign for Economic Democracy.[28] Reactions to Kennedy's appointment ran the gamut across party lines, from approval to incredulity to anger, and many Republicans and Democrats felt betrayed—the former by Schwarzenegger and the latter by Kennedy. But when the dust settled, there seemed to be a consensus that she was a disciplined, no-nonsense hand who could steady the governor's wayward ship.

I certainly shared that view, having worked with her for four years, and closely during the energy crisis. Her workplace persona combined the tempered bark of a demanding boss and the scathing wit of a prickly professor polished in her craft. Gubernatorial appointees in and outside of Davis's office dreaded the brow beating that often came their way in conversations with Kennedy that became back-and-forth exchanges, but she also didn't hesitate to commend the staff for good work. At the CPUC, as Bradley noted, a more pronounced "pro-business" inclination emerged from Kennedy as she controversially sought to repeal a consumer-friendly cell phone bill of rights and pushed for the expansion of direct access. However, environmental and consumer advocates praised Kennedy for her work on the state's first two Energy Action Plans which prioritized, first and foremost, energy efficiency and conservation, along with renewable resources and infrastructure improvements to enhance reliability.[29]

Before Kennedy left CPUC at the end of December to work for Schwarzenegger, she added her vote to a unanimous decision to take the first step to establish the California Solar Initiative (CSI), the commission's version of the governor's Million Solar Roofs proposal. Kennedy declared that the commission needed to step "into the breach" after SB 1 "got bogged down in politics in Sacramento."[30] However, the vote to fully fund the CSI from 2007 to 2016 with an additional $2.9 billion came a month later, with Kennedy's replacement, Rachelle Chong, casting the deciding vote in the 3–1 decision. Another new member, John Bohn, recused himself due to a potential conflict of interest. The lone "no" vote came from Geoffrey Brown, a Davis appointee who had almost always voted with Peevey and Kennedy in a majority bloc, but cost concerns overtook his general support for the CSI. "We have put our enthusiasm before our prudence," he observed, while other critics proved harsher. "This is a victory of public relations and popular press over good policy," economist Severin Borenstein declared, "because solar power right now is massively uneconomic." Nevertheless, support from environmental groups and the broader public proved strong, and Schwarzenegger hailed the commission's action as "a great day for California."[31]

The main goal of the CSI was to add 3000 MW of non-IOU solar generation, mainly from rooftop panel installations, while creating a self-sustaining solar industry with no ratepayer subsidies by 2017. "Our plan is to offer a [ratepayer] subsidy now to push the deployment of an important part of our sustainable energy future in the long run," Peevey maintained. Fellow commissioner Dian Grueneich added that the CSI "is a major tool in the State's promise to address climate change and meet the Governor's goal to reduce greenhouse gas emissions." The CPUC set aside 10 percent of the program's funds for "low-income customers and affordable housing installations."[32] Bernadette Del Chiaro, a clean energy advocate for Environment California, proclaimed: "We have a big, bold, meaningful solar program that's going to reduce costs and make this more than just a boutique technology for millionaires and backward hippies." The commission estimated that the average cost to residential IOU customers without solar would be about $12 per year, though critics, including TURN, contended that the cost would be higher than that due to additional metering needs and other expenses.[33]

***

The CSI became the first of Schwarzenegger's key goals in his 2003 Environmental Action Plan to be established by the state and served as a bellwether for the tilt of the rest of his 2006 agenda, including his ambitious goal to enact legislation to further reduce GHG emissions across California's economic sectors. Tamminen, the driving gubernatorial staff force behind this effort, asked Bob Epstein, the co-head of the advocacy group Environmental Entrepreneurs (E2), to help gather business support for this effort in late 2005. E2 members were mainly engaged in energy technology investments and innovations, and many were based in or near Silicon Valley. Tamminen told Epstein, a key backer of Pavley's AB 1493, that the governor's June EO that set targets for GHG emission reductions in California "needed the full force of law to be effective."[34] Indeed, an EO alone could initiate regulatory action by state entities, but lacking a legislative mandate, the scope of broader actions would be limited and the EO itself could be rescinded by the stroke of a succeeding governor's pen.

A partner of the NRDC, E2 issued a position paper in January 2006 titled "Solving Global Warming One State at a Time," which reflected the absence of action on the federal level. The paper primarily highlighted the economic benefits of reducing GHG emissions and the dire consequences of not doing so based on assessments by the Union of Concerned Scientists and other experts. Released around the same time, former vice president Al Gore's award-winning climate change documentary, *An Inconvenient Truth*, helped raise the perils of a warming planet to a new level of public awareness which was bolstered by the devastation of New Orleans during and after Hurricane Katrina in 2005.[35] Gore attributed Katrina's destructive intensity to climate change. Nevertheless, while global warming grew as a topic of discussion and concern, major disagreements over its causes continued, particularly over the role of man-made and induced GHG emissions as opposed to the change being part of a "natural" meteorological cycle.

When Schwarzenegger signed the climate change EO, he had declared that "the debate is over. We know the science; we see the threat. The time for action is now."[36] But the debate over the best ways to reduce GHG emissions from different sectors was far from settled and often contentious. In accordance with the EO, the CalEPA took the lead in forming the state's Climate Action Team (CAT), which included the Energy Commission, CPUC, CARB, and other state entities. After getting many stakeholder comments on a draft action plan released in December, the CAT issued a final report in March in which it recommended "a path that will build on the voluntary actions of California business, local government and community actions, and State incentives and regulatory programs." The report commended the 60 large companies that were already voluntarily reporting their emissions, along with the "dozens" of Silicon Valley firms that had committed to reducing their carbon footprints. However, the CAT used a broad brush regarding potential regulatory actions, noting the need for a "multi-sector, market-based program which considers trading, emissions credits, auctions and offsets." While the report recommended an emissions "cap" to help achieve the governor's reduction targets, a cap-and-trade program—similar to the Emissions Trading System established in the European Union in 2005—received scant attention given the opposition of environmental justice (EJ) groups and big business.[37]

EJ advocates opposed GHG emissions trading due to strong skepticism of the efficacy of "market mechanisms" in the wake of the electricity crisis, and because of concerns over "hotspots" in which conventional criteria air pollutants—such as nitrogen oxides and sulfur oxides—could increase, unintentionally or otherwise, due to these transactions. Given that many of the heavy industries that would be directly subjected to the cap and emissions trading were in or near lower income and minority communities, EJ representatives argued that those communities could be disproportionately impacted by hotspots. However, the California Chamber of Commerce's members included many of those large corporate GHG emitters. The Chamber made clear that any legislation that sought to establish emissions trading or a mandatory cap would be at the top of their ominous "Job Killer" list,[38] which had long served as the kiss of death for major "anti-business" bills. Though the CAT Report did not specifically identify a need for legislation, the Chamber nevertheless strongly objected to its "nonvoluntary" recommendations despite the dearth of specific actions in the report. When it became clear in early 2006 that a serious effort to pass AB 32 would take place, the Chamber's president, Allan Zaremberg, would lead business opposition to the bill.

As introduced at the outset of the 2005 legislative session, AB 32 directed the California Climate Action Registry, a nonprofit public benefit entity that certified voluntary corporate GHG emissions reductions, to prepare the appropriate protocols and procedures that could facilitate mandatory emissions reporting by major emitters from numerous industrial sectors. However, Pavley stopped short of having the bill actually impose that mandate or establish a cap, so it didn't attract much attention and passed easily out of the assembly on a bipartisan vote in April. Seven weeks later Schwarzenegger issued his EO on GHG emissions reductions at the UN's World Environment Day in San Francisco. Tamminen attended the event, as did his good friend Pavley. He had co-hosted her first fundraiser when she ran for the Assembly in 2000, and Pavley had consulted with Tamminen on the Environmental Action Plan he prepared for Schwarzenegger in 2003. Pavley and Tamminen continued to stay in touch after he became Schwarzenegger's CalEPA secretary and, at Tamminen's request, the governor appointed Anne Baker, Pavley's key staff member on AB 1493, to be an advisor at CalEPA.[39] In August of 2005, Pavley amended AB 32 in the senate to incorporate the emission reduction targets in the governor's EO, and she announced that she would work with stakeholders on amendments and seek to pass the bill when the legislature resumed its session in 2006.

***

When Schwarzenegger chose Kennedy as his chief of staff in November, the governor's office was so riven by Republican hyper-partisanship driven by key staff members that it proved "corrosive" to comradery for those outside of that power circle, and especially for Tamminen.[40] In December, after Schwarzenegger moved Tamminen from his powerful Cabinet Secretary post to become his adviser on energy and environmental issues, a reporter for the

Los Angeles Times observed that the "more liberal" and "eclectic" Tamminen "never quite fit in."[41] However, while he may not have "fit in" as cabinet secretary— the same position Kennedy held under Gray Davis—he never would've gotten that job if he had not forged a close relationship with the governor, who decided instead to deploy him as the point person for his signature climate agenda. In that regard, Tamminen's new job was not really a "demotion," as some described it, but a reshuffling of the deck to allow him to work in his strong suit.

Whatever concerns the governor reportedly had with Tamminen's performance as cabinet secretary, he was much more concerned with the entrenched conservative policy and communications perspectives of other key advisors who were ambivalent at best about his climate change and energy goals. They included Pat Clarey, whom Kennedy replaced, and Communications Director Rob Stutzman, Legislative Secretary Richard Costigan, and Press Secretary Margarita Thompson.[42] To right his listing ship, Schwarzenegger granted Kennedy the sole power to hire and fire staff. And everyone understood that she would not hesitate to jettison personnel who proved unwilling, or even reluctant, to support the governor's goals and pledge to have "more bipartisan cooperation." Kennedy ensured that Tamminen could work on the governor's climate and energy priorities without internal resistance, but filling in the devilish details of those priorities posed a formidable challenge.

The governor's office hosted brainstorming sessions with CAT members, which included CARB Chair Robert Sawyer, a retired UC Berkeley energy engineer, and Executive Director Catherine Witherspoon, who oversaw the effort to establish the GHG emissions standards for the implementation of AB 1493. They touted carbon offset markets in which major GHG-emitting companies could buy credits that would offset their emissions by financing carbon sequestration projects that avoided deforestation and engaged in reforestation; innovative agricultural land management practices that enhanced sequestration offered another credit source and purchase option.[43]

The 1997 Kyoto Protocol included provisions for carbon offsets to help countries meet their emissions reduction targets, and by the time the Protocol took effect in early 2005, numerous offset markets had been established. However, while offset markets provided some GHG emissions reduction opportunities for big emitters, they were limited. There was no way a carbon market that only included offsets could achieve the scale of reductions needed to curtail climate change; and the difficulty of verifying GHG data from offset projects, and especially determining which results from that data went beyond what would likely have occurred anyway—in other words, curtailments outside of practices that were essentially "business as usual"—created a good deal of skepticism about their effectiveness.

It had been clear for some time to Tamminen and key NRDC and EDF advocates that a cap-and-trade market similar to the one that began operating in the European Union in January 2005 would be needed to meet the scope of the state's GHG emissions reduction task. Under the EU GHG Emission

Trading Scheme (ETS), member nations determined their emissions allowances through National Allocation Plans (NAPs) linked to their major power plants and heavy industries. The sum of these NAPs established the EU's cap which, in keeping with the EU's Kyoto commitment, aimed to cut emissions to 8 percent below 1990 levels by 2012. If the owner of a large emitter determined it would be too expensive to comply with the cap by minimizing emissions at the source, the owner (or proxy) could buy extra allowances from other businesses with surpluses in the ETS market.[44] Each allowance accounted for one ton of carbon dioxide emissions or its equivalent for other GHGs. In theory, the larger the market, and the greater the number of participants, the more likely it would be that the market would offer the lowest cost compliance option.

However, although California had the biggest population of any U.S. state and, by itself, was the world's sixth largest economy, any market created by AB 32 would only apply by law to the major emitters' facilities within the state. That would limit market participation and create the even thornier problem of emissions leakage, in which big companies could relocate or shift GHG emissions-intensive production out of state—and out of reach of California's cap-and-trade market and other regulations. Moreover, that prospect also included the likely loss of economic activity and jobs in the state, though AB 32 supporters countered that the bill's implementation would unleash the "clean" economy and grow sustainable industries and "green" jobs. In addition, with carbon-market foe George W. Bush leaving office in January 2009, there appeared to be a good chance that his successor, Democrat *or* Republican, would support a cap-and-trade market given the bipartisan support for one in Congress. Republican supporters included Arizona Senator John McCain, who many politicians and pundits considered to be the leading candidate for the GOP presidential nomination. The enactment of AB 32, therefore, could provide a cap-and-trade blueprint for a national market that would exponentially increase market participation and thereby all but vanquish the emissions leakage problem. But for that to have a chance to happen, the key California politicians in the global warming policy debate needed to get on the same page.

***

On April 11 in San Francisco, the governor held a major public summit to discuss the findings and recommendations of the CAT Report, and that discussion included environmental, academic, and business stakeholders. While there was considerable anticipation among supporters of AB 32 that Schwarzenegger would endorse the bill that contained his own GHG emission reduction targets, he stopped short of doing so. He implicitly endorsed mandatory reporting by large emitters, but he did not back the cap on emissions in AB 32 and warned that "we don't want to go after business and make business leave the state." Though that was a legitimate economic and emissions leakage concern, the statement disappointed AB 32 supporters and raised questions about how the state could reduce its carbon footprint to 2000 levels by 2010 as stipulated in the governor's 2005 EO. Bill Magavern, a lobbyist for the Sierra Club, complained that the governor had "punted" and pushed "the ball into the future." Karen Douglas, the director of EDF's climate programs, challenged Schwarzenegger to "walk the walk" and back AB 32.[45]

The governor had certainly raised expectations among the bill's backers that he would take that big step toward unprecedented action to curtail GHG emissions, but the scope of that ambition came with much more than the "market-based system" that he heralded in his summit press release. The release also noted the need for "regulatory solutions," though it didn't identify any of those "solutions" beyond mandatory emissions reporting.[46] His cautious comments at the event showed that while the "debate on the science" of climate change may have been over for him, the argument over how aggressive state policies should be was not. A month before the summit, the Chamber-led business coalition seeking "reasonable and responsible" state actions on climate change that would not negatively impact the economy, released a study criticizing the CAT Report as "'not convincing' due to its general lack of documentation and supporting data."[47] Indeed, given the novel and exceedingly difficult challenge of reducing GHG emissions, the CAT Report could not help but be speculative and presumptive. But it was also clear that without a cap, which the Report recommended, significant emissions reductions would be unlikely, and Schwarzenegger had to grapple with that and his broader alignment with the Chamber. A day after the summit, and after discussions with Tamminen and Pavley, the governor "clarified" that he supported a cap in keeping with Pavley's bill, but he would continue to highlight the prospective role of the market as the cornerstone of his approach.[48]

Schwarzenegger's position was bold, but Republicans in good part, in tandem with the Environmental Defense Fund, had earlier blazed the trail on emissions trading and the imposition of a cap when the administration of President George H.W. Bush tackled the long-standing problem of "acid rain" from power plant emissions. Smokestacks at these facilities belched out tons of sulfur dioxide which returned to earth in the form of acid rain which damaged forests, bodies of water, and even buildings. After talking with EDF President Fred Krupp about the potential advantages and effectiveness of emissions trading compared to command-and-control regulation, White House Counsel C. Boyden Gray, a conservative Republican, led the effort to persuade Bush to establish the program—with a declining cap at the insistence of the EDF. In opposition, White House Chief of Staff John Sununu maintained the cap would hammer the economy. However, Bush not only disagreed but chose to back an ambitious emissions reduction target. As such, emissions trading, combined with a cap, was added to the Clean Air Act Amendments of 1990. After the cap took effect in 1995, the program proved highly successful.[49] In California, the South Coast Air Quality Management

District in 1993 established its own program, the Regional Clean Air Incentives Market (known as RECLAIM). By 1996, emissions from the 353 participants in the program, which included numerous industrial sectors, were about 20 percent lower than from facilities regulated by command-and-control regulations, and program participants realized substantial cost savings.[50]

Following the success of the acid rain markets, "cap-and-trade"—a term that first appeared in print in 1995—became the basis for the EU ETS, and in 2003, governors from nine northeastern states initiated discussions on a regional cap-and-trade program to reduce GHG emissions from power plants. When Schwarzenegger subsequently announced California's more ambitious GHG emissions reduction targets in his 2005 World Environment Day speech, the EDF likened his commitment to President Kennedy's exhortation to the nation in 1962 to put a man on the moon by the end of the decade. The EDF added that the targets needed to be "met efficiently and fairly, using cap and trade mechanisms perfected in the control of acid rain." But the challenges of reducing global GHG emissions went far beyond those of the regional efforts to mitigate acid rain, which focused mostly on utility power providers. While the EDF rightly noted that California's leadership in taking on climate change would "help create new economic opportunities" for the state's businesses,[51] it also would necessitate major downscaling of the fossil-fuel sector that had provided robust economic and job growth for decades. Trying to find a macroeconomic equilibrium between the promise of new technological innovations to reduce GHG emissions and the few effective near-term "sustainable" options was not easy without undue optimism. And even if California somehow achieved significant reductions over time, the state only accounted for roughly 1 percent of global GHG emissions. In other words, even that unlikely achievement, in itself—dissimilar to many of the state's other pioneering environmental accomplishments with local and regional benefits—would have no discernible impact on reducing global climate-change threats.

These daunting realities notwithstanding, Arnold Schwarzenegger appeared ready for the biggest role of his life: He would firmly grasp the mantle of leadership in the fledgling effort in the U.S. to address climate change. Indeed, it became the *raison d'etre* for him and his administration as he ramped up his reelection campaign. But the penultimate scene in this mission would play out in the legislature as the governor waited largely in the wings to cap his grand achievement.

***

When Schwarzenegger hosted the climate-change summit on the CAT Report, Pavley's bill had yet to be heard by a senate committee and had not been amended since the August 2005 addition of the governor's GHG emissions reduction targets. Despite her prominence as an environmental champion after the enactment of AB 1493, Pavley, a former middle school teacher, knew that she would need help from Núñez to pass AB 32, just as Núñez's predecessor, Speaker Herb Wesson, had provided critical support to round up votes for AB 1493 in the assembly. In early April she asked Núñez to jointly author the bill. It already was all but certain that she had enough votes to pass the bill out of the senate, but, as with AB 1493, the decisive battle would be in the assembly. After Pavley told the speaker that she had "about 30" solid votes between the two of them and other Democratic assemblymembers, Núñez, after a brief pause, said, "'I'll get those last eleven.'"[52]

On April 18, a week after the governor's summit, AB 32 was extensively amended by joint authors Núñez and Pavley, and they added a new title: The California Global Warming Solutions Act of 2006. The number of co-authors had expanded from five to 21 and included five senators. The bill directed the CARB to, by no later than January 1, 2008, "adopt regulations that will reduce statewide [GHG] emissions to 1990 levels by 2020," and included all GHG emissions from electricity generation "consumed in California, whether generated in-state or imported." In addition, the CARB would "systematically attack the serious problem caused by motor vehicles, which is the major source of air pollution in many parts of the state."[53] Though the bill did not lack ambitious goals, details on just how they would be reached proved scarce. It was understood that the bill's brevity was in good part by design to give stakeholders the leeway to negotiate more detailed amendments and because many specific elements would be determined in regulatory implementation proceedings. Still, the bill made no mention whatsoever of the "market-based system" prized by the governor. The lone reference to "emission allowances" focused more on equitable allocation than economics, and the CARB was not directed to even consider an allowance transaction platform or mechanism in its regulatory process.

EJ advocates had leaned on Núñez and Pavley to minimize market opportunities for large GHG emitters to "pay to pollute" given EJ concerns about hotspots, the efficacy of cap-and-trade programs, and enforcement issues in Southern California's RECLAIM market. The phrase "pay to pollute" had a pejorative meaning to EJ groups, and that carried over to numerous environmental organizations, including the influential Sierra Club California. But that phrase essentially captured how a cap-and-trade-market functioned. When a government imposes fees or taxes on "bad" polluting behavior, incentives are created to reduce that behavior by requiring the polluter to pay for its so-called negative externalities—in this case, for the carbon emissions released into the atmosphere that, in the absence of regulation, would be free, despite the costs to the environment and public health.[54] EJ groups and the Sierra Club preferred the more direct command and control approach, which would also likely include greater reductions in criteria pollutants such as nitrogen oxides and microscopic particulate matter. A key problem with this approach, however, was that, unlike reducing criteria pollutants with smokestack scrubbers and other technologies designed for that specific purpose, there were no feasible technological equivalents for reducing GHG emissions.

That glaring shortcoming notwithstanding, the speaker remained reluctant to add market mechanisms to the bill, though he understood the dilemma. I had numerous conversations about this matter with Núñez's policy director, Arnie Sowell, who had worked with me in the Davis administration, and Pavley's AB 32 staff lead, Adrienne Alvord. I conveyed to them what my energy crisis advisors, economists Severin Borenstein and Frank Wolak, had told me when the effort to pass AB 32 gained serious traction: While implementing an effective cap-and-trade program for California alone posed considerable challenges, if it was done right, it could still provide the lowest cost way for many industries to reduce their GHG emissions while minimizing potential emissions leakage and job losses. Sowell eventually asked me to set up a meeting with Borenstein and Wolak for him, Alvord, and a few other key staff members. I also asked another UC economist, Michael Hanemann, and UC engineering professor Alex Farrell, to join the conversation given that they had been working with the administration on climate issues and supported cap and trade. These four academics highlighted the economic perils of a command-and-control approach compared to cap and trade. They also argued that, to the extent, the legislative goal was to offer a model for a national climate-change program—which they believed should be the bill's primary purpose—a command-and-control approach would be rejected out of hand and make California an outlier rather than a trail blazer.

Alvord, Sowell, and I understood that broader political dynamic, as did anyone else who was being realistic about national climate-change policy prospects. But the ultimate purpose of the meeting was to hear from highly regarded academic experts that cap and trade could actually reduce GHG emissions and that it would not function as a "pay to pollute" ruse that EJ and other critics of that ilk claimed. Several days after the meeting, Núñez and Sowell talked with me and my boss, Assemblymember and "Mod Dem" principal, Joe Canciamilla. Núñez had been briefed on the meeting's discussions, and he said he felt more comfortable with market mechanisms. How that would factor into the final stretch of the AB 32 debate remained to be seen.

***

In late June, Linda Adams, a former legislative advisor to Gray Davis and Kennedy colleague, met with Schwarzenegger in the governor's office courtyard, which featured a "smoking tent" for the former actor and well-known cigar aficionado. Chosen by Kennedy to be the Secretary of the California Environmental Protection Agency, Adams had only met with Schwarzenegger briefly before beginning the job on June 1, and she was a bit nervous as she approached the iconic tent to discuss AB 32 with him. Núñez and Pavley had amended the bill on June 22 and added "market mechanisms" to it to provide "flexible compliance" to the large businesses that would be subject to the GHG emissions reduction regulations. However, Adams made clear to the governor that in the newly amended bill, market mechanisms could only be "considered" for utilization after the CARB completed a cost-and-benefit analysis of their potential use and provided it to the legislature; and the legislature implicitly had the prerogative to prohibit these mechanisms after reviewing the report. Clearly unhappy with these legislative limitations, the governor shouted "get Fabian" to another aide, and the speaker soon joined him, Adams, and Kennedy to discuss the need for amendments that clearly authorized the use of market mechanisms. Núñez and Schwarzenegger had developed a degree of comradery, and the speaker agreed to address his concerns with the bill during the legislature's summer recess in July.[55]

Schwarzenegger headed into July with additional momentum from a unanimous June 13 agreement by governors at the Western Governors Association annual meeting to develop more regional clean energy resources and improve efficiency and reliability. Schwarzenegger and Tamminen had spearheaded this initiative; and before the legislative session resumed in August, they set out to make an even bigger sustainability splash with international ramifications by meeting with British Prime Minister Tony Blair and Lord John Browne, the head of Britain's largest energy company, British Petroleum (BP).[56]

Initially billed as a CEO forum on climate change hosted by Browne at a BP terminal in the Port of Long Beach, Blair's attendance added a much higher profile contrast to the divergent views of Schwarzenegger and Bush on the topic. The governor declared that "California will not wait for our federal government to take strong action on global warming" and would "be a world leader" in that regard. His aides maintained that he was not trying to bypass the Bush administration, and Adams noted that the CalEPA had remained in "constant contact" with U.S. EPA officials on global warming issues. However, she acknowledged that her team had not consulted with Bush representatives on the "groundbreaking" agreement that Blair, a champion of the Kyoto Protocol, and Schwarzenegger signed at the event. The governor's office proclaimed that the two leaders pledged "to become partners and act aggressively to address climate change and promote energy diversity." The agreement committed California and the U.K. to collaborative efforts to "evaluate and implement market-based mechanisms that spur innovation," conduct clean technology research, and produce "mitigation strategies and adaptation measures."[57]

Though Blair and Schwarzenegger dominated media coverage of the event, Browne garnered some of the spotlight given his strong support of markets in curtailing GHG emissions—even for big oil companies. In a May 1997 speech at Stanford University, Browne had clearly acknowledged the threat of climate change and announced that BP would establish its own internal ETS to reduce its GHG emissions by 10 percent below 1990 levels by 2010. Browne triumphantly returned to Stanford five years later to declare that BP had already reached its goal. In a speech at MIT in early 2006, he maintained that government should "price externalities such as carbon in ways which encourage the development of innovation and alternatives," and he reiterated that belief when Blair and Schwarzenegger signed their agreement.[58] The Western States Petroleum Association, which represented California's major oil companies, remained officially opposed to AB 32 after the agreement was signed. Nevertheless, the head of the association, Catherine Reheis-Boyd, expressed tepid appreciation that the agreement "recognizes the importance of using market-based mechanisms to address the challenging issues of climate change."[59] In contrast, whatever hesitations the governor may have had regarding cap and trade prior to meeting with Blair and Browne, he made clear he was all-in on that approach afterward.

Though the optics of the Blair-Schwarzenegger summit proved positive, the event hardly generated a juggernaut of support for market mechanisms among Democrats when the legislature reconvened on August 7th. The moderate Democrats understood that most business interests outside of Silicon Valley did not even want mandatory GHG emissions reporting, much less a declining emissions cap with allowance purchases and trading. But with two-thirds of Californians expressing support for AB 32, and given that the bill had been "speakerized"—that is, not only strongly backed by Núñez, but authored by him as well—most mods leaned toward voting for it as long as market mechanisms could be utilized. In the same vein, "Progressive" Democrats, who aligned more with EJ interests and the Sierra Club, came to accept the market proposition of the EDF and NRDC: The legislature shouldn't *require* the entity implementing the bill to use market mechanisms, but the implementer should be permitted to do so if, after careful deliberation and consideration, it decided such mechanisms were sound and necessary.

Ultimately agreeing with this "compromise" approach, Núñez and Pavley amended AB 32 on August 23, with just over a week left in the legislative session, so that the implementers "*may* adopt market-based mechanisms" to help achieve "the maximum feasible reductions" to meet the state's cap limit. However, Schwarzenegger and Kennedy quickly insisted that the bill needed to be further amended to eliminate the discretion of the implementer in the bill so that it "*shall*" adopt market-based mechanisms instead of "may." But Núñez made clear he would "not send a bill to the governor that the environmental community doesn't support," and that the governor's demand crossed that line.[60] In addition, the governor wanted a GHG "Reduction Council," led by the CalEPA, to implement AB 32, while Democrats strongly preferred to have the CARB lead that effort. The last sticking point was the administration's request, pursuant to the concerns of the Chamber and other business groups, to grant the governor sole authority to suspend the enforcement of GHG emission reduction regulations in the event of extraordinary circumstances, such as a steep economic downturn. Many environmental groups opposed that provision.

The newly amended bill also had 40 assembly coauthors who, combined with Núñez and Pavley, would provide the 41 votes needed to pass the bill on the assembly floor and send it to the governor. Therefore, the only option Schwarzenegger had was to threaten to veto the bill unless the legislature acceded to his amendment demands. He did just that, but not without an onslaught of criticism led by his 2006 Democratic gubernatorial election opponent, Treasurer Phil Angelides. The treasurer accused the governor of "doing the bidding of corporate special interests" by seeking to "gut" the bill that Angelides said he supported "as is." The *Los Angeles Times* encouraged the governor to sign the bill given the growing climate-change challenge and to "promote the kind of innovation for which the state is famous."[61] In the capitol, AB 32 advocates utilized both critical and encouraging rhetoric in beseeching the governor to sign the bill as they worked with legislative staff on final amendments to fine-tune the governor's authority to suspend emission regulations and determine who would formulate and implement them. Changing "may" to "shall" was not under consideration.

On the second-to-last day of the session, Bob Epstein and several other key AB 32 supporters gathered with the speaker in his conference room as they waited for the official amended bill language from the legislature's legal counsel. The speaker, who had met with the governor earlier that morning, soon received a call from him, and Núñez went into his private office to take it. The governor and his top advisors had reviewed the amendments, and Schwarzenegger reiterated his veto threat given the absence of the key may-to-shall change, but Núñez refused to budge on the matter and indicated that the legislature would pass and send the bill to him with the final amendments. While Kennedy had joined the governor on the call with Núñez, she spoke with Núñez one-on-one shortly after that call had ended. Speaking with self-described brinksmanship, she told him that the veto threat was no bluff if he would not agree to change "may" to "shall." In steadfast response, Núñez said he would not do it because that would remove the linchpin of the deal legislators had made with environmental groups, and support for the bill would collapse. Frustrated but convinced that this deal was indeed ironclad, Kennedy concluded the call with no indication of what the governor would ultimately do, and Núñez conveyed that to the bill's backers.[62]

Schwarzenegger then huddled with Kennedy, Tamminen, and Bonnie Reiss, another key environmental advisor, to determine his ultimate decision on the bill. The big may/shall matter aside, the final amendments included the administration's request for the governor to have sole authority to suspend AB 32 regulations for a limited time, but the implementation responsibilities were shifted to the CARB, though the bill acknowledged that the governor's Climate Action Team would continue to coordinate "overall climate policy." Reiss cogently argued that even though the bill did not mandate the use of market mechanisms, the governor appointed all the CARB's voting members, including its chair, and could replace members who opposed utilizing them. Reiss's observation qualified more as realpolitik than an epiphany, but it proved to be enough to convince the governor to not only sign the bill but also to quickly issue a press release announcing that a deal had been reached on it which would make "California a leader in the effort to reduce carbon emissions."[63]

After being informed of the governor's decision, Núñez provided the good news to the bill's supporters in his office who were then asked to appear at a celebratory press conference with the speaker, senate leader Don Perata, and Pavley.[64] Later that night, Perata presented the bill on the senate floor; needing 21 votes, it passed with 23. The next day the bill passed in the assembly by a seven-vote margin.

In a high-profile ceremony, Schwarzenegger signed the bill on Treasure Island in San Francisco Bay on September 26th. Joined by George Pataki, the Republican governor of New York, and by Tony Blair via video conference, the governor, with a beaming smile and hearty handshakes, greeted the attendees and heralded the monumental moment as the beginning of "a bold new era of environmental protection in California that will change the course of history."[65]

Figure 7.1 Governor Schwarzenegger signs AB 32 as coauthors Pavley (second from left) and Núñez look on, along with Governor Pataki (behind Núñez).

Source: Photo by John Decker/Office of the Governor.

Notes

1 Canciamilla quoted in Mark Baldassare and Cheryl Katz, *The Coming Age of Direct Democracy: California's Recall and Beyond* (Lanham, MD: Rowan & Littlefield Publishers, Inc., 2008), 134.
2 Governor Schwarzenegger, State of the State Speech, January 5, 2005.
3 Schwarzenegger quoted in https://www.wsfa.com/story/1920811/arnold-schwarzeneggers-reaction-to-reagans-death/
4 Governor Schwarzenegger, "Governor Schwarzenegger Calls Upon Lawmakers to Stop the Red Ink," *Press Release*, February 23, 2005.
5 Michael Hiltzik, "Gov. Shuns Most Obvious Fiscal Remedy," *Los Angeles Times*, January 13, 2005.
6 Núñez quoted in George Skelton, "The Governor Owes Schools an Apology – and $2 Billion," *Los Angeles Times*, April 14, 2005.
7 Peter Nicholas, "Governor Drops Pension Revamp," *Los Angeles Times*, April 8, 2005.
8 Mark Baldassare, "Special Survey on Education," PPIC, Press Release, April 28, 2005; Staff Writer, "This isn't a good way to govern," *The Stockton Record*, June 13, 2005.
9 Campbell quoted in Governor Schwarzenegger, "Governor Schwarzenegger Announces One Million Solar Roofs by 2018," Press Release, February 28, 2005.
10 Marc Lifsher, "Groups Fueling Ad Blitz for LNG;" *Los Angeles Times*, December 13, 2004; Schwarzenegger quoted in Christian Berthelsen, "Governor's Close Ties to Gas Lobby," *San Francisco Chronicle*, August 15, 2005.
11 Marc Lifsher, "Groups Fueling Ad Blitz for LNG;" Christian Berthelsen, "Governor's Close Ties to Gas Lobby."
12 Marc Lifsher, "Groups Fueling Ad Blitz for LNG."
13 Michael Collins, "U.S. Could Take Over LNG Siting," *Ventura County Star*, December 1, 2004.
14 Marc Lifsher, "Panel Urges Rejection of Energy Plan," *Los Angeles Times*, June 24, 2005.
15 Ryan quoted in Mark Martin, "Governor Acts to Curb State's Gas Emissions," *San Francisco Chronicle*, June 2, 2005; Newsom in Josh Fecht, "San Francisco Mayor proclaims urban environmental movement," http://www.culturalecology.info/cons_hist/2005.UrbanEnvironmentalAccords.html
16 LaMalfa quoted in Martin, "Governor Acts to Curb State's Gas Emissions."
17 Miguel Bustillo, "Gov. Vows Attack on Global Warming," *Los Angeles Times*, June 2, 2005.
18 Tamminen quoted in Miguel Bustillo, "Gov. Vows Attack on Global Warming;" interview with Terry Tamminen, May 31, 2023.
19 All quotes in Lynda Gledhill, "Schwarzenegger, Top Lawmakers Reach Budget Deal," *San Francisco Chronicle*, July 6, 2005.
20 Campbell quoted in Christian Berthelsen, "Assembly Panel Oks Solar Bill," *San Francisco Chronicle*, August 26, 2005.
21 Lifsher, "Panel Urges Rejection of Energy Plan."
22 Finkelstein quoted in Lifsher, "Panel Urges Rejection of Energy Plan."
23 Levine quoted in Lifsher, "Panel Urges Rejection of Energy Plan."
24 Leno quoted in Amanda Little, "Schwarzenegger's Solar Roof Plan Could Get Sidelined by Partisan Squabbling," *Grist*, June 24, 2005.
25 Kerr and Schwarzenegger quoted in Michael Finnegan and Robert Salladay, "Voters Reject Schwarzenegger's Bid to Remake State Government," *Los Angeles Times*, November 9, 2005.

26 Schwarzenegger quoted in Staff, "Arnold Vows Cooperation, Denies He's Firing Anyone," *Capitol Weekly*, November 10, 2005; Bill Bradley, "Saving Arnold," *LA Weekly*, December 8, 2005.
27 Perata quoted in "Voters Reject Bid to Remake State Government"; interview with Tamminen.
28 Governor Schwarzenegger, "Governor Schwarzenegger Appoints Susan Kennedy Chief of Staff," Press Release, November 30, 2005; Bradley, "Saving Arnold."
29 Governor Schwarzenegger, "Governor Schwarzenegger Appoints Susan Kennedy Chief of Staff;" Bradley, "Saving Arnold;" Peevey and Wittenburg, *California Goes Green*, 81–82.
30 Kennedy quoted in Mark Lifsher, "PUC Approves 11-Year Solar Plan," *Los Angeles Times*, December 16, 2005.
31 Brown, Borenstein, and Schwarzenegger quoted in Elizabeth Douglass, "Solar Subsidy Plan Is Passed," *Los Angeles Times*, January 13, 2006; Michael Peevey, "Michael R. Peevey: An Entrepreneur in Business, Energy, Labor, and Politics." Conducted by Roger Eardley-Pryor, Oral History Center, The Bancroft Library, University of California, Berkeley, 2019, 334–36.
32 CPUC Press Release, "PUC Creates Groundbreaking Solar Energy Program," January 12, 2006.
33 Del Chiaro quoted in Douglass, "Solar Subsidy Plan Is Passed."
34 Bob Epstein, "Environmental Entrepreneurs Update," October 26, 2006 (copy provided to the author by Epstein).
35 Bob Epstein, "Environmental Entrepreneurs Update," October 26, 2006.
36 Schwarzenegger quoted in Bustillo, "Gov. Vows Attack on Global Warming."
37 Climate Action Team, "Executive Summary: Climate Action Team Report to Governor Schwarzenegger and the California Legislature," March 2006.
38 Michael Hanemann, "How California Came to Pass AB 32, the Global Warming Solutions Act of 2006," UC Berkeley Working Paper, March 1, 2007, 16–20.
39 Fran Pavley, "Hon. Fran Pavley: Member of the California State Senate from the 23rd and 27th District, 2008–2016." Conducted by Todd Holmes for the California State Government Oral History Program, Oral History Center, The Bancroft Library, University of California, Berkeley, 2022, 46; interview with Tamminen.
40 Interview with Susan Kennedy, August 3, 2023.
41 Peter Nicholas, "Gov. Demotes Deputy, Puts 2 Republicans in Key Roles," *Los Angeles Times*, December 10, 2005.
42 Peter Nicholas, "Gov. Demotes Deputy, Puts 2 Republicans in Key Roles."
43 Interview with Dennis Albiani, August 1, 2023.
44 Jeffrey Ball, "California Emission Plan Needs Allies," *The Wall Street Journal*, September 1, 2006.
45 All quotes in Marc Lifsher, "Gov. Calls for Curbs on Emissions," *Los Angeles Times*, April 12, 2006.
46 Governor Schwarzenegger, "Gov. Schwarzenegger Hosts Climate Action Summit," Press Release, April 11, 2006.
47 California Chamber of Commerce, "Alert: Chamber-led Coalition Seeks Clarification of Emission-Reduction Economic Analysis," March 10, 2006.
48 Interview with Albiani; interview with Tamminen; interview with Adrienne Alvord, August 11, 2023; Epstein, "E2 Update."
49 Richard Conniff, "The Political History of Cap and Trade," *Smithsonian Magazine*, August 2009.
50 Richard Schmalensee and Robert N. Stavins, "Policy Evolution under the Clean Air Act," *Journal of Economic Perspectives*, Vol. 33, No. 4 (Fall 2019): 39.
51 Jennifer Witherspoon, "Governor Schwarzenegger Takes On Global Warming," EDF Press Release, 2005.

52 Núñez quoted by Pavley in "Hon. Fran Pavley" interview by Holmes, Bancroft Library; interview with Arnie Sowell, August 2, 2023; interview with Alvord.
53 AB 32 as amended on April 18, 2006.
54 Sarah E. Light, "The New Insider Trading: Environmental Markets within the Firm," *Stanford Environmental Law Journal*, Vol 34. No. 3 (April 2015): 13.
55 Interview with Linda Adams, June 17, 2023; unpublished 2021 interview with Adams by Todd Holmes, UC Bancroft Library (provided to the author by Adams).
56 Terry Tamminen, *Cracking the Carbon Code: The Key to Sustainable Profits in the New Economy* (New York: Palgrave MacMillan, 2011), 2–3.
57 Governor Schwarzenegger, "Gov. Schwarzenegger, British Prime Minister Tony Blair Sign Historic Agreement to Collaborate on Climate Change," Press Release, July 31, 2006; Adams cited in Deborah Schoch and Janet Wilson, "Governor, Blair Reach Environmental Accord," *Los Angeles Times*, August 1, 2006.
58 David C. Victor and Joshua C. House, "BP's Emissions Trading System," *Energy Policy*, Vol. 34, No. 15 (October 2006): 2100–12; Tamminen, *Cracking the Carbon Code*, 4.
59 Reheis-Boyd quoted in Schoch and Wilson, "Governor, Blair Reach Environmental Accord."
60 Núñez quoted in Associated Press, "Global Warming Bill Stalls in Calif.," *CBS News*, August 23, 2006.
61 Treasurer Philip Angelides, "Angelides Slams Schwarzenegger's Attempts to gut Climate Change Bill," Press Release, August 9, 2006; Editorial, "Be a Cool Leader," *Los Angeles Times*, August 13, 2006.
62 Interview with Kennedy.
63 Interview with Tamminen; Schwarzenegger quoted in Felicity Berringer, "Officials Reach California Deal to Cut Emissions," *The New York Times*, August 31, 2006.
64 Epstein, "E2 Update."
65 Schwarzenegger quoted in Ben Margot, "Schwarzenegger Takes Center Stage on Warming," *NBC News*, September 27, 2006.

8 The End of a Foundational Decade and the Beginning of a Challenging Path Forward

On November 18, 2008, Governor Schwarzenegger welcomed hundreds of attendees from across the country and the world to his Global Climate Summit at the posh Beverly Hilton Hotel, less than a mile from the luxury retail establishments on Beverly Hills' famed Rodeo Drive. Holding the summit in an iconic locale for American affluence and conspicuous consumption during the depths of the Great Recession seemed incongruently indulgent. But Schwarzenegger elevated the event to one akin to a blockbuster Hollywood premiere as only he could, declaring that "through this collaboration, we are sending a powerful message to the rest of the world" that reducing GHG emissions will preserve the planet and increase prosperity.[1]

As much as the attendees appreciated and applauded the governor's opening remarks, he would not be the biggest star in his own production given the brief speech that followed from President-elect Barack Obama, who had embraced California's approach to sustainability during his 2008 campaign. Schwarzenegger had endorsed Obama's Republican opponent, Arizona senator John McCain, but the governor's wife, Maria, prominently supported Obama along with her uncle, Democratic senator Edward Kennedy of Massachusetts, a strong backer of federal climate-change legislation. Schwarzenegger's support for McCain aside, he told the crowd before Obama spoke that he would now be "in synch" with the White House on climate change and that "our revolution now does have soldiers and is spreading around the globe."[2]

Speaking by video, Obama—now in the vanguard of those "soldiers"—promised that his presidency would "mark a new chapter in America's leadership on climate change that will strengthen our security and create millions of new jobs in the process. That will start with a federal cap and trade system." He pledged to invest $15 billion annually "to bring about a clean energy future" that would help "transform our industries and steer our country out of this economic crisis by generating five million new green jobs that pay well and can't be outsourced." Upon taking office, he vowed to "help lead the world toward a new era of global cooperation on climate change."[3]

DOI: 10.4324/9781003518150-9

The excitement at the summit in response to Obama's speech and America's earnest reengagement in international climate discussions was palpable; but Schwarzenegger also basked in the limelight for another victory lap touting California's sustainability accomplishments which now included an executive order, signed the day before the summit, to increase the state's RPS requirement to 33 percent by 2020. Carter Roberts, CEO of the World Wildlife Fund, said that Schwarzenegger had assembled a "Dream Team" that included four other governors and representatives from 22 other states, along with officials from the EU, Mexico, Canada, Australia, Brazil, China, India, Indonesia, and the United Nations. CBS News correspondent Scott Pelley, who moderated several panel discussions, stated, "Never in the course of the history of the world has it come together on a global level to solve a global crisis. We are separated by language but united by this issue of global climate change."[4]

In his closing remarks, Schwarzenegger briefly but tersely admonished environmentalists advocating lifestyle constraints: "Technology is what needs to power change. Guilt trips don't work. We should still be able to drive the car we want but it should be powered by solar or electric." At the same time, he thanked the ardent yet pragmatic environmentalist Terry Tamminen for "inspiring" him to be more passionate about his climate agenda while leading the Golden State, whose "reach is like that of a continent's."[5]

***

The governor's admonition to eco-minimalists at the close of the summit reflected the tension that had developed between him and numerous environmental groups, particularly those to the left of the NRDC and EDF such as the Sierra Club, during the AB 32 negotiations and after the bill's enactment. Even though Schwarzenegger trounced Phil Angelides in his reelection bid shortly after he signed the landmark legislation, many environmental organizations, including the Sierra Club and the Planning and Conservation League, had endorsed Angelides. The governor clearly had benefited politically from his signature legislative accomplishment, but he upset many environmentalists and Democratic state legislators when he issued an executive order shortly before the election making CalEPA Secretary Linda Adams the "statewide leader for California's greenhouse gas reduction programs," including AB 32.[6] Environmental and legislative leaders derided the EO as an attempt to usurp the CARB's statutory authority to implement the bill. Moreover, it directed Adams to establish a Market Advisory Committee (MAC) "to make recommendations" to the CARB on the creation of a "market-based compliance program." Contrary to AB 32, the EO left little wiggle room for an outcome in which market mechanisms would not be significant components in the bill's implementation.

When the legislature began its new session in January 2007, Don Perata, the president pro tempore of the senate, led the resistance to the governor's pro-market maneuvers. The previous year Perata had authored, and Schwarzenegger signed, SB 1368, which established a GHG emissions performance standard for California electric utilities that essentially disallowed new long-term contracts with "dirty" coal-fired power plants (all of which were in other states). Perata also had secured the necessary Democratic votes for AB 32 in the Senate but was not a market-mechanism enthusiast. As such, in February he introduced several bills that required stricter regulation of GHG emissions and sharply criticized the governor for his market mantras. "The implementation of AB 32 is getting bogged down in arcane discussions of international trading schemes, carbon markets, and 'free' credits," Perata inveighed. Invoking the electricity crisis, he asserted, "that may work for Wall Street traders and Enron economists, but it doesn't work for Californians." Adams responded that "we are moving forward with [command and control] regulatory approaches as well as market-based approaches" because "we need every possible tool."[7] Indeed, roughly 60 percent of the GHG emissions reductions by 2020 were estimated to come from the RPS and Pavley's AB 1493, and only about 20 percent would result from cap and trade. But the latter did not have much of a track record for effectively reducing GHG emissions, and early problems with the EU ETS provided fodder for critics who maintained that the California carbon market was a dubious proposition.

Those criticisms, however, did not diminish the governor's revitalized political stardom which arguably reached an apex in April 2007 when he appeared on the cover of *Newsweek* magazine spinning a globe on his finger, with the caption: "Save the planet—or else!" His eco-prominence notwithstanding, Schwarzenegger lamented then that the environmental movement needed to go "mainstream" in a keynote speech at a conference hosted by the venerable Council on Foreign Relations in New York City. He maintained that environmentalists were "like prohibitionists at the fraternity party," and after a few more jabs that drew laughter from the audience, he asserted:

> The environmental movement is, to use a popular term, at a tipping point right now. I believe the tipping point will occur when the movement is no longer seen as a nag or a scold, but as a positive force in people's lives. And I don't know when the tipping point occurs, but I know where, and that is in California.[8]

Schwarzenegger's reference to "movement" environmentalists as nags and scolds came in part from his experience with demonstrators who had showed up at his campaign events in 2003 questioning his environmental *bona fides*. They chanted "a Hummer isn't green" in reference to his favorite motor vehicle, the hulking and gas-guzzling Hummer, built by General Motors.[9] He had pledged to convert at least one of his Hummers to run on hydrogen during the campaign, but the cost and technological challenges proved so great that, to get a street-legal, non-fossil fuel model, he converted one to run on biodiesel, which furthered his interest in reducing GHG emissions through biofuels. In his 2007 State of the State Address, the governor proposed "that California be the first in the world to develop a low carbon fuel standard that leads us away from fossil fuels." A week later he signed an executive order directing the CARB to develop a Low Carbon Fuel Standard (LCFS) "to reduce the carbon intensity of California's transportation fuels by at least 10 percent by 2020."[10]

The CARB enlisted two UC engineers, Dan Sperling from Davis and Berkeley's Alex Farrell, to devise the LCFS, and it emerged as a key "early action" measure to reduce GHG emissions pursuant to AB 32 before the launch of the cap-and-trade program in 2012. EDF President Fred Krupp, who had provided critical support for establishing a cap-and-trade market to mitigate acid rain impacts, hailed the LCFS "as the beginning of a whole new era for fuels and for renewable energy."[11] In February 2007, John McCain, who had not yet formally declared his presidential candidacy, joined with Schwarzenegger in calling for a national LCFS as they toured the Port of Long Beach. In May, the governor met with Ontario Premier Dalton McGuinty in Toronto to sign an agreement to jointly promote innovative, low-carbon technology, and McGuinty pledged that Ontario would adopt California's LCFS.[12] In addition, Barack Obama, who as a senator from Illinois had already formally declared his presidential candidacy, introduced legislation that proposed to enact California's LCFS nationally. Speaking at an event at a Los Angeles gas station in June, Obama touted the bill, and his campaign office cited research estimating that a national LCFS would cut GHG emissions by 180 million metric tons by 2020, equivalent to taking 30 million cars off the road.[13]

By the summer of 2007, 54 percent of Californians, a majority for the first time, believed that global warming posed a very serious threat to the Golden State's future economy and habitability. In addition, they expressed overwhelming support (84 percent) for the state's seminal clean energy and climate change efforts initiated in 2002 by Byron Sher's Renewable Portfolio Standard bill and Pavley's tailpipe emissions legislation. Seventy-eight percent supported AB 32, a 12 percent increase over the previous year, and 77 percent supported the LCFS.[14] The momentum for further government climate and clean energy actions in California and other states inclined to follow its lead appeared strong, and perhaps strong enough to establish national programs. But the road was about to get rockier for Schwarzenegger as the integrity and feasibility of his market-based approach to mitigate climate change came under increased scrutiny.

***

It had been evident for a while that friction between the governor's office and the CARB over the implementation of AB 32 had been growing, and it came to a head on June 29 when the governor fired the board's chair, Robert Sawyer. A spokesperson for the governor claimed that the dismissal occurred because Sawyer and CARB Executive Director Catherine Witherspoon were not moving aggressively enough on AB 32's early action items and on addressing air pollution in the San Joaquin Valley. Countering that contention, Sawyer accused the governor's office of an unprecedented "level of interference" in the board's activities which included tightening the reins on early action items.[15] He gave reporters access to a voice mail from Schwarzenegger's Cabinet Secretary Dan Dunmoyer telling him that "the direction from the governor's office" was "to stick to the three [early action items] we believe are vetted well," despite Sawyer's belief that the board could and should do more. Several days after firing Sawyer, Schwarzenegger indicated he needed a new chair who understood that "the only way to fight global warming is through a cap-and-trade system," and that "we've got to be extremely sensitive toward business here." An angry Fabian Núñez noted that the CARB's job was to implement the bill "to the letter of the law" and lamented the administration's interference. He vowed to hold a hearing "to get to the bottom of this."[16]

A few days later, Witherspoon, who had been in the administration's crosshairs longer than Sawyer given her "independence," resigned in protest over her former boss's dismissal and elaborated on his interference complaints. What had begun as a row with Sawyer's firing now seemed to border on rebellion; but a few days later Schwarzenegger largely quelled the brouhaha when he announced that Mary Nichols, a former CARB chair appointed by Jerry Brown, would succeed Sawyer, who magnanimously praised the appointment. Nichols, an environmental attorney who also had served as secretary of the state Resources Agency under Gray Davis, had lauded Schwarzenegger as a master communicator in 2006 but also said that his environmental "action has not matched his rhetoric."[17] The NRDC's government affairs director, Annie Notthoff, who had worked with Nichols over the years, praised her environmental resume and contended that "she's not the kind of person you can push around." Other environmental leaders echoed that opinion, but as clean energy advocate John White noted, the Sawyer-Witherspoon episode "caused damage to the brand of Arnold."[18] While the damage proved far from devastating, it heightened skepticism of the governor's commitment to battling climate change in some political circles on the left and provided more grist for investigative reporting by news media.

Schwarzenegger's environmental "brand" now was essentially in the hands of a triumvirate of former Davis administration officials, with Kennedy flanked by Adams and Nichols. Moreover, the previous administration's reach extended to the MAC created by the governor's controversial executive order. Kennedy and Adams asked my one-time boss, former CalEPA Secretary Winston Hickox, to chair the committee, and my predecessor as the CalEPA deputy secretary for policy, Nancy Sutley, served as a member. Hickox made clear that the MAC believed in direct regulations for emissions reductions, but that cap and trade was needed as well. Devra Wang, director of the California Energy Program for the NRDC, echoed Adams in asserting that "a well-designed cap-and-trade program can be a useful tool in the toolbox." The MAC also endorsed the use of carbon emission offsets provided that the CARB used "very stringent criteria for determining whether activities qualify as offsets."[19] The vice-chair of the committee, Stanford University economist Larry Goulder, neatly described the complementary nature of the market approach: "To the extent that the direct regulations continue to restrict or reduce emissions, they help meet the aggregate cap. If the direct regulations' restrictions are not sufficient to bring total emissions down to the aggregate cap, the emissions allowance market will do the rest of the work."[20]

The strongest criticism of cap and trade continued to come from environmental justice groups which now often voiced their concerns through the Environmental Justice Advisory Committee (EJAC) established by AB 32.[21] Though stakeholder discussions on the bill's implementation in the "workshops" hosted by the CARB in 2007 were mostly diplomatic, the EJAC pressed the MAC and the board to broaden the scope of the effort to include criteria pollutants and related EJ concerns. The MAC pushed back, making clear that while the committee understood the desire of EJAC members to address other longstanding issues, the bill's statutory breadth was limited to ensuring that no "backsliding" occurred in the emission of non-GHG pollutants, including potential emissions "hotspots" in lower income and minority communities.

Harvard University economist Robert Stavins, a leading critic of several rosy macro-economic analyses on AB 32's impact that had gained currency, told the MAC that "it bears repeating that climate change is a global commons problem." As such, "there are no grounds" for EJ concerns "on the basis of GHG emission reductions themselves," and that "local air quality regulations will remain in effect with or without a cap-and-trade system." Stavins, the director of Harvard's Environmental Economics Program, emphasized the importance of "carefully monitoring" the impacts of a cap-and-trade program, which he supported, on local air quality but also noted that "climate policy is a terribly blunt instrument in trying to achieve reductions in non-GHG emissions."[22]

Stavins' arguments supporting cap-and-trade both informed and reflected those of the MAC and eventually most CARB members, but the EJAC remained adamantly opposed to a market approach during and after the stakeholder deliberations in 2007. In February 2008, an EJ coalition unveiled an "Environmental Justice Movement Declaration" pledging to "fight at every turn" any global-warming regulation that allowed industries to trade carbon emissions and "gamble on public health." The effort was led by EJAC co-chairs Jane Williams and Angela Johnson Meszaros, who contended that "cap and trade is a charade to continue business as usual." Williams lamented that offsets, backed by distant projects such as "planting trees in

Manitoba," would not help California's low-income communities. Representatives from 18 groups signed the declaration, but none of the signatories represented "mainstream" environmental groups such as the NRDC, Sierra Club, or Planning and Conservation League.[23] Nevertheless, the "Declaration" launched a lengthy and high-profile battle between EJ groups and the CARB over cap and trade and the use of offsets.

***

In March 2008 the editorial board of the *Los Angeles Times* also took issue with the development of a cap-and-trade program in California, describing it as a "staggeringly complex undertaking that will once again create opportunities for dishonest traders to manipulate the market" as they had during the electricity crisis. The *Times* favored a carbon tax on large GHG emitters.[24] However, the editorial board acknowledged the political resistance to a "tax." If AB 32 had included a carbon "tax" it would've required an unattainable two-thirds vote in both houses of the legislature. The potential "fees to be paid by the sources of GHG emissions" in the bill as passed and signed by Schwarzenegger only required straight majority votes in each house.[25]

In an earlier editorial, the *Times* had lamented the "nasty effect" cap and trade would have on "consumers' power bills." The editorial board maintained that "utilities would have to shovel more coal to produce more juice" during hotter weather, and that the increased electricity demand would cause GHG emissions credit prices "to skyrocket" and then be passed on to customer rates.[26] The *Times* neglected to mention that no California utility would be "shoveling more coal" than the Los Angeles Department of Water and Power, which got over 40 percent of its electricity from several large coal-fired plants in Arizona and Utah.

AB 32 required all "load-serving entities" providing electricity in California, including the LADWP and other municipal utilities, to account for GHG emissions from all electricity consumed in the state, and that included power imported from other states. The LADWP's heavy reliance on cheap coal-based generation, which had long helped keep its customer rates well below the IOUs' rates, meant that it would have to purchase a lot of emissions allowances in the cap-and-trade market being designed by the CARB. David Nahai, the head of the utility, maintained that the cost of those allowances would unfairly increase LADWP's rates: "This strategy is nothing short of a recipe for a cataclysmic wealth transfer," he warned in October. "It will divert billions of dollars from the people of Los Angeles and other Southern California cities to line the pockets of investor-owned utilities or marketers for carbon credits."[27] In December the LADWP charged that the prospective auction of allowances would be a tax in violation of the state's constitution. Other cap-and-trade opponents had made similar arguments, and even supporters conceded that any AB 32 regulatory effort that crossed state lines would be in violation of the U.S. Constitution's Commerce Clause which granted Congress the exclusive right to regulate interstate commerce.[28]

These challenges notwithstanding, environmental groups strongly supported the auction approach and chafed at the LADWP's request to be allowed to opt out of the cap-and-trade requirements. Terry Tamminen became one of the LADWP's most strident critics. He had left the Schwarzenegger administration after AB 32's enactment and in 2007 established the non-profit organization Seventh Generation Advisors, which sought to convince other states and jurisdictions abroad to copy California's clean energy and climate policies. In the summer of 2008, he called the LADWP's opposition to an auction-based cap-and-trade program "morally bankrupt." He declared that "it is time for those utilities [that] have put themselves in this position to step up and internalize the costs they have been foisting on the rest of us for decades" to protect "cheap electricity." At the same time, he understood that the many potential legal challenges to climate change initiatives in general loomed large, and especially for AB 32's market mechanisms.[29]

In June 2008 the CARB released the first draft of its AB 32 Scoping Plan which explained, often only in broad terms, how cap and trade and other key elements of AB 32 would work and estimated their economic impacts. The many conflicting interests among stakeholders and the complex economics made the draft-plan process a daunting and thankless task. Accordingly, the plan elicited numerous highly critical responses from economic policy experts. The Legislative Analyst's Office maintained that the "CARB failed to demonstrate the macroeconomic analytical rigor of its findings" that the state's GHG emission reduction effort would result in a modest overall benefit to the economy over time.[30] More bluntly, Robert Stavins asserted that "the economic analysis is terribly deficient in critical ways." Other economists, including Matthew Kahn of UCLA, highlighted the considerable evidence contradicting the CARB's claim that large industries would be minimally impacted by higher energy costs. Dallas Burtraw, with the non-profit group Resources for the Future, maintained that the models the CARB used underestimated costs and wrongly predicted a smooth and easy transition to clean energy sources.[31]

The breadth of the macroeconomic analysis required for the Scoping Plan was simply too much for the CARB's in-house team which, in terms of cost-benefit analytics, had been limited to estimating the direct cost-effectiveness of technologies and other approaches to reduce criteria pollution. The board neglected to request more money for AB 32's implementation to expand its staff's economic expertise beyond the two economists it already employed. However, the CARB did contact UC Berkeley economists in the summer of 2008 to initiate a peer review of the plan's economic analysis, but as the statutory deadline to approve the Scoping Plan by the year's end approached, the peer review process was still underway, and the board had to approve a final draft in December.[32]

On December 12, 2008, the board unanimously voted to approve the final iteration of the Scoping Plan and heralded it as a model for President-elect Obama, while the governor described it as "a roadmap for other states."[33] Those states potentially included members of the Western Climate Initiative established after the enactment of AB 32 in an effort coordinated by the Schwarzenegger administration. The WCI consisted of four Canadian provinces and seven Western states that had tentatively committed to reducing their GHG emissions through a cap-and-trade program linked to California's market, though the details on the distribution and auction of allowances would be established by each jurisdiction. Scheduled to begin in 2012, that allowance market remained a work in progress for the CARB. As acknowledged in the Scoping Plan, the board would continue to "seek input from a broad range of experts in an open public process regarding the options for [allowance] allocation and revenue use under consideration" during the two-year rulemaking process for the program.[34]

Environmental Justice groups aside, most environmental organizations supported the plan while a few were neutral. The business community proved much more divided. Amisha Patel, a lobbyist for the California Chamber of Commerce, maintained that "market structures like cap-and-trade are essential for businesses to meet their obligations until green technology comes to market." However, James Duran with the Hispanic Chamber of Commerce called the plan "an economic trainwreck waiting to happen" for small businesses, despite the board's insistence that the "implementation of the plan will have a positive impact on small business given robust economic growth" and energy efficiency gains. That rosy outlook was in keeping with the broader prediction that "the Scoping Plan will have a net positive impact on both the economy and public health."[35]

In strong support of the plan, E2's Bob Epstein noted that technology investors had already poured $2.5 billion into California in 2008, well above the $1.7 billion that came in during the entire previous year. "This plan is a clear signal to investors to invest in California," Epstein said, while the governor noted that with the nation in the grip of the Great Recession, "green tech is one of the few bright spots out there."[36] Obama had made clear in his remarks to attendees at Schwarzenegger's summit the month before that he agreed as he prepared to take office during the worst economic crisis since the 1930s.

***

Before Obama could undertake a serious effort to address climate change and public health care, another priority for his campaign, he had to immediately address the nation's economic emergency. However, the president-elect's transition office made clear that major energy and related investments would be part of his economic stimulus plan to help revive the economy and create green jobs. Speaker of the House Nancy Pelosi, a Democrat representing San

Francisco, announced in early December that rebuilding infrastructure and creating green jobs would be "the first order of business we will have" when Congress reconvened in January; and Schwarzenegger, one of the few prominent Republicans to back the nascent stimulus plan, told Obama that states were ready to move forward with $136 billion in infrastructure and energy projects that would create many new jobs over the next few years.[37] He too was a firm believer that sustainable energy projects should be an integral part of the federal government's investment.

Wind, solar, and other alternative energy projects faced major challenges because of the bank credit freeze in 2008 after the collapse of two prominent Wall Street investment banks, Bear Stearns and Lehman Brothers, due primarily to the sub-prime mortgage crisis. In addition, the price of oil and natural gas had plunged due to reduced global demand and more efficient extraction methods such as fracking in which water and chemicals are injected underground at high pressure to crack rock strata and release the oil or gas inside. These dynamics created a classic double whammy that, by late 2008, drove stock market shares of alternative energy companies down even more than the rest of the stock market. "Everyone is in shock about what the new world is going to be," said John White, who had long been one of the most prominent renewable energy advocates in California. "Surely, renewable energy projects and new technologies are at risk," he glumly observed, "because of their capital intensity."[38]

Obama convened a meeting in Chicago on December 16 that focused on the green components of what would become the American Recovery and Reinvestment Act (ARRA) after he became president in January. Though his commitment to sustainable energy policies didn't wane during the recession, Obama understood that the politics surrounding those policies had "actually worsened." David Axelrod, one of his top and most trusted advisors, bluntly noted that "nobody gives a shit about solar panels when their home's in foreclosure."[39] That truism notwithstanding, Obama and Vice President-elect Joe Biden outlined an aggressive plan at the Chicago meeting and bolstered the portfolio of Carol Browner, who the day before had been named the director of the new White House Office of Energy and Climate Change Policy. Browner had served as administrator of the U.S. EPA during both terms of the Clinton administration and earned the respect of numerous top executives from the companies she had regulatory battles with during that time.[40]

Along with Browner's appointment, Obama announced that the Nobel Prize-winning physicist and climate-change expert Steven Chu would be his Department of Energy (DOE) Secretary. Having been the director of the Lawrence Berkeley National Laboratory (LBNL) for four years when he was interviewed by Obama for the job, Chu wasn't sure that he wanted to leave that post to become a "bureaucrat." However, after speaking one-on-one with Obama for about an hour, a very impressed Chu phoned his wife and told her, "If this guy asks, I'm going to say yes." He thought it would be a "wonderful opportunity" to help Obama with his climate change agenda, even though the priority of that agenda had slipped. During the campaign, Obama had stated that, after enacting the stimulus legislation, dealing with climate change would be his top priority. Despite those statements, he told Chu during the interview that healthcare legislation would top his legislative agenda, followed by climate change. That did not rankle Chu, who greatly appreciated that during the interview Obama was "just willing to sit and listen, rather than telling me what he believed." Moreover, Chu realized that as the director of the LBNL, which had over 4000 employees, he was indeed already a bureaucrat and well suited to run the DOE.[41]

Chu helped shape the energy components of Obama's ARRA proposal, and his arguments in several instances prevailed over push back from Larry Summers, the chair of the White House Council of Economic Advisors, and Treasury Secretary Timothy Geithner. For example, both opposed the Chu-backed idea of a DOE loan guarantee program for renewable energy projects, contending that it encroached too much on the role of the private sector. However, Obama sided with Chu, and the program would receive $4 billion in the Stimulus bill. Moreover, Chu, a self-described "energy efficiency fanatic," found Obama to be a kindred spirit. The ARRA appropriated almost $20 billion for efficiency, including $5 billion for low-income home weatherization and $3.2 for green building grants.[42]

Reflecting the urgent need for action to address the economic malaise, the ARRA passed after intense negotiations barely three weeks after Obama became president. Altogether, the $787 billion stimulus package appropriated $90 billion for Obama's "clean energy transformation," including $26.6 billion for renewable energy projects. In addition to energy efficiency, the other top dollar appropriations went to transportation, which received $18.1 billion for public transit and high-speed rail; $10.5 billion for grid modernization, including "smart meters"; and $6.1 billion for advanced vehicles and fuels. To buttress the commitment to job creation, the ARRA included $3.5 billion for green innovation, clean manufacturing, and job training.[43] The bill also appropriated large funds for healthcare, education, financial assistance to families and small businesses, and "traditional" transportation infrastructure such as bridge replacements and retrofits.

Democrat Harry Reid of Nevada, the senate majority leader, praised the ARRA's passage as "a team effort," but he diligently managed to get three Republican senators to support the bill and thereby prevented a GOP filibuster to block it from a vote on the senate floor. Though as many as 20 moderate house Republicans had appeared likely to vote for the ARRA, not one did so after immense pressure from conservative groups raised fears of political retaliation. John Boehner of Ohio, the Republican minority leader in the house of representatives, stated that the bill was "bad policy" that would "drive up the debt and put all of this cost on our kids and grandkids.... I hope it works, but I surely have my doubts."[44]

Obama decided to sign the bill at the Denver Museum of Science where a local company, Namaste Solar, had installed roof-top solar panels. In comments made at the event, the company's CEO said that because of the stimulus dollars, he expected his firm to grow by 40 percent through 2011.[45] In addition to acknowledging Namaste in his remarks, Obama maintained that the clean-energy funding was "an investment that will double the amount of renewable energy produced over the next three years" by providing loan guarantees and other subsidies. He also touted the government funds that would help "create a newer, smarter electric grid that will allow for the broader use of alternative energy" and lay "the groundwork for a new green energy economy."[46]

***

Professor Dan Kammen, an energy engineer and director of the Renewable and Appropriate Energy Laboratory at UC, Berkeley, had campaigned for Obama for president and became a climate science advisor to his administration. A lead author of the Nobel Prize-winning 2007 climate report by the UN's Intergovernmental Panel on Climate Change, Kammen told members of the American Association for the Advancement of Science the day after the stimulus bill had passed that California served as a model for Obama's energy vision. "A version of California's plan, scaled up to the size of the nation," he observed, "is Obama's evolving federal plan. The endpoint numbers are about the same."[47] Having advised the Schwarzenegger administration on climate change and clean energy, in addition to promoting the renewed emphasis on efficiency and conservation during Davis's tenure, Kammen clearly understood the centrality of California's pioneering efforts—as did Obama.

On Earth Day 2007, nine months before the Iowa Caucuses formally launched the 2008 presidential nomination process for each party, Senator Obama visited the University of Iowa. He pledged to model his climate-change plan on California's and to provide incentives for new green technologies and manufacturing. Two years later, after touring a wind energy equipment factory in Newton, Iowa, on Earth Day, President Obama remarked that the "choice we face is not between saving our environment and saving our economy. The choice we face is between prosperity and decline." He subsequently hailed the Golden State: "I want everybody to think about this," he said. "Over the last several decades, the rest of the country, we used 50 percent more energy; California remained flat...even though they were growing just as fast as the rest of the country—because they were more energy efficient." Reminiscent of a pep talk by a sports coach, the president declared, "if California can do it, then the whole country can do it. Iowa can do it."[48]

Obama also very much appreciated California's political support for the stimulus legislation, especially from Schwarzenegger, whom he commended for being one of the few leading Republicans "out there consistently promoting the plan," when the president addressed the National Governor's Association in late February. Like Obama, Schwarzenegger strongly supported energy efficiency and criticized fellow Republicans who had taken aim at ARRA provisions to make federal buildings more efficient. "Some of my Republican colleagues are questioning how does it create jobs when you green government buildings. Well, let me tell you, you don't green government buildings by just looking at it; you have to put a lot of people to work to green all those buildings."[49] After the ARRA's enactment, the governor took that perspective to Sunday news talk shows. At a packed Obama town hall meeting in Los Angeles in March, Schwarzenegger gushed that the president "is so well informed" and "very philosophic... I think it's beautiful." Asked how he felt about backing a stimulus package most Republicans did not, he responded: "You know me. I don't look at things as a Republican. If it's good for California, it's good for me."[50]

For large-scale renewable energy development, it proved to be very good not only for California but for the country and its clean energy future. The procurement obligations of PG&E and Southern California Edison pursuant to the state's RPS created the demand for five utility-scale solar projects supported by DOE loan guarantees (through the department's 1705 Program). Once these five projects closed their financing in 2011, the doors opened wide for private financing of utility-scale solar projects in the U.S.[51]

Figure 8.1 President Obama speaks to an enthused audience at a Townhall in Los Angeles on March 19, 2009.

Source: Photo: Mandel Ngan/Getty Images.

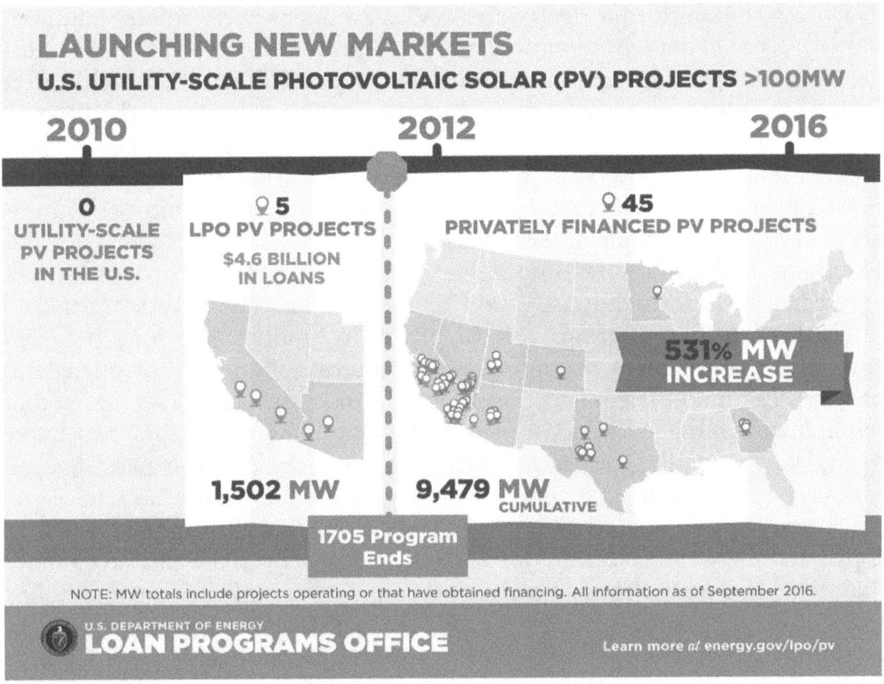

Figure 8.2 "Powering New Markets": October 2016 Update, Loans Program Office[52].
Source: Courtesy of U.S. Department of Energy.

In addition, another ARRA program administered by the Department of the Treasury provided $26 billion in grants (in lieu of investment tax credits) for companies installing a wide variety of clean energy generation technologies. By the time Obama left office in 2017, this funding had supported the installation of 34.6 GW of generation capacity—enough to power over 8 million homes. Over 56 percent of the energy came from wind projects.[53]

To promote and advance aggressive energy efficiency efforts, Chu, along with Obama's White House science advisor, Harvard University physicist John Holdren, utilized California's programs as a model and motivation. In the summer of 2009, Chu told *Science Magazine* that "energy efficiency isn't just low-hanging fruit; it's fruit lying on the ground." Both Chu and Holdren had worked with LBNL's legendary energy efficiency pioneer Art Rosenfeld while they were at UC, Berkeley. Chu told John Stewart, the comedic television host of *The Daily Show*, that Rosenfeld was "a local hero" to him[54]—as he was to me and so many others who had worked with him to optimize efficiency and conservation as far back as Governor Jerry Brown's first term in the mid-1970s. The "Rosenfeld Effect"—the name given to the flattening of the energy demand curve through efficiency and conservation measures—became an increasingly important metric in the first decade of the 21st century.

During the California energy crisis, Vice President Dick Cheney had infamously asserted that conservation may be "a personal virtue" but it provided no basis "for a sound, comprehensive energy policy." The Rosenfeld Effect in California belied that assertion, and the state's residents, on the heels of Cheney's statement, showed once again in the summer of 2001 how important efficiency and conservation efforts could be. In 2009 these efforts became federal priorities, moving from the Bush administration's backburner to front and center under Obama and the ARRA.

Despite being a key feature of the ARRA's clean-energy provisions, energy efficiency efforts did not get off to a good start. Home weatherization, the highest profile program with $5 billion in funding, had long been exempt from government prevailing wage requirements for labor on federal projects. But union-friendly congressional Democrats had quietly added that requirement in the ARRA. Given that the Department of Labor had never formulated prevailing wages for weatherization, the program was delayed for six months due to that time-consuming process and soon became a media meme for bureaucratic bungling.[55] Still, once this effort got on track, it supported the weatherization of over 800,000 sites by 2013 and saved more than 5 million metric tons of carbon emissions, in addition to saving money for weatherized households.[56] Perhaps the most notable efficiency "success" came from the acceleration of rulemaking for improving energy-use standards for appliances such as refrigerators, washers and dryers. This action reversed a pattern of missed deadlines for appliance efficiency rulemaking dating back to the 1990s. By the end of Obama's first term, the DOE estimated that the new standards established during and since January 2009 would save about 800 million metric tons of carbon emissions by 2030.[57]

***

At the end of September 2009, the governor convened his second global climate summit in Los Angeles which featured U.S. EPA Administrator Lisa Jackson in the keynote speaker slot that Obama had filled the year before. In her speech, Jackson mentioned her previous job as commissioner of the New Jersey Department of Environmental Protection, when "we joined the Regional Greenhouse Gas Initiative [RGGI] and stepped-up state efforts on clean energy." She then lauded California for having been "out front on energy efficiency, greenhouse gas reduction, [and] transportation innovation," and noted that "the country once again is catching up" with the Golden State. "That is literally true," she declared, "with one of President Obama's signature initiatives—a groundbreaking agreement on national fuel economy and greenhouse gas standards for vehicles."[58] Jackson highlighted the critical role that California's actions had played as the catalyst for this agreement, just as Obama had done when he announced the deal in May.

The implementation of Fran Pavley's AB 1493—the incipient force behind the agreement—had been held up for seven years by the Bush administration because California needed a waiver from the U.S. EPA for the state to exercise its long-held authority under the Clean Air Act to issue its own regulatory standards. Though waivers had never been denied by any previous administration, Bush's EPA refused to grant the waiver. That denial prompted California to file a lawsuit against the agency in 2008. When Obama took office, he directed Jackson to issue the waiver, and that put California in a position to implement the AB 1493 standards along with 14 other states that had joined as plaintiffs in the lawsuit. However, White House and other administration officials had been secretly negotiating with the big automakers to accept California's standards as national regulations which would eliminate state-by-state differences in addition to increasing fuel efficiency and GHG emissions reductions across the country. Most automakers had joined with the Bush administration in opposing AB 1493's implementation; but given that General Motors and Chrysler corporations had received billions of dollars from the ARRA to keep them solvent, Obama had leverage in the negotiations.[59] At Schwarzenegger's summit, Jackson announced that "15 days ago, the secretary of transportation and I signed a formal proposal setting standards of 35.5 MPG by 2016, and containing the first ever national action to significantly control greenhouse gas emissions from vehicles." (Subsequent rulemaking pursuant to the agreement established an average of 54.5 MPG by 2025.)[60]

Citing Obama's pledge at the 2008 summit that the U.S. would begin "a new chapter in America's leadership on climate change," Jackson extolled the "comprehensive legislation" that had already passed in the house of representatives "from LA's own Congressman Henry Waxman and Massachusetts' Ed Markey," both Democrats. That bill featured a cap-and-trade program and mandated increases in renewable energy and efficiency to achieve a 17 percent cut in GHG emissions by 2020 and 83 percent by 2050. While her speech was overwhelmingly upbeat, she also acknowledged the staunch opposition to the legislation and related Obama administration efforts. "Very soon," she said dismissively, "we'll hear about doomsday scenarios—with EPA regulating everything from cows to the local Dunkin' Donuts."[61] In fact, those scenarios had already surged significantly as foreboding Republican critiques of Obama after he defeated McCain, and they reached a fever pitch in the house debate over the Waxman-Markey bill.

On June 26, the day the bill passed in the house by one vote, John Boehner called it "the biggest job-killing bill that's ever been on the floor of the House of Representatives." Although the Congressional Budget Office estimated that the bill would raise household electricity prices by $175 per year, many Republicans contended that the increase would be as much as $3000 and called the price hike an "energy tax."[62] Only eight "moderate" Republicans voted for the legislation, and 44 Democrats, mostly from coal-producing and heavy manufacturing states, voted against it, even after amendments were added to water-down some of the most controversial provisions. Still, the bill's passage proved to be a landmark accomplishment for Obama and

Speaker Nancy Pelosi who were joined by Al Gore and Secretary of State Hillary Clinton in rounding up the requisite votes. Obama heralded the house for taking a "bold and necessary step" and challenged the senate "to take the next step." Conversely, the Republican National Committee issued a press release targeting two dozen vulnerable house Democrats for their "ongoing crusade against economic recovery."[63]

At his summit three months later, Schwarzenegger, speaking before Jackson's address, announced that he planned to attend the UN climate conference in Copenhagen in December and proclaimed: "Today there was great action in Washington with the introduction of the climate change legislation in the senate." Slipping momentarily into a popular caricature of himself that originated on the comedy TV show *Saturday Night Live*, he told the crowd "I am here today to pump you all up" with "some strong muscles." The reason "we need all those muscles is because there is a lot of pushback" from people who "don't believe in what we're saying here." He told the "experts and leaders from around the world" that they needed to continue to work together to meet the challenge which he likened to pushing a boulder up a hill: "When you get up there with this boulder on top of that hill, on the other side it rolls down and it will gain momentum. That's exactly the way it will happen with the environmental movement, fighting global warming."[64]

Alas, the boulder would never get to the top of that hill. Moreover, the Governors' Global Climate Summit of 2009 would be the last full-fledged hurrah in the decade-long trajectory of progress and promise of sustainability in America—all the fits and starts and regionalism notwithstanding.

* * *

While expectations on the chances for notable progress at the Copenhagen climate summit varied, by the time the conference had ended, the consensus among news media and environmentalists was that it was a missed opportunity and ultimately a failure. Obama dazzled a few of his top aides with his extensive knowledge of the issues and by corralling the elusive Chinese Premier Wen Jiabao for "meaningful" discussions,[65] but the U.S. was widely criticized for offering only a 4 percent reduction of its GHG emissions by 2020. With the world still economically reeling from the Great Recession, the biggest GHG-emitting countries, led by the U.S. and China, proved averse to binding commitments, and that rippled through the conference. Lumumba Di-Aping, chief negotiator for a group of 130 developing countries, described the summit's flimsy agreement as having "the lowest level of ambition you can imagine" and said, "Obama has eliminated any difference between him and Bush."[66] Despite hailing the "Copenhagen Accord" as an "unprecedented breakthrough" before leaving the summit, Obama subsequently acknowledged it was a non-binding "political declaration" that fell well short of what was needed.[67]

Meanwhile, Schwarzenegger had arrived in Copenhagen with his usual star power, though that glow dimmed when he began downplaying expectations for the conference. One reporter described the governor's speech touting the progress on climate change at the sub-national level as "shockingly defeatist" and "tricked out with sunny language about private-sector innovation."[68] Maintaining his sunny perspective, a few days later Schwarzenegger contended that the conference was not a failure because "it brought the focus to the world that something has to be done."[69]

Obama had hoped to sign the climate change bill before the Copenhagen Conference, even though he had prioritized the enactment of his Affordable Care Act (ACA, i.e., "Obamacare") over climate change legislation.[70] Behind an extraordinary effort by Obama and top White House staff, the ACA passed along party lines 60–39 in the senate on December 24, and House Democrats eked out a partisan 219–212 victory to send the bill to the president on March 21st. However, the Democrat's filibuster-proof majority in the senate vanished in January when Massachusetts Republican Scott Brown shockingly defeated his Democratic opponent to fill the senate seat of Ted Kennedy, who had died in 2009. As a result, Massachusetts's other senator, Democrat John Kerry, and Connecticut independent Joe Lieberman (who caucused with the Democrats), began pursuing their Republican colleague, Lindsey Graham of South Carolina, to support the climate change legislation. Though he had initially expressed conceptual support for a climate change bill, Graham sought numerous concessions, and the expansion of offshore oil drilling topped his list. Lieberman, Kerry, and Browner talked extensively with environmentalists about this possible drilling "trade off" to get a climate bill passed, but it became increasingly clear after the ACA had passed that Graham would not likely be able to deliver Republican votes, and perhaps not even his own. As Obama later recalled, the "political price for cooperating with my administration" had become "too high" for Republicans who had been besieged by powerful Waxman-Markey opponents and the GOP's right wing.[71]

Any chance of salvaging a climate change bill ended after a major pipe explosion at BP's *Deepwater Horizon* oil rig in the Gulf of Mexico on April 20—two days before Earth Day—began spewing tens of thousands of barrels of oil into the gulf 52 miles south of Venice, Louisiana. The environmental groups that had been reluctantly and cautiously receptive to the potential drilling-expansion trade-off pulled back, and Obama realized that "my already slim chances of passing climate legislation before the midterm elections had just gone up in smoke."[72]

The demise of the Waxman-Markey bill and its senate counterpart became the source of much debate, acrimony, and finger-pointing among supporters of the legislation. While it would be an overstatement to say that this ambitious effort was destined to fail, it would not be by much. After the stimulus bill passed, Republican leaders in Congress dug in on their efforts to obstruct the passage of Obama's big legislative priorities. While they failed to sink the ACA, from the time Obama took office, Republicans contributed to and benefitted from a decline in public interest in climate change. By the fall of 2009, only 57 percent of Americans believed there was "solid evidence" of "global warming" compared to 71 percent in April 2008. While this belief declined even among Democrats, it plunged among Republicans and independents.[73] Though concerns about climate change had consistently ranked at or near the bottom of the public's issue priorities, by early 2010, just 28 percent considered the matter to be a top priority—less than half the prioritization of health care—and down from 38 percent in 2007.[74] By the time the senate introduced its climate bill, even Democratic legislators found scant support for a climate change bill among their constituents as the economy remained very sluggish and concerns about energy and other consumer cost increases grew. As crestfallen as many environmental advocates were about the legislative failure, Bill McKibben, who in 2008 had co-founded 350.org, an activist group promoting climate-change action, later noted that the effort at that time "wasn't politically possible. The lift was much, much too heavy."[75]

***

Many Californians were of course disappointed by the fruitless legislative endeavor in Congress, but a similar outcome, for all intents and purposes, loomed in the Golden State: AB 32 opponents, backed by big oil companies, had gathered enough petition signatures to place an initiative on the November 2010 general election ballot to all-but repeal the bill. Though the public's belief in solid evidence of global warming and the need for government action to mitigate it was stronger in California than in the rest of the country, the state had been hammered hard by the Great Recession. Proposition 23 proposed to delay the implementation of AB 32 regulations until California's unemployment level dropped to or below 5.5 percent for a year. Given that unemployment in the fall of 2010 was above 12 percent and that reaching and maintaining a 5.5 percent level—a rarity then even in good times—was an exceedingly unlikely prospect in the near term, Proposition 23 would suspend the bill indefinitely. The proposition's backers called it the "California Jobs Initiative" and contended it would also prevent residents from facing higher energy costs both directly "and indirectly as businesses pass higher costs for [GHG emissions] reduction on to consumers."[76] Schwarzenegger led the opposition to the initiative and mocked the "black-oil hearts" of its primary sponsors, Texas-based Valero and Tesoro corporations, and their purported concern for jobs. "This is like Eva Braun [Hitler's long-time companion] writing a Kosher cookbook," he declared. "It's not about jobs," it was about "their profits."[77]

Though summer polls on Proposition 23 indicated it had a chance of passing in November, by fall polls showed voter support declining. Schwarzenegger provided the *coup de grâce* by enlisting James Cameron, who also donated $1 million to fight the proposition, to star in an ad against it. Sitting in an office surrounded by movie memorabilia, Cameron highlighted the stakes at hand in a personal parable:

> I've made movies about a cyborg assassin sent to annihilate humanity, an unsinkable ship on a collision course with an iceberg, and about a mineral-rich alien moon facing environmental destruction. Those are movies. But we face a real threat right now in California. Two oil companies from Texas are pushing Prop 23. This deceptive ballot measure would be the ultimate real-life disaster, terminating our air pollution standards, sinking our clean energy economy and exploiting our environment for profit. We can say no on Prop 23, to stop the dirty energy proposition. Tell your friends and family, cyborgs, and avatars, to vote no on 23 before it's too late.[78]

By election day, the results showed that Californians had been receptive to this message—and to bringing back an old, familiar face to succeed the termed-out Schwarzenegger.

Having helped former governor Jerry Brown during his 2010 campaign to reclaim that office, I joined other Brown supporters on election night at the Fox Theater in Oakland for a widely expected victory celebration. Brown eventually took the stage and told the crowd that, while many ballots still needed to be counted, "it looks like we're going back."[79] Joined onstage by his wife, Anne Gust, Brown also mentioned that the San Francisco Giants had won their first World Series that night—over the Texas Rangers, no less. And it was also clear that California voters had steamrolled the Texas oil companies and Proposition 23. Though Democratic candidates across the country suffered crushing defeats in what proved to be a Republican "wave" election, California became true "blue" as Democrats won every constitutional office in the state and maintained control of the legislature.

Appropriately enough, Schwarzenegger would pass the gubernatorial baton to the guy who embraced Art Rosenfeld's ideas and by and large started California's move toward renewable energy in the 1970s, as quixotic as those efforts were then. Now, Brown would continue Schwarzenegger's role as a leading climate change ambassador by orchestrating a global accord among cities, states, and countries to limit GHG emissions, and he aggressively increased the state's commitment to renewable energy and efficiency.[80] Moreover, the slowly receding mire of the Great Recession notwithstanding, Brown forged ahead in implementing a cap-and-trade program even though the other states in the Western Climate Initiative that had tentatively committed to do the same withdrew in the wake of the collapse of the federal legislative effort. California's program launched in November 2012 without notable glitches. In 2017 it was tweaked and extended by the legislature and Brown to run through 2030. While criticisms of the program's efficacy accompanied the operation of its market, the CARB-run GHG emission-credit auctions raised about $25 billion (through 2023) for a wide variety of efforts to mitigate climate change through the state's Greenhouse Gas Reduction Fund. As economist James Bushnell has noted, the cap-and-trade market "has been through its ups and downs," but it has generally been a success.[81]

In addition, California's RPS proved to be a great success, not only within the state but through a ripple effect in others. Unlike California in 1996, Massachusetts enacted the first "modern" RPS as part of its electricity restructuring effort in 1997, and Texas followed suit in 1999.[82] However, when California enacted its more ambitious RPS in 2002, it was in large part a reaction to the failure of restructuring in the state due to the electricity crisis, and that failure led to a backlash against electricity "deregulation" elsewhere in the nation and an RPS boom. From 2004 to 2009, 22 states (and Washington, DC) authorized binding RPS targets, including seven of the ten largest states after California and Texas. (Two additional states established non-binding standards.)[83] The Obama administration in 2016 recognized the importance of state RPS programs in the "dramatic growth" of renewable energy, noting that "since 2008, electricity generation from wind has more than tripled, and electricity from solar has increased 30-fold."[84] Unlike most states, California was already utilizing a significant amount of green energy when the ARRA became law. As this graph of California's utility-scale renewable energy growth shows, driven by its RPS, the state almost tripled its capacity in eight years. It led all states in total renewable energy generation at the end of the decade.

And despite the notoriety of the 2011 failure of the solar panel manufacturer Solyndra, the first recipient of a DOE loan guarantee, by the time

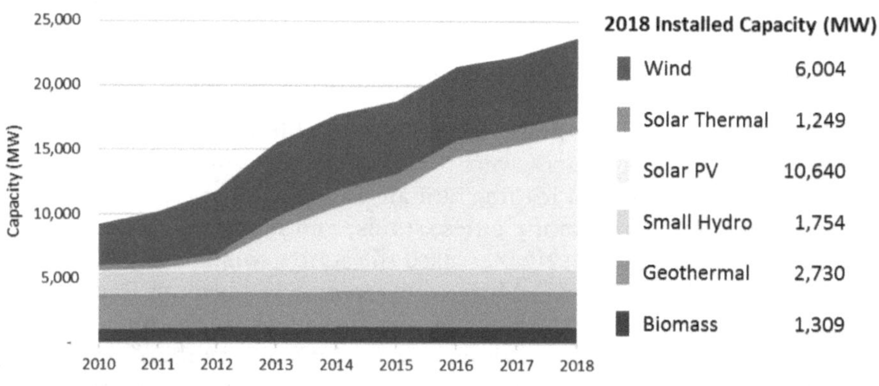

Figure 8.3 Cumulative installed large-scale renewable energy capacity in California from 2010 to 2018.

Source: CEC (2019).[85] (Graphic by Energetics).

Obama left office that DOE program had received $30 million more in interest payments than it had lost in defaults.[86]

The "dramatic growth" in clean energy and the corresponding research, development, and deployment-driven cost reductions in renewable technologies occurred despite strong economic headwinds created by the Great Recession and plummeting natural gas prices due to fracking. From 2009 to 2023 the cost of wind power dropped by more than half while solar energy costs declined by 83 percent; and the cost of lithium-ion battery cells, which are critical to storing renewable energy due to its intermittency, fell 97 percent since the mid-1990s.[87] Moreover, a 2023 analysis by the global financial services firm Lazard estimated that the "unsubsidized levelized cost" of utility-scale photovoltaic solar and "onshore" wind—that is, the revenue required to build and operate this type of generation over a specified cost recovery period—was below the cost of "conventional generation technologies" using nuclear and fossil fuels. In 2021 renewable energy surpassed both coal-based and nuclear energy to become the nation's second leading electricity generation source behind natural gas.[88] A major increase in wind and solar power drove this growth. In 2022 those two sources accounted for 14 percent of the generation from the nation's electric power sector and double that percentage in California, not including the thousands of non-utility solar panel installations less than 1 MW.[89]

Campaigning in California shortly before the state's 2020 Democratic presidential primary (and the Covid-19 pandemic), former vice president Joe Biden praised the "green" provisions in the ARRA and lauded the state's pioneering sustainability efforts, saying that "everyone sort of had an epiphany here." Commenting on the earlier failure of California-based Solyndra, which Republicans repeatedly highlighted, Biden maintained that in the ongoing effort "to get us to net zero emissions, there's going to be mistakes made. But that can't turn us back from the commitment."[90]

After winning the presidential election, Biden followed through on that commitment. In 2022, he and his administration spearheaded the successful effort to enact the Inflation Reduction Act (IRA) which allocated $369 billion for climate and clean energy endeavors—almost three times the inflation-adjusted amount appropriated through the ARRA in 2009. On the one-year anniversary of the passage of the IRA, *Time* magazine proclaimed that it had already "Reshaped the U.S.—and The World" and cited Biden advisor John Podesta's contention that the Act was driving "a transformation of the economy."[91] Time will tell if the IRA and the state and local sustainability efforts buttressed by it will generate the green wave that pushes clean energy past natural gas as the nation's primary source of electricity. That would surely be a fitting and monumental complement to the topsy-turvy and catalytic power trip that transpired in the first decade of the new century.

Figure 8.4 Former Governors Davis, Schwarzenegger and Brown at the swearing-in ceremony for California Governor Gavin Newsom in January 2019.

Source: Photo: Paul Kitagaki Jr./*The Sacramento Bee*.

Notes

1 Schwarzenegger quoted in Samantha Young, "Schwarzenegger Opens Climate Summit with Obama," *San Diego Union Tribune*, November 18, 2008.
2 Schwarzenegger quoted in Betsy Reed, "Obama Opens New Green Chapter for U.S. on Climate," *The Guardian*, November 18, 2008.
3 Obama speech: https://www.americanrhetoric.com/speeches/barackobama/barackobamaglobalclimatesummit.htm
4 Roberts and Pelley quoted in Paige Donner, "Governors' Global Climate Summit: Thinking as One Planet," December 21, 2008. https://www.huffpost.com/entry/governors-global-climate_b_145299
5 Schwarzenegger quoted in Paige Donner, "Governors' Global Climate Summit: Thinking as One Planet."
6 Governor Schwarzenegger, Executive Order S-20-06, October 18, 2006.
7 Perata and Adams quoted in Janet Wilson, "Senate to Turn Up Heat on Gov. to Fight Global Warming," *Los Angeles Times*, February 22, 2007.
8 Schwarzenegger's remarks in "Twenty-First Century Environmentalism: How Protecting Our Environment Will Create Economic Growth," Council on Foreign Relations, April 12, 2007; accessed at Cfr.org.
9 Joe Motavalli, "Special Order: A Green Hummer," *The New York Times*, October 5, 2003.
10 Governor Schwarzenegger, State of the State Address, January 9, 2007; Executive Order S-01-07; interview with Tamminen.
11 Krupp quoted in Marc Lifsher, "Next Schwarzenegger Target: Fuel Emissions," *Los Angeles Times*, January 9, 2007.
12 Reuters Staff, "Schwarzenegger, McCain Back Low Carbon Fuel," *Reuters.com*, February 21, 2007; https://www.ctvnews.ca/schwarzenegger-brings-green-message-to-canada-1.243214
13 Reuters Staff, "Barack Obama Endorses Low Carbon Fuel Standard," *Reuters.com*, June 12, 2007.

14 Mark Baldassare, et al., "Californians and the Environment," PPIC Statewide Survey, Press Release, July 2007.
15 Janet Wilson, "State Air Resources Board Chief Fired," *Los Angeles Times*, June 29, 2007.
16 Dunmoyer, Schwarzenegger and Núñez quoted in Steve Harmon, "Schwarzenegger Pressured Air-Quality Board, Democrats Charge," *The San Jose Mercury News*, July 2, 2007.
17 Nichols quoted in Tim Reiterman, "Governor, Rival Both Profess to Lean Green," *Los Angeles Times*, October 28, 2006.
18 Notthoff and White quoted in Jesse McKinley, "Schwarzenegger May Lose a Bit of His Eco-Luster," *The New York Times*, July 6, 2007.
19 Wang quoted in Sarah Jane Tribble, "California Cap-and-Trade Program Endorsed to Fight Global Warming," *The San Jose Mercury News*, June 1, 2007; MAC comment on offsets in *Recommendations for Designing a Greenhouse Gas Cap-and-Trade System for California: Market Advisory Committee Recommendations to the California Air Resources Board*, June 30, 2007, p. H-10.
20 Lawrence H. Goulder, "California's Bold New Climate Policy," *The Berkeley Electronic Press*, September 2007.
21 For a good analysis of the years-long battle between environmental justice groups and the CARB over cap and trade and offsets, see Alice Kaswan, "Climate Change and Environmental Justice: Lessons from the California Lawsuits," *San Diego Journal of Climate & Energy Law*, Vol. 5, No. 1 (2013–2014): 2–42.
22 Stavins to Winston Hickox, Chair, Market Advisory Committee, "Comments on the Recommendations of the Market Advisory Committee to the California Air Resources Board," June 15, 2007, accessed at Harvard.scholar.edu/files/stavins.
23 Johnson Meszaros and Williams quoted in Margot Roosevelt, "Groups to Fight Plan for Trading Carbon Emissions," *Los Angeles Times*, February 20, 2008. Regarding EJ critiques that the program would exacerbate pollution in disadvantaged communities, economists Kyle Meng and Danae Hernandez-Cortez "estimate that the program lowered GHG, PM2:5, PM10, and NOx emissions by 3-9% annually between 2012-2017 for sample industrial facilities regulated only by the carbon market." Meng and Hernandez-Cortez, "Do Environmental Markets Cause Environmental Injustice: Evidence From California's Carbon Market" (November 2022). https://www.nber.org/system/files/working_papers/w27205/w27205.pdf
24 Editorial Board, "Deregulation déjà vu," *Los Angeles Times*, March 10, 2008.
25 The California Chamber of Commerce legally challenged the claim by the State of California that the revenues raised through the CARB's quarterly emission-credit auctions were fees, arguing instead that the auction revenue constituted a tax. However, in 2017 the California 3rd District Court of Appeal rejected the Chamber's claim. https://www.scientificamerican.com/article/court-upholds-californias-cap-and-trade-program/
26 Editorial Board, "Time to Tax Carbon," *Los Angeles Times*, May 28, 2007.
27 LADWP, "LADWP Denounces CPUC/CEC Cap and Trade Proposal as a Recipe for Wealth Transfer," Press Release, October 6, 2008.
28 Steven Ferry, "Auctioning the Building Blocks of Life: Carbon Auction, the Law, and Global Warming," *Notre Dame Journal of Law, Ethics & Public Policy*, Vol. 23, No. 2, Art. 1 (2009): 343, 361.
29 Tamminen quoted in Steven Ferry, "Auctioning the Building Blocks of Life: 343, 361.
30 Mac Taylor to Roger Niello, "LAO's Critique of the AB 32 Scoping Plan Economic Analysis," November 26, 2008.
31 Stavins, Kahn and Burtraw cited in Editorial Board, "Dishonest Debate," *The San Diego Union-Tribune*, December 8, 2008.
32 Taylor, "LAO's Critique of the AB 32 Scoping Plan Economic Analysis."

33 Schwarzenegger quoted in Margot Roosevelt, "State Orders Big Cuts in Gases," *Los Angeles Times*, December 12, 2008.
34 California Air Resources Board, *Climate Change Scoping Plan: A Framework for Change*, December 2008, 69.
35 Patel and Duran quoted in Roosevelt, "State Orders Big Cuts in Gases"; *Climate Change Scoping Plan*, 85, 2.
36 Epstein and Schwarzenegger quoted in Roosevelt, "State Order Big Cut in Gases."
37 Pelosi quoted and Schwarzenegger cited in John N. Broder, "Proposal Ties Economic Stimulus to Energy Plan," *The New York Times*, December 3, 2008.
38 White quoted in Clifford Krauss, "Momentum Slows for Alternative Energy in U.S.," *The New York Times*, October 21, 2008.
39 Axelrod quoted in Barack Obama, *A Promised Land* (New York: Crown, 2020), 490.
40 Carol Browner interview by Dov Weinryb Grohsgal, Obama Presidency Oral History Project, Columbia University, July 2020, 31–32; Michael Hirsch, "What Climate Czar Carol Browner Really Does," *Newsweek*, April 3, 2009.
41 Steven Chu interview by Keith A. Wailoo, Obama Presidential Oral History Project, Columbia University, October 2020, 4–6.
42 Steven Chu interview by Keith A. Wailoo, 19–20; appropriations cited in White House Council of Economic Advisors, "The Economic Impact of the American Recovery and Reinvestment Act of 2009: Supplement to the Third Quarterly Report," April 2010.
43 "The Economic Impact of the ARRA of 2009," April 2010.
44 Reid and Boehner quoted in David Rogers, "Senate Passes $787 Billion Stimulus Bill," *Politico*, February 13, 2009.
45 Michael Grunwald, *The 'New' New Deal: The Hidden Story of Change in the Obama Era* (New York: Simon & Schuster, 2012), 242.
46 "Obama's remarks on signing the stimulus plan," *CNN*, February 17, 2009.
47 Kammen quoted in Robert Sanders, "The Pluses and (Mostly) Minuses of Biofuels," *Phys.org*, February 23, 2009. https://phys.org/news/2009-02-pluses-minuses-biofuels.html
48 Obama quoted in William Bradley, "Obama's Earth Day Energy Declaration: California May be the Model He Says, but It's Not Enough," *Huffington Post*, May 24, 2009. https://www.huffpost.com/entry/obamas-earth-day-energy-d_b_190677
49 Schwarzenegger quoted in Ronald Brownstein, "President Obama's Top Republican Ally," *The Atlantic*, February 19, 2009.
50 Schwarzenegger quoted in Carol E. Lee, "Arnold on Obama: 'Beautiful'," *Politico*, March 19, 2009.
51 Varun Sivaram, "The American Recovery & Reinvestment Act and the Rise of Utility-Scale Photovoltaics," Bipartisan Policy Center, June 2020. https://bipartisanpolicy.org/download/?file=/wp-content/uploads/2020/06/The-Successful-Demonstration-of-Utility-Scale-PV.pdf
52 "Powering New Markets": https://www.energy.gov/lpo/articles/powering-new-markets-utility-scale-photovoltaic-solar
53 Department of the Treasury, "Final Overview of the Section 1603 Program," March 1, 2018. https://home.treasury.gov/system/files/276/P-Status-overview-2018-03-01.pdf
54 Chu quoted in Dan Charles, "Leaping the Energy Efficiency Gap," *Science Magazine*, August 14, 2009; and on *The Daily Show*, Comedy Central, July 21, 2009. https://www.cc.com/video/7y64wv/the-daily-show-with-jon-stewart-steven-chu
55 Grunwald, *The 'New' New Deal*, 306-07.
56 Office of President Barack Obama, *A Retrospective Assessment of Clean Energy Investments in the Recovery Act*, February 2016, 22.
57 Andrew deLaski, "Appliance Standards in President Obama's Climate Plan," Appliance Standards Awareness Project, June 26, 2013. https://appliance-standards.org/blog/appliance-standards-president-obamas-climate-plan

58 Administrator Lisa P. Jackson, "Remarks to the 2nd Annual Governors' Global Climate Summit," September 30, 2009. https://www.epa.gov/archive/epapages/newsroom_archive/speeches/dfb9d60add641fac852576410070a78d.html
59 Ann E. Carlson, "The President, Climate Change, and California," *Harvard Law Review Forum*, Vol. 26, No. 5 (March 2013): 157.
60 Jackson, "Remarks to the 2nd Annual Governors' Global Climate Summit;" Carlson, "The President, Climate Change, and California," 157.
61 Carlson, "The President, Climate Change, and California, 157.
62 Boehner quoted in Lisa Lerer and Patrick O'Conner, "House Passes Climate Change Bill," *Politico*, June 28, 2009.
63 Obama and the RNC quoted in Lisa Lerer and Patrick O'Conner, "House Passes Climate Change Bill".
64 Schwarzenegger quoted in "excerpts" from "Governor Calls for Climate Action at Second Annual Global Summit," *The Planning Report*, November 3, 2009. https://www.planningreport.com/2009/11/03/governor-schwarzenegger-calls-climate-action-second-annual-global-summit
65 Browner interview by Dov Weinryb Grohsgal, 26–28; author interview with Nancy Sutley, June 9, 2023.
66 Di-Aping quoted in Staff, "Low Targets, Goals Dropped: Copenhagen Ends in Failure," *The Guardian*, December 18, 2009.
67 Obama quoted in Mark Hertsgaard, "The Ugly Truth about Obama's 'Copenhagen Accord'," *Vanity Fair*, December 21, 2009.
68 Amanda Little, "Schwarzenegger Lowers Expectations for Copenhagen," *Grist*, December 16, 2009.
69 Schwarzenegger quoted in Andrew S. Ross, "Schwarzenegger Weighs in at Copenhagen," *San Francisco Chronicle*, December 16, 2009.
70 Obama, *A Promised Land*, 503.
71 Obama, *A Promised Land*, 560.
72 Obama, *A Promised Land*, 560.
73 Tom Rosentiel, "Fewer Americans See Solid Evidence of Global Warming," Pew Research Center, October 22, 2009.
74 Staff, "Public's Priorities for 2010: Economy, Jobs, Terrorism," Pew Research Center, January 25, 2010.
75 Interview with Bob Epstein, April 27, 2023; Bill McKibben interview by Dov Weinryb Grohsgal, Obama Presidency Oral History Project, Columbia University, June 2021, 53.
76 Proponent argument quoted in Laura Cueva, "Poll Shows Proposition 23 Losing Support in California," *Daily Trojan*, October 13, 2010 (University of Southern California).
77 Schwarzenegger quoted in Darren Samuelsohn, "Arnold's Last Hurrah in Calif.," *Politico*, October 21, 2010.
78 Cameron quoted in Todd Woody, "Schwarzenegger and James Cameron Team up to Terminate Prop 23," *Grist*, October 29, 2010.
79 Brown quoted in Anthony York, "Brown Stops Short of Declaring Victory in Speech to Oakland Crowd," *Los Angeles Times,* November 2, 2010.
80 Governor Brown, "Governor at World Economic Forum Summit: "Climate Change Does Not Recognize Sovereignty," Press Release, September 25, 2018. https://archive.gov.ca.gov/archive/gov39/index.html
81 James Bushnell, "California's Cap-and-Trade Market Enters its Teen-Age Years," *Energy Institute Blog*, UC Berkeley, November 27, 2023. https://energyathaas.wordpress.com/2023/11/27/californias-cap-and-trade-market-enters-its-teen-age-years/
82 Leah Cardamore Stokes, *Short Circuiting Policy: Interest Groups and the Battle over Clean Energy and Climate Policy in the American Policy* (New York: Oxford University Press, 2020), 101.

83 On the backlash to further restructuring, see Severin Borenstein and James Bushnell, "The U.S. Electricity Industry After 20 Years of Restructuring," Energy Institute at Haas, Working Paper 252R (September 2014): 2; state RPS data in "State Renewable Portfolio Standards and Goals," National Conference of State Legislatures, August 13, 2021. https://www.ncsl.org/energy/state-renewable-portfolio-standards-and-goals#me
84 Obama, "A Retrospective Assessment of Clean Energy Investments in the Recovery Act,"16.
85 Harrison Schwartz and Sabine Bruske, "Utility-Scale Renewable Energy Generation Technology Roadmap," CEC Publication Number: CEC-500-2020-062, p. 81.
86 Shannon Osaka, "Obama's Recovery Act breathed life into renewables. Now they need Rescuing," *Grist*, June 1, 2020.
87 David Gelles, Brad Plummer, Jim Tankersley and Jack Ewing, "The Clean Energy Future is Arriving Faster than You Think," *The New York Times*, August 17, 2023.
88 Lazard, "Levelized Cost of Energy Analysis—Version 16.0," April 2023; U.S. EIA, "Levelized Costs of New Energy Sources," *Annual Energy Outlook 2022*, March 2022. https://www.eia.gov/outlooks/aeo/pdf/electricity_generation.pdf; Brad Plumer, "U.S. Carbon Emissions Fell in 2023 as Coal Use Tumbled to New Lows," *The New York Times*, January 10, 2024. Plumer cited an analysis by the Rhodium Group that included hydropower in the renewable category, which the U.S. EIA does as well.
89 U.S. EIA, "Short-term Energy Outlook," January 9, 2024; California Energy Commission, "2022 Total System Generation." https://www.energy.ca.gov/data-reports/energy-almanac/california-electricity-data/2022-total-system-electric
90 Biden quoted in Guy Marzorati, "With California Voters Focused on Climate, Biden Touts Obama-Era Energy Investments," *KQED*, February 5, 2020. https://www.kqed.org/news/11799776/with-california-voters-focused-on-climate-biden-touts-obama-era-energy-investments
91 Justin Worland, "How the Inflation Reduction Act Has Reshaped the U.S.—and The World," *Time*, August 11, 2023.

Appendix

Author Interviews

The dates of the interviews are when I initially spoke to that interviewee. In many cases, but not all, I had follow-up discussions or correspondence with interviewees.

Linda Adams—17 June 2023
Dennis Albiani—1 August 2023
Lorraine Paskett —21 October 2021
Ken Alex—8 March 2022
Adrienne Alvord—11 August 2023
BB Blevins—3 January 2022
Severin Borenstein—18 July 2021
James Bushnell—26 July 2021
Ralph Cavanagh—16 July 2021
Randy Chinn—7 December 2022
Kevin Civale—26 August 2022
Governor Gray Davis—16 August 2023
Kari Dohn—22 June 2021
Daniel Douglass—17 January 2022
Shannon Eddy—17 June 2023
Bob Epstein—25 August 2023
Mike Florio—1 July 2021
Matthew Freedman—11 June 2021
Tim Gage—17 August 2022
Pete Garris—3 November 2021
Lenny Goldberg—29 June 2021
Chuck Goldman—19 December 2023
Vincent Harris—26 February 2022
Winston Hickox—2 November 2022
Mike Jaske—7 July 2022
Daniel Kammen—15 November 2023
Fred Keeley—17 December 2021
Susan Kennedy—3 August 2023

William Kissinger—9 April 2022
Lawrence Lingbloom—7 December 2022
Dan Morain—8 August 2021
Annie Notthoff—17 September 2023
Arthur J. O'Donnell—13 October 2021
Dorothy Rothrock—8 June 2021
Rick Simpson—3 August 2021
Jan Smutny-Jones—19 July 2021
Garry South—1 July 2021
Arnie Sowell—2 August 2023
Nancy Sutley—9 June 2023
Terry Tamminen—31 May 2023
Nancy Vogel—21 June 2021
V. John White—29 July 2021
Frank Wolak—14 December 2021

Interviews Conducted by Arthur J. O'Donnell

The following interviews were provided to the author in 2021 by Energy Overseer/Arthur O'Donnell:

Interview with Joe Dunn, 2003
Interview with Mike Florio, 2002
Interview with S. David Freeman, 2002
Interview with Michael Kahn, 2003
Interview with Jan Smutny-Jones, 2002
Interview with Terry Winter, 2002

Oral Histories

"Oral History Interview with Carol Browner 2020" by Dov Weinryb Grohsgal, Obama Presidency Oral History Project, Columbia University, Incite @ Columbia University, New York City.

"Oral History Interview with Steven Chu 2020," by Keith A. Wailoo, Obama Presidency Oral History Project, Columbia University, Incite @ Columbia University, New York City.

"Oral History Interview with Bill McKibben 2021," by Dov Weinryb Grohsgal, Obama Presidency Oral History Project, Columbia University, Incite @ Columbia University, New York City.

"Hon. Fran Pavley: Member of the California State Senate from the 23rd and 27th District, 2008–2016." Conducted by Todd Holmes for the California State Government Oral History Program, Oral History Center, The Bancroft Library, University of California, Berkeley, 2022.

"Michael R. Peevey: An Entrepreneur in Business, Energy, Labor, and Politics." Conducted by Roger Eardley-Pryor, Oral History Center, The Bancroft Library, University of California, Berkeley, 2019.

References

Abraham, Spencer, et al. 2001. Abraham Nomination Hearing before the Committee on Energy and Natural Resources. U.S. Senate. 107th Congress, First Session. January 18.
Baldassare, Mark. 2002. *A California State of Mind: The Conflicted Voter in a Changing World*. Berkeley, CA: University of California Press.
Baldassare, Mark. 2002. *PPIC Statewide Survey: Californians and Their Government*. San Francisco, CA: Public Policy Institute of California (PPIC). February.
Baldassare, Mark. 2002. *PPIC Statewide Survey: Special Survey on Californians and the Environment*. San Francisco, CA: Public Policy Institute of California (PPIC). June.
Baldassare, Mark. 2002. *PPIC Statewide Survey: Californians and Their Government*. San Francisco, CA: Public Policy Institute of California (PPIC). October.
Baldassare, Mark. 2003. *PPIC Statewide Survey: Californians and Their Government*. San Francisco, CA: Public Policy Institute of California (PPIC). February.
Baldassare, Mark. 2003. *PPIC Statewide Survey: Special Survey on Californians and the Environment*. San Francisco, CA: Public Policy Institute of California (PPIC). July.
Baldassare, Mark. 2007. *PPIC Statewide Survey: Californians and the Environment*. San Francisco, CA: Public Policy Institute of California (PPIC). July.
Baldassare, Mark, and Cheryl Katz. 2008. *The Coming Age of Direct Democracy: California's Recall and Beyond*. Lanham, MD: Rowan & Littlefield Publishers, Inc.
Blumstein, Carl, L. S. Friedman, and Richard Green. 2002. "The History of Electricity Restructuring in California." *Journal of Industry, Competition and Trade* 2: 9–38
Bohn, Sarah, and Eric Schiff. 2011. *The Great Recession and Distribution of Income in California*. San Francisco, CA: Public Policy Institute of California (PPIC).
Bonfante, Jordan. 1991. "The Endangered Dream." *Time*, November 18.
Borenstein, Severin. 2002. "The Trouble with Electricity Markets." *Journal of Economic Perspectives* 16: 191–211.
Borenstein, Severin, and James Bushnell. 1999. "An Empirical Analysis of the Potential for Market Power in California's Electricity Industry." *The Journal of Industrial Economics* 47: 285–323.
Borenstein, Severin, and James Bushnell. 2014. "The U.S. Electricity Industry After 20 Years of Restructuring." UC, Berkeley. Energy Institute at Haas, Working Paper 252R. https://haas.berkeley.edu/energy-institute/
Borenstein, Severin, James Bushnell, Ed Kahn, and Steve Stoft. 1995. "Market Power in California Electricity Markets." *Utilities Policy* 5: 219–36.
Borenstein, Severin, James Bushnell, and Frank Wolak. 2000. "Diagnosing Market Power in California's Restructured Wholesale Electricity Market," National Bureau of Economic Research, Working Paper 7868. September. https://www.nber.org/papers/w7868
Borenstein, Severin, James Bushnell, and Frank Wolak. 2002. "Measuring Market Inefficiencies in California's Restructured Wholesale Market." *The American Economic Review* 16: 1376–1405.

Bradley, Bill. 2001. "Master of Disaster." *LA Weekly*, February 14.
Bradley, Bill. 2001. "Light and Darkness." *LA Weekly*, September 6.
Bradley, Bill. 2005. "Saving Arnold." *LA Weekly*, December 8.
Bradley, William. 2009. "Obama's Earth Day Energy Declaration: California May Be the Model He Says, but It's Not Enough." *Huffington Post*, May 24.
Bradley, William. 2015. "Jerry Brown, Arnold Schwarzenegger, or Gray Davis? Which Governor Spearheaded California's Climate Change Program?" *Huffington Post*, July 29.
Breslau, Karen. 2001. "As the Megawatts Turn." *Newsweek*, April 6.
Brown, Governor Jerry. 2018. "Governor at World Economic Forum Summit: "Climate Change Does Not Recognize Sovereignty." Press Release, September 25, 2018. Governor Brown's Media Archives for 2011–2019; can be accessed at https://archive.gov.ca.gov/archive/gov39/index.html
Brownstein, Ronald. 2009. "President Obama's Top Republican Ally." *The Atlantic*, February 19.
Bushnell, James. 2023. "California's Cap-and-Trade Market Enters Its Teen-Age Years." *Energy Institute Blog*. Energy Institute at Haas, November 27.
Bushnell, James, and Carl Blumstein. 1994. *A Reader's Guide to the Blue Book: Issues in California's Electric Industry Restructuring and Regulatory Reform*. Berkeley: UC Energy Institute.
California Air Resources Board. 2008. *Climate Change Scoping Plan: A Framework for Change*, December.
California Assembly Committee on Energy Costs and Availability. 2001. Analysis of SB 78 (Second Extraordinary Session), August 23.
California Assembly Joint Oversight Committee. 1994. "Assembly Joint Oversight Committee on Lowering the Cost of Electric Services." October 14. http://digitalcommons.law.ggu.edu/caldocs_joint_committees/48
California Assembly Utilities and Commerce Committee. 2004. Analysis of SB 199, August 25.
California Chamber of Commerce. 2006. "Alert: Chamber-Led Coalition Seeks Clarification of Emission-Reduction Economic Analysis." March 10. https://advocacy.calchamber.com/wp-content/uploads/alert/2006/Alert_03-10-2006.pdf
California Climate Action Team. 2006. "Executive Summary: Climate Action Team Report to Governor Schwarzenegger and the California Legislature." March.
California Energy Commission. 2022. "2022 Total System Generation." https://www.energy.ca.gov/data-reports/energy-almanac/california-electricity-data/2022-total-system-electric-generation
California Environmental Protection Agency. 2007. *Recommendations for Designing a Greenhouse Gas Cap-and-Trade System for California: Market Advisory Committee Recommendations to the California Air Resources Board*, June 30.
California LAO. 2008. "LAO's Critique of the AB 32 Scoping Plan Economic Analysis." November 26.
California Legislative Analyst's Office (LAO). 1983. "Summary of Legislative Action on the Budget Bill 1983–84 Fiscal Year." August.
California Public Utilities Commission (CPUC). 1994. *The Blue Book* (R.94-04-031).
California Senate. 1999. Office of Senate Floor Analyses. "Unfinished Business." Senate Bill 96, August 30.
California Senate Energy, Utilities and Communications Committee. 2000. "California's Energy Supply: Preparing for Summer 2000 & Beyond." March 14. (Video Available for Purchase from the California State Archives.)
California State Auditor. 2001. "Energy Deregulation: The Benefits of Competition Were Undermined by Structural Flaws in the Market, Unsuccessful Oversight, and Uncontrollable Competitive Forces." March.

Carlson, Ann E. 2013. "The President, Climate Change, and California." *Harvard Law Review Forum* 26: 156–59.
Charles, Dan. 2009. "Leaping the Energy Efficiency Gap." *Science Magazine*, August 14.
Chen, Allan. 2001. "*Myth: California Is an Energy Hog Ranking Low in Energy Efficiency*." *Sciencebeat*, Lawrence Berkeley National Laboratory. https://www2.lbl.gov/Science-Articles/Archive/energy-myths1.html
Chilcott, Leslie, and Allen Hughes. 2023. *ARNOLD*. Netflix Documentary.
Chu, Steven. 2009. *The Daily Show* Interview. Comedy Central, July 21. https://www.cc.com/video/7y64wv/the-daily-show-with-jon-stewart-steven-chu
Clarion Energy. 2001. "Gov. Davis Announces Plan to Increase State's Renewable Energy Generation." *Power Engineering*, July 31. https://www.power-eng.com/renewables/california-gov-davis-announces-plan-to-increase-states-renewable-electricity-generation/
Clark, Charles S. 2013. "Reinventing Government – Two Decades Later." *Government Executive*, April 26. https://www.govexec.com/management/2013/04/what-reinvention-wrought/62836/
Conniff, Richard. 2009. "The Political History of Cap and Trade." *Smithsonian Magazine*, August.
Consumer Watchdog. 1998. "Sierra Club condemns Use of Name against Prop. 9, Demands Retraction." https://consumerwatchdog.org/newsrelease/sierra-club-condemns-use-name-against-prop-9-demands-retraction
Cooper, Marc. 2002. "California's Gray Politics: Davis May Win Reelection Only because the GOP's Simon Is Such a Loser." *The Nation*, August 19.
California Public Utilities Commission (CPUC). 1997. "Pacific Gas & Electric Company's Divestiture of Electric Assets: Environmental Review." Decision 97-10-058, October 22. https://ia.cpuc.ca.gov/environment/info/esa/divest-pge-one/chapters/attachb.htm
Davis, Governor Gray. Gray-Davis.com. 1999–2003. This online archive mainly covers Davis's gubernatorial years and contains press releases, event transcripts, speeches, statements, executive orders and correspondence cited in this book, as listed in the endnotes.
Davis, Governor Gray. 2000. Democratic Convention Speech Transcript. *PBS Newshour with Jim Lehrer*. https://www.pbs.org/newshour/spc/election2000/demconvention/davis.htm
deLaski, Andrew. 2013. "Appliance Standards in President Obama's Climate Plan." Appliance Standards Awareness Project. June 26. https://appliance-standards.org/blog/appliance-standards-president-obamas-climate-plan
Donner, Paige. 2008. "Governors' Global Climate Summit: Thinking As One Planet." *Huffington Post*, December 21.
Duane, Timothy P. 2010. "Greening the Grid: Implementing Climate Change Policy through Energy Efficiency, Renewable Portfolio Standards, and Strategic Transmission System Investments." *Vermont Law Review* 34: 711–80.
Earthjustice. 2001. "House Bill Introduced Yesterday Takes Aim at Clean Air & Water, Species and More." May 2. https://earthjustice.org/news/press/2001/house-bill-introduced-yesterday-takes-aim-at-clean-air-water-species-and-more-a-polluter-gift-package
Eichenwald, Kurt. 2005. *Conspiracy of Fools: A True Story*. New York: Broadway Books.
Epstein, Bob. 2006. "Environmental Entrepreneurs Update." October 26.
Farrell, Alexander E., and W. Michael Hanneman. 2009. "Field Notes on the Political Economy of California Climate Policy." In *Changing Climates in North American Politics: Institutions, Policymaking and Multilevel Governance*, edited by Henrik Selen and Stacy D. VanDeveer, 87–109. Cambridge, MA: MIT Press.

Fecht, Josh. 2005. "San Francisco Mayor Proclaims Urban Environmental Movement." May 15. http://www.culturalecology.info/cons_hist/2005.UrbanEnvironmental-Accords.html
Federal Energy Regulatory Commission. 2004. "Order on Further Development of California ISO's Market Redesign and Establishing Hearing Procedures." Docket No. ER02-1656-017, et al. June 17.
Ferry, Steven. 2004. "Soft Paths, Hard Choices: Environmental Lessons in the Aftermath of California's Electric Deregulation Debacle." *Virginia Environmental Law Journal* 23: 251–351.
Ferry, Steven. 2009. "Auctioning the Building Blocks of Life: Carbon Auction, the Law, and Global Warming." *Notre Dame Journal of Law, Ethics & Public Policy* 23: 317–79.
Fessler, Dan. 1994. Testimony before the Subcommittee on Energy and Power of the Committee on Energy and Commerce. U.S. House of Representatives. One Hundred Third Congress, Second Session, July 14.
Fineman, Howard. 2002. "Bill Simon Jr., California Governor." *Newsweek*, February 27.
Fisher, Jolanka V., and Timothy P. Duane. 2001. "Trends in Electricity Consumption, Peak Demand, and Generating Capacity in California and the Western Grid, 1977–1998." POWER Working Paper-085. UC Energy Institute.
Galbraith, Kate, 2011. "Texplainer: Why Does Texas Have Its Own Power Grid?" *The Texas Tribune*, February 8.
Garrett, Major. 2001. "Power of Advertising Fights Energy Rate Caps." *CNN*, June 10.
Gerston, Larry N., and Terry Christensen. 2004. *Recall! California's Political Earthquake.* New York: Routledge.
Gibney, Alex. 2008. "Larry Summers' Enron Problem." *Daily Beast*, November 12.
Gibney, Alex, Matt Houser, and John McCullough. 2005. *Enron: The Smartest Guys in the Room.* USA (Documentary).
Gilbert, Richard J., editor. 1991. *Regulatory Choices: A Perspective on Developments in Energy Policy.* Berkeley, CA: University of California Press.
Goulder, Lawrence H. 2007. *California's Bold New Climate Policy.* The Berkeley Electronic Press, September.
Grunwald, Michael. 2012. *The 'New' New Deal: The Hidden Story of Change in the Obama Era.* New York: Simon & Schuster.
Guliasi, Les. 2018. *The Evolution of the Regulatory State: Energy Policy and Regulatory Reform in California.* Doctoral dissertation. Santa Barbara: Department of Sociology, University of California.
Hanneman, Michael. 2007. "How California Came to Pass AB 32, the Global Warming Solutions Act of 2006." UC, Berkeley Working Papers. https://escholarship.org/uc/item/1vb0j4d6
Harvey, Scott M., and William W. Hogan. 2001. "On the Exercise of Market Power Through Strategic Withholding in California." Working Paper, April 24. https://lmpmarketdesign.com/papers/Mkt_Pwr_CA_HH_042401.pdf
Hebert, Curt. 2001. Interview by Ray Suarez. "Wholesale Electricity Price Limits." *PBS Newshour*, June 18.
Hertsgaard, Mark. 2009. "The Ugly Truth about Obama's 'Copenhagen Accord'." *Vanity Fair*, December 21.
Hickox, Winston. 2001. Letter to Diane Feinstein. Congressional Record (Bound Edition), Senate Vol. 147: March 28.
Hirsch, Michael. 2009. "What Climate Czar Carol Browner Really Does," *Newsweek*, April 3.
Hirsch, Richard F. 1999. "PURPA: The Spur to Competition and Utility Restructuring." *Electricity Journal* 12: 60–72.
Isser, Steve. 2015. *Electricity Restructuring in the United States: Markets and Policy from the 1978 Energy Act to the Present.* Cambridge: Cambridge University Press.

Jackson, Lisa P. 2009. "Remarks to the 2nd Annual Governors' Global Climate Summit." September 30. https://www.epa.gov/archive/epapages/newsroom_archive/speeches/dfb9d60add641fac852576410070a78d.html

Jacobs, Meg. 2016. *Panic at the Pump: The Energy Crisis and the Transformation of American Politics in the 1970s*. New York: Hill & Wang.

Jones, Geoffrey. 2018. *Varieties of Green Business: Industries, Nations and Time*. Cheltenham: Edward Elgar Publishing Limited.

Joskow, Paul. 2001. "California's Electricity Crisis." *Oxford Review of Economic Policy* 17: 365–88.

Joskow, Paul, and Ed Kahn. 2001. "Identifying the Sources of Market Power: Refining the Estimates." July 5. https://economics.mit.edu/sites/default/files/2022-09/Identifying%20the%20Exercise%20of%20Market%20Power%20Refining%20the%20Estimates.pdf

Joskow, Paul, and Richard Schmalensee. 1983. *Markets for Power: An Analysis of Electrical Utility Deregulation*. Cambridge, MA: MIT Press.

Kahn, Debra. 2017. "Court Upholds California Cap-and-Trade Program." *Scientific American*, April 7. https://www.scientificamerican.com/article/court-upholds-californias-cap-and-trade-program/

Kahn, Michael, and Loretta Lynch. 2000. "California's Electricity Options and Challenges: Report to Governor Gray Davis." https://docs.cpuc.ca.gov/word_pdf/REPORT/report.pdf

Karapin, Roger. 2016. *Political Opportunities for Climate Policy: California, New York, and the Federal Government*. New York: Cambridge University Press.

Kaswan, Alice. 2013–2014. "Climate Change and Environmental Justice: Lessons from the California Lawsuits." *San Diego Journal of Climate & Energy Law* 5: 2–42.

Knapp, Don. 2000. "San Francisco Heat Blamed for Deaths, Blackout." *CNN*, June 15.

Kolstadt, Jonathan T., and Frank Wolak. 2003. "Using Environmental Emission Permit Prices to Raise Electricity Prices: Evidence from the California Electricity Market." *National Bureau of Economic Research*. May 28. https://users.nber.org/~confer/2003/si2003/papers/ee/wolak.pdf

Lazard. 2023. "Levelized Cost of Energy Analysis—Version 16.0." April.

Lee, Carol E. 2009. "Arnold on Obama: 'Beautiful'." *Politico*, March 19.

Leopold, Jason, and Utne.com. 2003. "Arnold's Enron Connection." *Utne Reader*, August 1. https://www.utne.com/community/arnolds-enron-connection/

Lerer, Lisa, and Patrick O' Conner. 2009. "House Passes Climate Change Bill." *Politico*, June 28.

Light, Sarah E. 2015. "The New Insider Trading: Environmental Markets within the Firm." *Stanford Environmental Law Journal* 34: 3–56.

Little, Amanda. 2005. "Schwarzenegger's Solar Roof Plan Could Get Sidelined by Partisan Squabbling." *Grist*, June 24.

Little, Amanda. 2009. "Schwarzenegger Lowers Expectations for Copenhagen." *Grist*, December 16.

Llanos, Miguel. 2003. "Green Hummer for Schwarzenegger?" *NBC News*, October 5. https://www.nbcnews.com/id/wbna3180817

Lloyd, Alan. Dr. 2001. Testimony. House Subcommittee on Energy and Air Quality. Congressional Record (Bound Edition), Senate Vol. 147. March 22.

Lockyer, Bill Attorney General. 2004. "Attorney General's Energy White Paper: A Law Enforcement Perspective on the California Energy Crisis." https://oag.ca.gov/sites/all/files/agweb/pdfs/antitrust/publications/energywhitepaper.pdf

Lopez, Steve. 1999. "Gray Davis: The Most Fearless Governor in America." *Time*, October 11.

Los Angeles Department of Power and Water. 2008. "LADWP Denounces CPUC/CEC Cap and Trade Proposal as a Recipe for Wealth Transfer." Press Release, October 6.

Lynch, Loretta. 2001. Interview with *FRONTLINE* and *The New York Times* for the documentary Blackout (PBS).

Margot, Ben. 2006. "Schwarzenegger Takes Center Stage on Warming." *NBC News*, September 27.
Marzorati, Guy. 2020. *With California Voters Focused on Climate, Biden Touts Obama-Era Energy Investments*. KQED, February 5. https://www.kqed.org/news/11799776/with-california-voters-focused-on-climate-biden-touts-obama-era-energy-investments
McCullough, Robert. 1998. "California's Electricity Market: Are Customers Necessary? Why Competitive Energy Suppliers See Retail Consumers as a Burden under the Current Rules." *Public Utilities Fortnightly* July 15: 36–41.
McLean, Bethany, and Peter Elkind. 2003. *The Smartest Guys in the Room: The Amazing Rise and Scandalous Fall of Enron*. New York: Portfolio.
Meng, Kyle, and Danae Hernandez-Cortez. 2022. "Do Environmental Markets Cause Environmental Injustice: Evidence from California's Carbon Market." *National Bureau of Economic Research*. https://www.nber.org/system/files/working_papers/w27205/w27205.pdf
Mullman, Jeremy. 2001. "Contract Killings: How the State's Contracts with Crucial Electric Power Providers Actually Encourage Them to Gouge Us." *SF Weekly*, May 30.
National Conference of State Legislatures. 2021. "State Renewable Portfolio Standards and Goals." August 13. https://www.ncsl.org/energy/state-renewable-portfolio-standards-and-goals#me
Natural Gas Intelligence (NGI) Staff. 1999. "CA Fights FERC for Control of ISO and PX." *NGI*, March 15.
NGI Staff. 2000. "San Diego Power Prices Capped Through 2003." *NGI*, September 4.
NGI Staff. 2000. "CAL-ISO to Consider Imposing Wholesale Caps." *NGI*, October 4.
NGI Staff. 2001. "California Hits Stage Three; Narrowly Averts Blackouts." *NGI*, January 12.
NGI Staff. 2001. "CA Gears Up for Implementation of Edison Agreement." *NGI*, April 17.
NGI Staff. 2001. "CA Governor, Generators Meeting 'Cordial'." *NGI*, May 11.
NGI Staff. 2001. "California Hammers Out a Deal with QFs." *NGI*, June 18, 2001.
NGI Staff. 2002. "CA Power Authority Releases Draft Plan for Future Energy Projects." *NGI*, January 28.
NGI Staff. 2002. "CA Power Authority Focuses on State Reserve Levels." *NGI*, December 2.
Navarro, Peter. 1996. "Electric Utilities: The Argument for Radical Deregulation." *Harvard Business Review* January–February: 112–25.
O'Donnell, Arthur J. 2003. *The Soul of the Grid: A Cultural Biography of the California Independent System Operator*. New York: iUniverse, Inc.
Obama, Barack President-Elect. 2008. Transcript and Video of Speech to the Governors' Global Climate Summit, November 18. https://www.americanrhetoric.com/speeches/barackobama/barackobamaglobalclimatesummit.htm
Obama, Barack Office of President. 2016. *A Retrospective Assessment of Clean Energy Investments in the Recovery Act*, February. https://obamawhitehouse.archives.gov/sites/default/files/page/files/20160225_cea_final_clean_energy_report.pdf
Obama, Barack. 2020. *A Promised Land*. New York: Crown.
Olmstead, James L. 2008. "The Global Warming Crisis: An Analytical Framework to Regional Responses." *Journal of Environmental Law and Litigation* 23: 128–89.
Osaka, Shannon. 2020. "Obama's Recovery Act Breathed Life into Renewables. Now They Need Rescuing." *Grist*, June 1.
Osborne, David, and Ted Gaebler. 1992. *Reinventing Government: How the Entrepreneurial Spirit Is Transforming the Public Sector*. Boston, MA: Addison-Wesley.

Peevey, Michael R., and Diane O. Wittenberg. 2017. *California Goes Green: A Roadmap to Climate Leadership*. North Charleston, SC: CreateSpace.

Pellegrini, Frank. 2001. "Bush Turns on the Megawatt Charm for California." *Time*, May 29.

Pew Research Center. 2010. "Public's Priorities for 2010: Economy, Jobs, Terrorism." January 25.

Porter, Kevin. 1995. "A Summary of the California Public Utilities Commission's Two Competing Electricity Restructuring Proposals." Golden, CO: National Renewable Energy Laboratory. https://www.nrel.gov/docs/legosti/old/8330.pdf

Rawls, James J., and Walton Bean. 2008. *California: An Interpretative History*. 9th ed. New York: McGraw-Hill.

Reason, Tim. 2001. "Ring Around the Subsidiary." *CFO Magazine*, October 1.

Renewable Energy World Staff. 2000. "California Group Argues for Mandatory Renewable Energy." December 12. https://www.renewableenergyworld.com/solar/california-group-argues-for-mandatory-renewable-energy-5046/

Richardson, Bill. 2001. Interview with *FRONTLINE* and *The New York Times* for the documentary Blackout (PBS).

Rilinger, Georg. 2020. *Toward a Sociology of Economic Engineering: The Creation and Collapse of California's Electricity Markets between 1993 and 2001*. Doctoral dissertation, Department of Sociology, University of Chicago.

Rodriguez, Joe Fitzgerald. 2021. "What Lessons Can California Learn from Its Energy Crisis 20 Years Ago." KQED, July 17. https://www.kqed.org/news/11881207/what-lessons-can-california-learn-from-its-energy-crisis-20-years-ago

Rogers, David. 2009. "Senate Passes $787 Billion Stimulus Bill." *Politico*, February 13.

Romm, Joseph. 2011. "Reagan Helped Save the Ozone Layer but Ruined America's Leadership in Clean Energy." *Grist*, February 8.

Rosentiel, Tom. 2009. "Fewer Americans See Solid Evidence of Global Warming." *Pew Research Center*. October 22.

Russell, Ron. 2001. "Dim Bulbs." *SF Weekly*, March 7.

Sanders, Robert. 2009. "The Pluses and (Mostly) Minuses of Biofuels." *Phys.org*., February 23. https://phys.org/news/2009-02-pluses-minuses-biofuels.html

Schmalensee, Richard, and Robert N. Stavins. 2019. "Policy Evolution under the Clean Air Act." *Journal of Economic Perspectives* 33: 27–50.

Schuparra, Kurt. 1998. *Triumph of the Right: The Rise of the California Conservative Movement, 1945–1966*. New York: Routledge.

Schwartz, Harrison, and Sabine Bruske. 2020. "Utility-Scale Renewable Energy Generation Technology Roadmap." CEC Publication Number: CEC-500-2020-062.

Schwarzenegger, Arnold. 2003. *Larry King Live* interview. *CNN*, September 17.

Schwarzenegger, Governor Arnold. 2003–2011. Press releases, event transcripts, speeches, statements, executive orders and correspondence cited in this book were accessed through the *Wayback Machine Internet Archive* unless otherwise noted.

Schwarzenegger, Governor Arnold. 2007. "Twenty-First Century Environmentalism: How Protecting Our Environment Will Create Economic Growth." Council on Foreign Relations. April 12; accessed at Cfr.org.

Sierra Club California, San Diego Chapter. 2001. "Myth vs. Fact." http://fbaum.unc.edu/lobby/_107th/126_CAFE_Standards_2/Organizational_Statements/SC/SC_San_Diego_Chapter_Myth_Vs_Fact.htm

Sivaram, Varun. 2020. "The American Recovery & Reinvestment Act and the Rise of Utility-Scale Photovoltaics." *Bipartisan Policy Center*. June. https://bipartisanpolicy.org/download/?file=/wp-content/uploads/2020/06/The-Successful-Demonstration-of-Utility-Scale-PV.pdf

Smeloff, Ed, and Peter Asmus. 1997. *Reinventing Electric Utilities: Competition, Citizen Action, and Clean Power*. Washington, DC: Island Press.
Smith, Terence. 2003. "California Recall Revelations." *PBS NewsHour*, October 3.
Stavins, Robert N. 2007. "Comments on the Recommendations of the Market Advisory Committee to the California Air Resources Board." June 15; accessed at https://scholar.harvard.edu/stavins/publications/comments-recommendations-market-advisory-committee-california-air-resources
Stokes, Leah Cardamore. 2020. *Short Circuiting Policy: Interest Groups and the Battle over Clean Energy and Climate Policy in the American States*. New York: Oxford University Press.
Stravos, Richard. 2002. "California: Beginning Anew." *Fortnightly Magazine*, February 15.
Tamminen, Terry. 2011. *Cracking the Carbon Code: The Key to Sustainable Profits in the New Economy*. New York: Palgrave MacMillan.
Teece, David, et al. 2001. "Manifesto on California's Energy Crisis," Institute of Management, Innovation & Organization. UC, Berkeley, January 26. https://silo.tips/download/manifesto-on-the-california-electricity-crisis
U.S. Department of the Treasury. 2018. "Final Overview of the Section 1603 Program." March 1. https://home.treasury.gov/system/files/276/P-Status-overview-2018-03-01.pdf
U.S. Energy Information Agency. 2022. "Levelized Costs of New Energy Sources." *Annual Energy Outlook*. March.
U.S. Energy Information Agency. 2024. "Short-Term Energy Outlook." January 9.
Victor, David C., and Joshua C. House. 2006. "BP's Emissions Trading System." *Energy Policy* 34: 2100–12.
Vogel, David. 2018. *California Greenin': How the Golden State Became an Environmental Leader*. Princeton, NJ: Princeton University Press.
Wang, Xi. 2014. *The Emergence of the Renewable Portfolio Standard in the U.S.: A Case Study of Negotiating Power in California*. Masters thesis, Department of Environmental Studies, University of Colorado.
Wasserman, Harvey. 2001. "California's Deregulation Disaster." *The Nation*, January 26.
Weare, Christopher. 2003. *The California Electricity Crisis: Causes and Policy Options*. San Francisco, CA: Public Policy Institute of California (PPIC).
White House Council of Economic Advisors. 2010. "The Economic Impact of the American Recovery and Reinvestment Act of 2009: Supplement to the Third Quarterly Report." April.
Windpower Monthly Staff. 1996. "Crumbs for Wind Out of a Cruel Hoax." *Windpower Monthly*, October 1. https://www.windpowermonthly.com/article/956913/crumbs-wind-cruel-hoax
Windpower Monthly Staff. 2002. "California Considers Renewable Mandate." *Windpower Monthly*, May 31. https://www.windpowermonthly.com/article/953620/california-considers-renewables-mandate
Wiser, Ryan, and Charles Allen Goldman. 1996. "California Renewable Energy Policy and Implementation Issues: An Overview of Recent Regulatory and Legislative Action." Lawrence Berkeley National Laboratory, Energy and Environment Division. https://www.researchgate.net/publication/236397785_California_renewable_energy_policy_and_implementation_issues_An_overview_of_recent_regulatory_and_legislative_action
Witherspoon, Jennifer. 2005. "Governor Schwarzenegger Takes on Global Warming." Environmental Defense Fund. Press Release. https://www.edf.org/media/governor-schwarzenegger-takes-global-warming
Wolak, Frank. 2003. "Diagnosing the California Electricity Crisis." *The Electricity Journal* 16: 11–31.
Wolak, Frank, and James Bushnell. 1999. "Reliability Must-Run Contracts for the California Electricity Market." http://web.stanford.edu/group/fwolak/cgi-bin/sites/default/files/RMR_Report_Bushnell.pdf

Woodruff, Judy, et al. 2003. "California Governor to Face Recall Vote." *CNN*, July 25.
Woody, Todd. 2010. "Schwarzenegger and James Cameron Team Up to Terminate Prop 23." *Grist*, October 29.
Worland, Justin. 2023. "How the Inflation Reduction Act has Reshaped the U.S.—and The World." *Time*, August 11.
Yang, Carter M. 2001. "Energy Crisis Poses Political Quandary for Bush." *ABC News*, January 26. https://abcnews.go.com/Politics/story?id=121967&page=1
Zanjani, Nick. 2014. "A Brief History of the California Public Utilities Commission: Examining the Past to Help Shape the Future." CPUC Executive Division; accessed at CPUC.CA.Gov.

Index

FSC
www.fsc.org
MIX
Papier | Fördert
gute Waldnutzung
FSC® C083411

Kolibri 360 GmbH
Ferdinand-Jühlke-Straße 7
99095 Erfurt, Deutschland
produktsicherheit@kolibri360.de